Your Official America Online® Guide to Pictures Online

David Peal

AOL Press

Dulles, VA

Your Official America Online® Guide to Pictures Online
Published by

AOL Press

An imprint of Hungry Minds, Inc.

909 Third Avenue

New York, NY 10022

www.aol.com (America Online Web site)

Library of Congress Control Number: 00-104774

ISBN: 0-7645-3529-3

Printed in the United States of America

10 9 8 7 6 5 4 3 2

1B/QZ/QS/QR/IN

Distributed in the United States by Hungry Minds, Inc. and America Online, Inc.

For general information on IHungry Minds books in the U.S., please call our Consumer Customer Service department at 800-762-2974. For reseller information, including discounts and premium sales, please call our Reseller Customer Service department at 800-434-3422.

Welcome to AOL Press™

AOL Press books provide timely guides to getting the most out of your online life. AOL Press was formed as part of the AOL family to create a complete series of official references for using America Online as well as the entire Internet — all designed to help you enjoy a fun, easy, and rewarding online experience.

AOL Press is an exciting partnership between two companies at the forefront of the knowledge and communications revolution — AOL and IDG Books Worldwide, Inc. AOL is committed to quality, ease of use, and value, and IDG Books excels at helping people understand technology.

To meet these high standards, all our books are authored by experts with the full participation of and exhaustive review by AOL's own development, technical, managerial, and marketing staff. Together, AOL and IDG Books have implemented an ambitious publishing program to develop new publications that serve every aspect of your online life.

We hope you enjoy reading this AOL Press title and find it useful. We welcome your feedback at AOL Keyword: **Contact Shop Direct** so we can keep providing information the way you want it.

About the Author

David Peal teaches in the Educational Technology Leadership MA program at George Washington University in Washington, D.C. As the former editorial manager of AOL's Internet Connection, he developed forums about the Internet and helped create AOL's first comprehensive online source of Internet help. In addition to this book, David has written three other books for AOL: *America Online Internet Guide, Student's Guide to the Internet* (1998), and *Picture This* (1999). He wrote *Access the Internet* (1994–97) and edited the *Lycos Small Business Web Resource Guide* (1997), and developed one of the first newsletters devoted to the commercial use of the Internet (1994–95). He was a finalists judge for the education category in the 2000 Global Information Infrastructure (GII) awards.

Photo Credits

The following photographs were provided by Len Rizzi. The images are the property of the photographer and may not be reproduced without permission.

Figures 3-3, 3-5, 3-6, 3-7, 3-9, 3-10, 3-12, 10-5, 10-6, 10-7, 10-8, 10-9, 14-2, 14-5, 14-6

Credits

America Online

Technical Editor:
Keith Fleming

Cover Design:
DKG Design, Inc.

Hungry Minds, Inc.

Senior Project Editor:
Nicole Haims

Acquisitions Editor:
Kathy Yankton

Senior Copy Editor:
Kim Darosett

Senior Copy Editor, Training:
Diana Conover

Proof Editor:
Jill Mazurczyk

Technical Editor:
Lee Musick

Permissions Editor:
Carmen Krikorian

Publishing Director:
Andy Cummings

Editorial Manager:
Leah Cameron

Media Development Manager:
Heather Heath Dismore

Editorial Assistants:
Seth Kerney, Candace Nicholson

Project Coordinators:
Valery Bourke, Maridee Ennis

Layout and Graphics:
Gabriele McCann, Kathie Schutte, Brian Torwelle, Erin Zeltner

Proofreaders:
Laura Albert, Laura L. Bowman, Susan Moritz, Marianne Santy

Indexer:
Sharon Hilgenberg

Acknowledgments

Many people helped in tangible ways in writing this book.

- ▶ Len Rizzi — friend and professional photographer — created and edited many of the photographs and figures in Chapters 3 and 10, and drafted the case study at the end of Chapter 14.

- ▶ Dave Marx and Jennifer Watson, esteemed authors of *Your Official America Online Tour Guide* (IDG Books Worldwide/AOL Press, 1999), drafted several chapters.

- ▶ Online sage Dona Patrick — formerly a student and now a friend — wrote Appendix A: "Online Digital-Imaging Resources."

- ▶ Denise Kennell — an AOL community leader and the person responsible for answering AOL members' questions about "You've Got Pictures" — was just the person to write the question-and-answer element in Chapters 4–6.

- ▶ Anyone familiar with *Picture This,* published by an earlier incarnation of AOL Press, might hear Jeff Borsecnik's echo in this book. He's the one who taught me about the Rule of Thirds.

At AOL, I relied on the support and information provided by John Dyn, Kathy Harper, Jen Consalvo, Thomas Kriese, Dan Pacheco, Dan Shilling, Janice Smith, Keith Fleming, and Blair Zervos.

At IDG Books, I am grateful for the continued support of Kathy Yankton and Andy Cummings. Nicole Haims, the book's Senior Project Editor, deftly managed a cranky author, large team, and impossible schedule. Special thanks for the painstaking editorial and production services of Kim Darosett, Senior Copy Editor; and Diana Conover, Senior Editor, Training. Lee Musick, Technical Editor, did a thorough job of reviewing the manuscript and contributed many suggestions for improving it.

Finally, thanks to Carol, the kids, and the friends and neighbors who were such good sports when I took all those pictures.

Dedication

For my mother, for supporting me all along.

Contents at a Glance

Table of Contents

Part III: Using Your Digital Darkroom   **127**

Part IV: Special Projects for Home and Work   233

Chapter 12: Projects for Home and School 235

Introduction

Just when you thought you had figured out the latest technology — cell phones, DVD players, your VCR, that new color printer, whatever — you're about to get ... pictures. *Digital* pictures, to be precise — photographs changed in a format that allows computers to display, store, and transmit them. With a host of new products and services, you can create and share digital pictures almost as easily as you can send e-mail. You can share your pictures with more people than was possible with just prints, and you can use them in ways undreamt-of in the world of traditional photography.

What This Book Is About

This book is about the emerging world of digital pictures — pictures you can share with friends, include in a family newsletter or homework assignment, and much more. You don't need anything except a computer, a film camera, and AOL to get digital pictures today. With all sorts of new easy-to-use home equipment — described in detail in this book — you can go as far into the new world of digital pictures as you want to go.

At the center of the new world of digital pictures, for America Online members, is a service called "You've Got Pictures." With this service, you take your rolls of film to be developed at the drugstore, as you ordinarily do. In addition to prints, you now get digital pictures posted directly to AOL. Accessing your pictures is as simple as accessing your e-mail.

Who This Book Is For

The new world of digital pictures has something for everyone, and so does this book:

▶ Anyone comfortable with any traditional camera — whether it's a Hasselblad, 35mm, or point-and-shoot — will want to check out AOL's "You've Got Pictures," the online storage space for your digital pictures.

▶ Anyone considering purchasing a digital camera can find out what features to look for in such a camera. And digital camera owners may want to know more about how to copy pictures from a digital camera to a computer, manage them on the computer, and upload them to AOL's "You've Got Pictures."

▶ Graphic artists and Web builders, especially newcomers to these fields, may want to learn the principles of resolution and get an introduction to the wonders of digital editing.

▶ Anyone who has a growing collection of digital pictures — whether they're from "You've Got Pictures," a digital camera, or a scanner — will want to use this book for its many tips on keeping track of pictures.

This book is different from other digital photo books in its focus on the digital-imaging mosaic and its many pieces, rather than this or that piece. The big-picture view makes it easier to master any piece of the mosaic.

What You Need

What you need to get started with digital pictures depends on what you want to do.

▶ If you have a film camera and just want to get digital pictures (for sharing or for use on the Web or in family trees), all you need is your computer, your existing film camera, and an AOL account.

▶ If you want to create home projects with your digital pictures, or if you have a small business or home office, you will likely need graphics software and a color printer.

▶ If you want the convenience of filmless photography or if you're primarily interested in creating digital pictures for the Web or to share via e-mail, consider buying a digital camera.

▶ If you have lots of photographic prints that you want to convert into digital pictures, you need a scanner.

What AOL Provides

Many of the technologies and services that make digital imaging possible are available right on AOL, as described in the following list:

▶ **"You've Got Pictures":** This is the online home for your digital pictures, where you can store and view your pictures and then share them with others. See Part II.

▶ **AOL Hometown:** The online place where AOL provides easy-to-use tools for sharing pictures and adding pages to a growing community of Web pages available to anyone on AOL and the Internet. See Chapter 13.

▶ **Groups@AOL:** The new AOL service for creating small communities of AOL and non-AOL members, with all sorts of communication tools and an easy method for sharing digital pictures. See Chapter 13.

▶ **AOL Picture Gallery:** AOL's tool for letting you edit and manage all the digital pictures stored on your hard drive. See Chapters 9 and 10.

▶ **E-mail:** E-mail is available on AOL, on the Web, and as part of "You've Got Pictures." With AOL, you can insert your digital pictures into messages or send them as attachments, to anyone on the Internet. See Chapter 5.

▶ **Online communities and information hubs devoted to *every* aspect of digital imaging:** These include CNET, AOL's Popular Photography Online, and countless Web sites. See Chapter 5.

Don't forget that AOL itself is the hub of countless communities, many of which support ongoing discussions about digital imaging in their message boards and chat rooms. Through AOL, you also have complete access to the world of information resources on the Web and elsewhere on the Internet.

How This Book Is Organized

This book is designed to introduce the entire mosaic of digital imaging — identifying the pieces, showing how they work together, and helping you rearrange them for your own purposes. Whatever your interests and background, you will want to skim the Quick Start and Part I, just to get a sense of this big picture. Beyond that, you can use this book as a reference, reading just the material you need.

Quick Start

This short opening section provides a glimpse into the new world of digital pictures. It defines digital pictures, indicates a few of their benefits, and lists the major things you can do with them.

Part I: Digital Imaging: An Introduction

Relax, you can read this part for an overview of digital imaging; you don't have to do anything quite yet. Chapter 1 introduces the major pieces of the digital-imaging mosaic — storing, editing, sharing, and having fun with digital imaging. Chapter 2 outlines the four sources of digital pictures: "You've Got Pictures" (if you use a film camera), digital cameras, scanners, and stock photography. And Chapter 3 explores the underlying subject for the whole book: taking pictures that you'll *want* to share with others.

Part II: What You Can Do with "You've Got Pictures"

Parts II and III look, respectively, at the online and offline methods of storing, viewing, and working with digital pictures. Chapter 4 covers the basics of "You've Got Pictures," from getting your film developed and posted on AOL, to storing your pictures. Chapter 5 is about sharing digital pictures by e-mail and as part of collections of pictures (albums). And Chapter 6 shows you how to share your pictures as gifts — coffee cups, mouse pads, and other things.

Part III: Using Your Digital Darkroom

Part III takes place closer to home — on your computer. It explores the key topics of choosing hardware and software, managing digital pictures, selecting image-editing software, editing them, and printing them. The creativity possible in your digital darkroom can bring much of the satisfaction of working with digital pictures.

Chapter 7 outlines what to look for if you're in the market for a digital camera or scanner. Chapter 8 helps you download your pictures from a scanner or digital camera and manage them on your computer. Chapters 9 and 10 explore image editing. Chapter 11 covers printing, a topic about as unsexy as it is indispensable.

Part IV: Special Projects for Home and Work

This part hints at the things you can do with digital pictures for school, home, and work. Chapter 12 gets you started making things with your digital pictures, Chapter 13 explores the white-hot subject of the World Wide Web, and Chapter 14 introduces the wealth of uses for digital pictures in small businesses and home offices.

Part V: Appendixes

The point of the appendixes is to make the book more complete and to give you tools for keeping up with several fast-changing areas. Appendix A is a useful guide to selected online resources, and Appendix B provides short definitions of the book's more-technical terms.

Using AOL Keywords

Keywords are AOL's shortcut to nearly everything online. I refer to keywords throughout this book. Keywords are indicated like this: AOL Keyword: **Pictures**. The boldface is for your convenience. Since keywords are not case sensitive, you can type in *pictures* or *Pictures*. This particularly useful keyword takes you to "You've Got Pictures" whenever you are online. *All* keywords work only when you're online.

After you know the keyword for an online area, you can jump there directly and immediately, by doing one of the following:

▶ Typing the keyword into the text box on the navigation bar at the top of your AOL window, and then clicking the Go button.

▶ Pressing Ctrl+K (Windows) or ⌘+K (Mac), typing the keyword in the Keyword window, and clicking the Go button.

Book Elements and Conventions

This book's goal is to show you how to make the new world of digital pictures a part of your life. The subject may be revolutionary, but the book itself is meant to be as familiar and easy-to-use as possible. That's the beauty of books. For now, at least, they're the most familiar way of learning *anything*.

You will find the following helpful icons sprinkled throughout the margins of this book:

These hints and suggestions aim to provide shortcuts or less-than-obvious hints.

Read the book's Caution icons to avoid frustration.

Less scintillating than Tips, less forbidding than Cautions, Notes contain information you really, really want to know.

This icon defines terms that may be new to you.

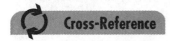

This icon indicates sections or chapters in this book that explore a specific topic in more detail.

This icon alerts you to an AOL area or Web site with insights into a topic in the text.

I'm happy to have enlisted the help of Denise Kennell in preparing this book. As the AOL community leader who answers AOL members' e-mail messages regarding "You've Got Pictures," she has created a set of concise questions and answers (concentrated in Chapters 4-5) that address the questions of greatest interest to people who frequent "You've Got Pictures."

Web Addresses

I've indicated the address of Web sites using strikethrough type, as follows: www. photoalley.com. I've left out the *http://* part because with the AOL browser you don't have to type it in. To visit PhotoAlley.com, part of AOL's Shop@AOL, type www.photoalley.com into the AOL toolbar's text box, and click Go.

Commands, Selections, and So Forth

Sometimes, I'll provide instructions for doing something. For example, in Chapter 10, you see the following text describing a process in PhotoSuite:

Choose Touchup⇨Touchup Filters⇨Fix Colors.

See the ⇨? That just means to do one thing and then do another; it's a shortcut. In this case, you click the Touchup button, then you click the Touchup Filters button, and then you select Fix Colors from the drop-down list.

Quick Start

From Traditional Photos to Digital Pictures

Cradle to grave, life seems to consist of photographs. About as soon as the cord is cut, most newborn babies are captured in a snapshot with a happy mom or proud dad. For many people, a vacation or wedding isn't fully experienced until they get back the pictures showing the highpoints of the ceremony or the presence of an old friend or cousin Claire. Perhaps you can see a photograph from where you are right now, or fumble around for one. That picture may be in the newspaper, on the wall, or in your purse or wallet. Or think of the family photo album, one of the first things many people think to remove from the house in an emergency. How can pictures of family members and loved ones be replaced, after all?

Pervasive in daily life, pictures are becoming ubiquitous in the online world as well. If you have ever done any Web surfing, you can't help noticing *digital pictures* everywhere you look. *Every* picture you see on the Web, in fact, is a digital picture.

To say that pictures are *digital* simply means they can be used by a computer. They can be saved on a hard drive, transmitted over AOL, printed out, modified in a hundred ways, and displayed on a standard computer monitor. Your computer is very good at handling all these aspects of digital pictures.

Aren't Digital Pictures for Technical People?

Computers make digital pictures possible, but you don't have to be technically inclined or even like computers to collect, share, and use these pictures. All you need is imagination. You can use your digital pictures in family newsletters or birthday invitations, and you can use them to adorn all sorts of things, like the coffee mugs and mouse pads available at "You've Got Pictures" (see Chapter 6).

 Note

In this book, *pictures* means images that originated in any kind of camera, old or new. The term does *not* mean clipart and the images created from scratch with graphics software.

 **Definition**

A *digital camera* is like a traditional film camera, except that it doesn't use film; instead, it creates files for computers to use. What looks like a digital picture to you is, to a computer, just another *file* to store, open, display, and transmit. A *scanner* works like a copy machine except that it produces computer files instead of paper copies. In other words, digital cameras *create* digital pictures directly. I have a lot more to say about these wonderful gadgets in Chapter 2 (how they work) and 7 (selecting all kinds of hardware).

Tip

On America Online, a key-word gives you direct access to an online area. To see a list of keywords, click the Keyword button on the navigation bar at the top of your AOL window. In the box that appears, click the Keyword List button. You can look at keyword lists alphabetically, by popularity, and by AOL channel. To visit an AOL area (and many Web sites) directly, type its AOL Keyword (such as **Hometown**) into the Keyword window and click Go.

Computers are also good at taking old-fashioned prints (snap-shots) and turning them into digital pictures, which can then be modified and shared. For example, Figure Q-1 shows a picture on the bulletin board by my computer. Figure Q-2 shows the same snapshot quickly transformed into a digital picture with a one-touch scanner. (You find out about scanners later in this book.) Here, I'm about to send the digital picture via e-mail using AOL's "You've Got Pictures."

Figure Q-1. My bulletin board with snapshots and assorted papers.

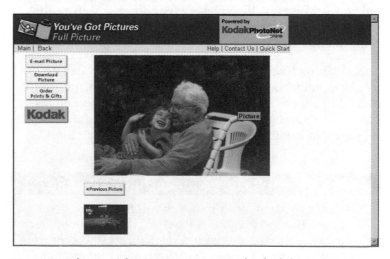

Figure Q-2. The picture shown in Figure Q-1, scanned, uploaded (copied) to AOL's "You've Got Pictures" area, and ready to send to anyone by e-mail.

Good Reasons to Get Your Pictures Online

The path from traditional pictures to digital pictures may seem daunting. But actually, it's direct and not particularly thorny. Here are some good reasons to try the digital world:

▶ **You can begin your adventure in digital photography with what you already have.** No matter what type of camera you have, you can scan your snapshots and then upload (copy) them to AOL (*scanning* is a big subject covered in Chapters 2, 7, and 8). Or, you can have your new rolls developed and delivered online. Or, if you have a digital camera, you can transfer your pictures directly from your camera to your PC. After they're on your computer's hard drive, it's a snap to upload pictures to AOL's "You've Got Pictures" area.

▶ **Digital pictures can be easier to share with others than traditional pictures — and in a variety of ways.** In addition to using the "You've Got Pictures" service, you can also use digital pictures with AOL's other tools and services. For example, you can insert pictures of the grandchildren into your next e-mail to grandma, as shown in Figure Q-3, or plaster them all over your Web page (use AOL Keyword: **Hometown**).

You don't have to have a digital camera to find the benefits of digital images — "You've Got Pictures" allows you to get digital pictures from your traditional film camera.

Try AOL Keyword: **Paperworks** to find a large selection of quality printing products, including business cards and résumé paper.

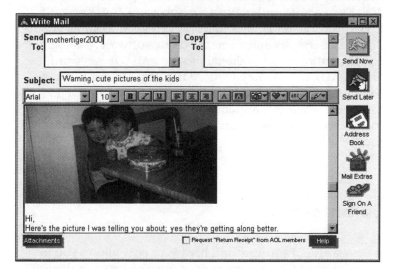

Figure Q-3. Here a digital picture has been added to AOL's familiar Write Mail window.

With "You've Got Pictures,"
every screen name has
unlimited room for pictures
from any source — scanners,
digital cameras, or developed rolls of film. You can
also manage your space by
downloading pictures and
storing them on your hard
drive, where you're limited
only by the amount of storage
space you have available.
Chapter 7 introduces you to
ways of storing pictures, and
Chapter 8 covers down-
loading and managing your
digital pictures.

▶ **Digital pictures lend themselves to a much wider range of uses than traditional prints.** Use digital pictures to promote a business, help a young student illustrate a report for school, add visual interest to a newsletter, and make party invitations, T-shirts, a home inventory, and personal stationery.

▶ **Digital pictures are easier to organize, store, and find when you need them.** With digital pictures, you can use your computer to help organize, store, and retrieve your pictures. Some of the places you can store your pictures are on your computer's hard drive, in digital albums, and in your space on the "You've Got Pictures" service.

▶ **Unlike traditional prints, you can enhance digital pictures with graphics software.** With graphics software packages like MGI PhotoSuite III and Adobe PhotoDeluxe, it is now possible to make all sorts of changes to your digital pictures, such as remove dust spots, bring out contrast, eliminate red eye, and much more. Chapter 10 explores many of the things you can do with graphics software.

AOL offers a complete range of resources to assist in all your activities with digital pictures. "You've Got Pictures" (AOL Keyword: **YGP**) makes it as easy as possible for AOL members to get digital pictures by providing the easy online tools for collecting, managing, using, and sharing digital pictures. At AOL Keyword: **Popular Photography** and AOL Keyword: **CNET**, you can find out as much as you want to know about digital cameras, scanners, image-editing software, photography, and the entire world of digital pictures. At AOL Keyword: **Shop@AOL** or AOL Keyword: **AOL Shop Direct**, you can shop for any kind of hardware or software. "Online Digital-Imaging Resources" (Appendix A) provides a guided tour to selected, useful digital-imaging resources on AOL and the Web.

Summary

A new world of software and hardware now allows you to take charge of the pictures in your life: You can edit them, share them, and use them for all sorts of new purposes.

"You've Got Pictures" gives you a single online place in which to store your digital pictures regardless of their source — scanners, digital cameras, traditional cameras, or something else. This book is your guide to the possibilities of digital pictures.

CHAPTER

1

GETTING STARTED WITH
DIGITAL PICTURES

A QUICK LOOK

Chapter 1

Getting Started with Digital Pictures

IN THIS CHAPTER

Finding out about "You've Got Pictures"

Storing your photos on your PC

Editing pictures in your own digital workshop

Using your digital pictures on Web pages

What microcomputers and word-processing software did to the world of *text* in the 1980s, digital imaging equipment and the Internet are doing right now to the world of *photographs*. For all sorts of reasons, the connected world is bracing for a flood of images:

▶ The huge popularity of e-mail and the World Wide Web creates a huge demand for digital pictures.

▶ Digital cameras, scanners, printers, and other gadgets are getting much easier to use and much more affordable.

▶ Easy-to-use software makes it even simpler to enhance and share digital pictures.

▶ All these services, hardware, and software are beginning to work smoothly together.

Online leader America Online and its many partners, including Kodak, have taken these pieces and created an integrated set of tools for creating, collecting, storing, editing, and sharing digital pictures.

Digital pictures, you might remember from the Quick Start, are simply photographs available in such a way that computers can store them and send them to other computers, located anywhere on the globe.

Neither pictures nor digital pictures are really "worth a thousand words." When put *with* words, pictures are easily worth much more than a thousand words. Would you prefer to read about your great-grandparents or see a portrait of them, with dates, an anecdote, and a capsule history? With the right equipment and software — fully described in this book — you, too, can make digital pictures and tell your own stories. With your photos in digital form, sharing digital pictures becomes as easy as exchanging text messages by e-mail. How do you take the first step?

Getting Your Pictures Online

The cornerstone of AOL's digital-imaging initiatives is the online area called "You've Got Pictures" (AOL Keyword: **Pictures**), shown in Figure 1-1. Here's where you start building your online collection of digital pictures.

Tip

On America Online, a keyword gives you direct access to an online area. For example, the AOL Keyword: **You've Got Pictures** (or simply **Pictures**) takes you to the "You've Got Pictures" area. To go to a keyword area, type the keyword in the text box on the navigation bar and click the Go button (which is located to the right of the text box).

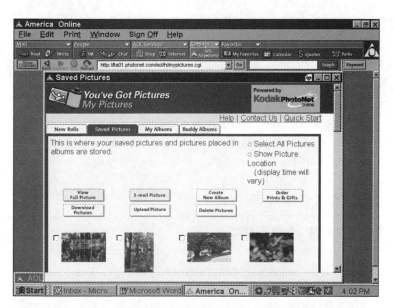

Figure 1-1. Start here to view, share, organize, and store your digital pictures.

To get digital pictures, you just check a box and provide an AOL screen name when you drop off your pictures at a designated PhotoNet outlet (most large drugstores and supermarkets are members) to have them developed. (See Chapter 4 for all the details.) A day or two later, your digital pictures are ready at "You've Got Pictures" for sharing, downloading, editing, and using in countless ways.

That's not all. Suppose you already have digital pictures on your computer. They may be pictures that someone else shared with you, or pictures you've scanned, or pictures you've taken with a digital camera — it doesn't really matter how you get them. If you're signed on to AOL, you can copy them (upload them) directly from your computer to "You've Got Pictures."

Definition

Uploading is the term commonly used for transferring an electronic document or picture from one computer to another, usually from a personal computer to an Internet-connected computer, sometimes called a *server* (AOL has about a zillion such computers), where many people can view the document or picture. (Appendix B consists of a glossary of important terms like *upload*.) *Downloading* is the opposite; it's the process of copying a file from an Internet-connected computer to your own computer, for archiving or other use.

My Pictures Are Online, Now What?

At "You've Got Pictures," you can do the following with your photos:

▶ Send an individual picture to anyone with an e-mail account, as well as include an electronic greeting or write a few words about your picture. Your picture and message arrive in the recipient's electronic mailbox (just the way you receive your e-mail).

▶ Group related pictures in an online photo *album* and share it with others.

▶ Have your photo emblazoned on a mug or other product, and share it with a special person.

▶ Download pictures from "You've Got Pictures" to your own computer.

Sharing Pictures

Think of how you share photographic prints: You can show them to people, one person at a time, or you can get duplicates or reprints and mail them to grandparents and whoever else may be interested, or you can arrange the prints in an album for posterity — a sure way of making sure that no one will see them except on special occasions.

Digital pictures lend themselves to hundreds of ways of sharing. Here are a few ideas to consider:

> ▶ At AOL Hometown (AOL Keyword: **Hometown**), you can create Web pages with your pictures so that anyone, anywhere, can see them.

> ▶ The Hometown Gallery highlights notable members' pages (AOL Keyword: **Gallery**), as shown in Figure 1-2.

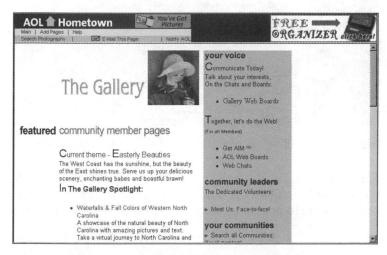

Figure 1-2. AOL Hometown's Gallery. The place to share Web pages.

> ▶ AOL areas such as AOL Keyword: **Traveler** provide additional opportunities to share your images. See Chapter 5 for more libraries where you can upload pictures.

> ▶ Genealogy.com's Family Tree Maker software makes it simple to create a family tree to post on the Web for everyone to see.

> ▶ The GatherRound Web site provides the opportunity to share pictures and albums with others and to chat about areas of common interest (www.gatherround.com). After you've registered, you can download free software for organizing your digital pictures. GatherRound is a free service from MGI, the makers of PhotoSuite III, an all-purpose graphics software program featured in several chapters of this book.

▶ The Kideo Web site (www.kideo.com), soon to become more closely integrated with "You've Got Pictures," offers a broad range of children's products on which you can feature your digital pictures (see Figure 1-3).

Figure 1-3. Kideo lets you create all sorts of gifts for kids with your digital pictures.

The upshot? Digital pictures are much easier to share than traditional snapshots. Once you start using digital images, you'll find new ways of sharing them and new people to share them with.

Storing Digital Pictures

It's important to realize early on that your digital pictures have two homes — two places where you can store them, share them, and create things with them. These two places are "You've Got Pictures" and your own PC.

Cross-Reference

Part II of this book is devoted to "You've Got Pictures," the online home for your digital pictures.

Storing Pictures Online

"You've Got Pictures" is the online collecting point for your pictures on AOL. You can do many things with "You've Got Pictures" (as described earlier). However, you can't enhance your pictures online with image-editing software, and you can't directly use those pictures in a Web page. If you want to use those images in a Web page, you must first download the pictures and then upload them to a different online place called AOL Hometown (AOL Keyword: **Hometown**), which is described in detail in Chapter 12.

Though you have unlimited storage space available online at "You've Got Pictures," you may want to consider a supplementary means of storing your digital pictures and reserve "You've Got Pictures" for only your most recent pictures. The next section describes this alternative storage place — your own computer.

Storing Pictures Offline

Your computer, in particular your hard drive, is the cavernous place in which to keep your digital pictures. Here are some reasons why you'd want to keep pictures on your computer instead of online:

▶ There's no limit to the number of pictures you can store on your computer, even if you don't use supplementary storage media, as described in Chapter 7.

▶ All the changes you make to individual pictures take place on your own computer. You can enhance images, remedy picture defects (like dust and scratches), and, for fun, add special effects.

▶ From your own PC, you can upload your digital pictures to many online places where you can share your pictures, such as AOL Hometown and non-AOL destinations as well.

▶ When you acquire digital pictures from a digital camera or scanner, you're really copying them to your PC, where you can store them or upload them to "You've Got Pictures" or *anywhere* online.

"You've Got Pictures" is the starting place for storing and sharing your digital pictures online. Your PC is the hub of activity for a great deal of what you *do* with digital pictures, online and offline.

Cross-Reference

Part III is devoted to storing pictures on your PC, the offline home for your digital pictures. Chapter 7, in particular, introduces storage equipment and the software you need for organizing your pictures.

Note

In this book, Web addresses appear in monofont, as in the following example: `www.aol.com`. To visit such a Web site, type the address into the text box on the AOL navigation bar, and click the Go button.

Putting Pictures on Web Pages

Of all the ways of sharing digital pictures, none is as pervasive as the World Wide Web. The beauty of the Web is that it is accessible, affordable, and fun. Web sites serve countless purposes, so there are no real limits to how you use your digital pictures. You can make as many Web pages as you want at AOL Hometown (AOL Keyword: **Hometown**). You can create, among other things, a Yellow Page–type listing for your business, a family tree, a community photo gallery, and a commemoration of a wedding or other event. You can even do the Seinfeld thing and make a Web page about nothing. You'll be in good company.

Cross-Reference

Chapter 13 has details and advice for planning your Web page and preparing your digital pictures for the Web.

AOL provides all the tools and services required to create Web pages with digital pictures and to share them with others. AOL's Web-creation tools — 1-2-3 Publish and Easy Designer — get you started. If you're already comfortable with Web building, you can use any HTML editor, or any major productivity application (like Microsoft Word, Publisher, and PowerPoint) to build a full-fledged site and make it available at AOL Hometown.

Cross-Reference

Chapters 9 and 10 go into detail about editing your pictures. You find out what features to look for in software, what you need to know about graphics, and how to use a specific program (MGI PhotoSuite III) to edit and improve your digital pictures.

Editing Digital Pictures

Using affordable software, you can make all sorts of changes to your digital pictures before sharing them, something you can't do with traditional prints. Here are a few examples of how you can edit digital pictures:

▶ Crop out part of the picture to highlight the subject.

▶ Fix common problems like red-eye, dust, and faulty color.

▶ Apply special filters and add special effects, as shown in Figure 1-4.

Figure 1-4. A special effect you can create in about a minute by using MGI PhotoSuite III. The Rain filter creates the effect of a streaky window on a drizzly day.

▶ Get your pictures ready for the Web — by reducing their file size, adjusting the number of colors they use, and putting them into the proper file format.

Buying Digital Cameras, Printers, and Scanners

To make full use of digital pictures, you may want to purchase some additional software and hardware. But don't feel like you need to rush right out and spend your money, because the longer you wait, the better and cheaper most of these products get. At the same time, the longer you wait, the longer you put off the pleasure of using this stuff. So now may be the time to take stock of what's available.

Tip

AOL Keyword: **AOL Shop Direct** (the same as AOL Keyword: **AOL Store**) takes you to AOL-tested and approved hardware and software.

Take, for example, high-end digital cameras, which offer enough resolution to compete nicely with the resolution of good film cameras; their only drawback is that they're still pretty pricey. Among the lower-resolution models — whose output is perfectly fine when you want to use digital pictures on the Web and in e-mail — the price is becoming affordable. You can find a good digital camera for online use for under $200.

You can find outstanding background information and product reviews for all major product categories and manufacturers at CNET's massive Web site (AOL Keyword: **CNET**), shown in Figure 1-5 (click the Hardware link to find the Cameras section). The digital camera product reviews provide in-depth information on the latest features in various cameras. CNET's Editors' Choices help you identify high-quality products, and categorize the products by price and manufacturer so you can make an informed choice. Finally, CNET's comparison pricing helps you identify what vendors sell particular scanners or printers at the lowest price, and then link to the online sites where you can purchase them online.

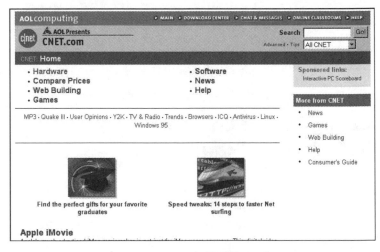

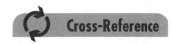

Cross-Reference

This book helps you understand what different types of products do (see Chapter 2) and gives you some tips for selecting digital cameras and scanners (see Chapter 7) and printers (see Chapter 11).

Tip

Use AOL Keyword: **Computing** for additional hardware and software resources and information.

Figure 1-5. CNET's Web site (AOL Keyword: **CNET**) provides an enormous amount of information about almost every type of computer product.

At AOL Keyword: **Personalogic**, you can find online Decision Makers — guides to help you select a printer, a digital camera, a scanner, and other consumer gear, based on your expressed preferences. These Decision Makers walk you through a series of decisions that help you narrow your choice to a product and price point that make sense for you.

Is It Safe to Buy Things Online?

Shopping online is safe and convenient at AOL's shopping channel, Shop@AOL (AOL Keyword: **Shop@AOL** or AOL Keyword: **Shopping**). Here are a few features of this channel:

▶ Products bought from AOL-certified merchants at Shop@AOL are backed by AOL's money-back guarantee.

▶ AOL protects you against credit-card fraud.

▶ AOL's Quick Checkout feature lets you enter credit-card information just once, so you can more quickly complete your future purchases at Shop@AOL.

▶ You can always reach AOL's customer service staff by chat, e-mail, message board, and phone.

When you're ready to make a purchase, check out Shop@AOL, AOL's online mega-mall, at AOL Keyword: **Shop@AOL**. The consumer electronics area contains so many large vendors — such as Egghead, Beyond.com, and Mattel.com — that you can search for specific products and then compare prices.

Summary

This chapter looked at the key aspects of digital pictures: how you get them and share them with your friends and family, how and where you can store them, how you can transform them with software, and what equipment you need to go further with them. For each aspect, you will find chapters and sections of this book where you can look for guidelines and step-by-step procedures. The next chapter looks at the specific types of equipment you need to create digital pictures.

GETTING DIGITAL PICTURES

A QUICK LOOK

Chapter 2

Getting Digital Pictures

No, you don't need to buy any new equipment to use "You've Got Pictures"; you can enter a new world of sharing images and creating fun projects by using the film camera you already have. After you take a roll of pictures, just have your film developed at your local photo lab, and the digital pictures will be sent directly to your AOL account. By investing in equipment beyond your film camera, however, you can greatly expand the sources from which you can acquire digital pictures — and have fun in the process.

Where Do Digital Pictures Come From?

Here are some types of equipment you may want to learn about if you want to do more with digital pictures:

▶ **A digital camera:** With a digital camera, you can take pictures just as with a traditional camera, but a major difference is that you can see your images right away. And as soon as you get back to your PC, you can transfer image files to your computer (more about that in Chapter 8), upload them to "You've Got Pictures," and start sharing them.

▶ **A scanner:** With a scanner, you can convert any old photographic print into a digital image (whether it's 100 years old or 1 day old), upload it to "You've Got Pictures," share it with others, and use it in other ways.

▶ **Video equipment:** Parts of the digital-video world are merging with the world of digital pictures. For your digital pictures, you can now draw upon both analog tapes (the kind made by your camcorder) and video files (the kind made by *digital-video* cameras, which I describe toward the end of this chapter).

▶ **Stock photographs:** With existing archives of stock photography and other sources of online photography, you can use digital pictures of people and places that you may never have the opportunity to photograph yourself.

All this equipment is continually becoming more affordable, better integrated, and more capable, so there's no rush to buy anything — unless you really need it. Now may be the time to take a look at what's out there and consider what you may want to purchase in the future. This chapter looks at each of these major sources of digital pictures.

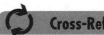
Cross-Reference

For more information about understanding and buying digital cameras, scanners, and video equipment, see Chapter 7.

Getting Digital Pictures from Digital Cameras

Using a digital camera is a simple, handy, and fun way to capture digital pictures. The best part is that you can view your pictures instantly so you can show off that big fish you just caught. Kids love to see pictures right away, so don't be surprised if they want to start using a digital camera right away,

2

Getting Digital Pictures

too. Digital cameras are becoming increasingly affordable, and offer convenience and options that film-based cameras can't match. Although they cost more than many traditional film cameras, you do save a considerable amount of money not having to pay processing costs. And although the picture quality is not 100% equal to that of film-based prints, digital cameras are more than adequate for any online use (e-mail and the Web). Figure 2-1 shows one of Kodak's digital cameras.

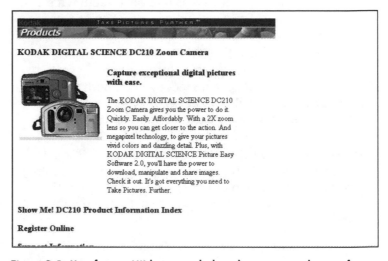

Figure 2-1. Manufacturers' Web sites are the best place to get complete specifications for just about every digital camera. For reviews and comparisons, start with AOL Keyword: **CNET** or one of the resources in Appendix A.

Using a digital camera is similar to using a traditional one. Many digital cameras even look just like film-based cameras on the outside, although some can be pretty funky-looking. On the inside, you usually have a choice of two or more resolution modes to use when capturing pictures. (*Resolution* refers roughly to sharpness, sometimes called *definition* in traditional photography. See Chapters 7 and 9 for more on resolution.) Finer resolution results in better-looking pictures, but the large files fill up your camera's memory more quickly.

Most digital cameras have a built-in viewer, called an *LCD screen* (see Appendix B), which allows you to see what your digital picture will look like before you take it. After you take the picture, you can quickly view the result in the same viewer. This feature enables you to delete not-so-good images to make room in your camera's memory for better ones. No more wasting money by developing pictures that you perhaps shouldn't have taken in the first place!

Instead of using film, digital cameras capture and store pictures electronically (see the sidebar "How Digital Cameras Work"). Because digital cameras let you start working with pictures right away, you avoid the delays and costs of the film-processing stage. Also unlike traditional cameras, you can easily edit your images by using software to improve or change the image. After they're edited, you can use the images in Web sites, upload them to "You've Got Pictures" and order prints, and e-mail them to friends and family.

How Digital Cameras Work

Traditional cameras record images on film coated with silver halide (a chemical that's highly sensitive to light). To retrieve the recorded image, the film must first be developed (creating negatives) and then printed (creating paper prints).

Digital cameras work differently. As with traditional cameras, you start with the click of a button, briefly admitting light through the camera's shutter. That's where the similarity stops. Images are recorded when the brief burst of light admitted through the shutter hits something called a charge-coupled device (CCD). The CCD converts light into a series of charges that are transmitted to the camera's memory, where they are stored.

A digital camera, like a computer, has *memory.* In memory, an image's color and tonal information is saved as tiny square picture elements, or *pixels.* If you're using a digital camera, the amount of memory determines how many pictures, of what file size (as determined by number of pixels per image), your camera can hold. When working with digital cameras, it's important to understand some of the relationships between pixels and image quality, a subject further discussed in Chapters 7 and 9:

Continued

How Digital Cameras Work *(continued)*

▶ A digital picture's resolution is measured in the number of pixels in the image (for example, 640 x 480).

▶ The number of dots (pixels) per *inch* (dpi) determines how big (in inches) an image of a certain resolution will be when printed out on a piece of paper.

▶ The resolution of a user's computer monitor (whether it's 800 x 600 or 1024 x 768, for example) determines how big that image will be on the monitor.

▶ A camera with a high resolution (1 million pixels per inch, for example) is not necessarily better than a camera with a lower resolution *if* your goal is to create online photo albums and make Web pages.

To transfer digital pictures from the camera's memory to your PC requires an adapter or a cable or card (which are all discussed in Chapter 7). After transferring the pictures to your PC, you can view and edit them, upload them to "You've Got Pictures" to order prints, share them, and so on.

Cross-Reference

Chapter 7 includes a detailed guide to scanner features, plus a list of shopping tips.

Getting Digital Pictures from Scanners

You can convert your existing photographs into digital pictures by using a scanner. A *scanner* is a piece of hardware that works like a photocopy machine. Instead of making a paper copy of a picture, however, the scanner makes a file that you can manipulate with your computer — you can view, edit, share, and publish the file online.

Scanning has gotten easy and inexpensive in the past few years. Very good scanners are quite affordable — to the $100 price point and below. Figure 2-2 shows an affordable scanner. With a scanner, you can convert just about anything available in print into a file that your computer understands and that you can share over AOL.

Figure 2-2. A simple, flatbed scanner available at AOL Keyword: **AOL Shop Direct**.

Scanners do more than create computer files of images. Many can be used to make copies and send faxes, as well as to scan photographic prints and documents. Most include a special kind of software, called OCR (optical character recognition), that can take a single image representing text (on a fax, for example) and convert it into text that you can actually edit with a word processor. A type of multifunction hardware mentioned in Chapter 7 delivers a scanner, printer, fax, and copy machine in one convenient package, often saving you money and always saving you space.

2

Getting Digital Pictures

To use a standard, flatbed scanner, you place your photo face down on the scanner's glass surface and press a button. You can usually also operate a scanner from your computer by using the scanner's software. (See Chapter 7 for more about types of scanners.) A light is drawn across your picture, creating a series of charges that are then converted line by line into a file — in most cases a JPG, just as with digital pictures (see Chapter 9 for more on file types). When the scan is complete, the scanner's graphics software usually opens automatically (unless you're using it to operate the scanner in the first place), allowing you to edit the new file, save it, or convert it to a different format. Chapter 8 provides an example of scanning an image.

AOL's Picture Gallery, discussed in Chapters 8–9, gives you the capability of starting and managing a scan with software (not a physical button).

Cross-Reference

Anything you do with video requires lots of hard-drive and other disk storage space. According to CNET, an hour's worth of digital video requires 13GB (gigabytes) of storage space. Chapter 7 reviews some of your storage options in this area.

Getting Digital Pictures Using Video Cameras

You're probably familiar with camcorders — cameras you use to take movies — and VCRs, which you use to play videos and record TV shows. With a video card (a gadget described shortly) and some video-editing software, you can convert your traditional videotapes into digital video suitable for e-mail and the Web. With a digital-video camera, it's even easier to import, edit, and use digital video.

Regardless of the source, video consists of many frames, each of which is a sort of digital picture (often called a *still*). Although video may seem like a tremendous source of digital pictures, it's important to remember that the video-camera lenses (digital and otherwise) lack the quality of still-camera lenses; the resolution is often less than you'd expect even with a digital camera intended primarily for Web and e-mail use. Also, there's no good way to compose or adjust the exposure of a single still. Digital videos offer real differences in quality over camcorders, but for the best digital pictures, you need a traditional camera or digital camera. Figure 2-3 shows you the Canon GL1 digital-video camera.

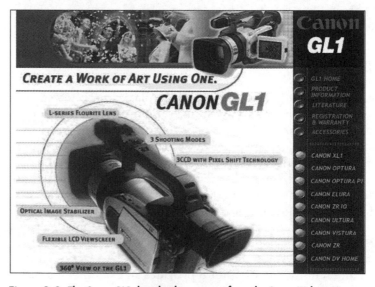

Figure 2-3. The Canon GL1 digital-video camera, from the Canon Web site (www.dvcanon.com).

Video stills can be used as digital pictures for cases where authenticity and documentation are more important then resolution and composition.

Video consists of many frames, each of which is a digital picture. Sort of. Although video may seem like a tremendous source of still pictures, it's important to remember that the lenses of video cameras (digital and otherwise) lack the quality of still-camera lenses. Furthermore, the resolution is often much less than you'd expect even with a digital camera intended primarily for Web and e-mail use. Have fun with digital video, but remember that you create the best digital images from traditional film cameras or from digital cameras with good image quality.

Using Stock Pictures

If you need a digital picture, you don't have to take it yourself. Sometimes, you can't take it yourself — if you need an image of a mountain or a person you've never seen, for example. Sometimes, you want a generic image conveying a business, educational, home, health-club, or other setting. Numerous companies supply *stock photography*, making available high-quality images of a wide range of subjects. Most such companies make their images available on the Web, on AOL, and via CD. On AOL and the Web, you can find many general sources of images to use in your own work. Here are a few sources you may want to check out:

> ▶ At AOL Keyword: **Photography** (in the AOL Interests Channel), the Photography Libraries (currently in the channel's list box) contain dozens of images you can help yourself to. This service does not really count as stock photography because it's not commercial; however, it does illustrate the occasional value of using others' images.

> ▶ On the Web, hundreds of stock-photography sites contain millions of images that you can use — sometimes for free, sometimes upon payment of a licensing fee. In every case, make sure to read the fine print about usage conditions and restrictions. One such site is Philip

Note

Chapter 4 has more to say on copyright issues, but for now, keep in mind that not every image you find on the Web is in the *public domain*. Except for the public-domain images at AOL Keyword: **Photography**, assume that all other images can be downloaded and used only with the express permission of the person who created the image. If your purposes are remotely commercial, it's especially important to get the appropriate written permission! For more information about your responsibilities in this area, visit AOL Keyword: **Copyright**.

Find It Online

For a guide to the dozens of specialized collections of digital pictures on the Web, one of the most valuable starting places is the Digital Librarian (`www.servtech.com/~mvail/images.html`).

Tip

To uncover stock photography sources, use AOL Search. Here's how: In the text box on the navigation bar, type **stock photography** and then add additional words (like **bird**) to focus your search. Click the Go button to see the sites returned by your search.

Greenspun's Stock Photography page (`db.photo.net/stock`), shown in Figure 2-4. Greenspun is a gifted photographer and an extremely informative writer about photography, and he makes his images available to "publishers, kids doing school projects, people who want have a polar bear as their screen background, et al." Make sure you read his detailed and interesting copyright notice before using any images.

▶ For professional jobs, you may want to look into a commercial source like EyeWire (`www.eyewire.com`).

Stock Photography

from Philip Greenspun

OK, well not exactly stock photography (no business guys standing in front of Venetian blinds, for example). But I have 6000 on-line images and I make them available to publishers, kids doing school projects, people who want to have a polar bear as their screen background, et al.

- Search
- Browse

- happy users of my images

Just about everything in this library is copyright Philip Greenspun.

Under the Hood

This is yet another of my RDBMS-backed sites. The underlying RDBMS is the old Illustra system (which Informix bought and rolled the features into Informix Universal Server but I haven't quite moved all of my stuff yet). The Web server is the AOLserver, which is why I was able to build this entire site in about an hour (in Tcl code written for the AOLserver API).

Figure 2-4. Philip Greenspun's Stock Photography archive (`db.photo.net/stock`).

Corbis: A Leading Stock Photography Source on the Web

One of the largest stock photographers is Corbis (`www.corbis.com`), a company that licenses tens of millions of images for personal and professional use. When you need high-quality images of obscure subjects and are willing to pay a few bucks per image, Corbis may be the place to start. You'll also find areas on Corbis devoted to projects you can make with digital pictures. Enjoy exploring this rich site.

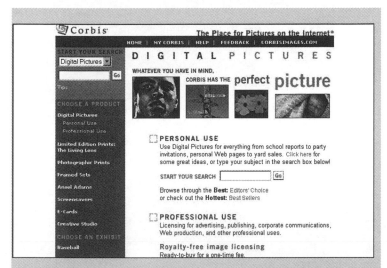

For example, say your daughter's doing an assignment on Native Americans of the Pacific Northwest. A Corbis search for **Makah**, a local tribe, brings up more than 20 digital pictures. To use such images, your child must provide the source of any image she uses.

Summary

Many people are perfectly happy with having their rolls of film developed and posted on "You've Got Pictures"; it's hard to match the convenience and simplicity. This chapter looked at some other sources of digital pictures: digital cameras, scanners, digital-video cameras, and stock-photography services. For the more adventurous types, digital cameras and scanners are a great source of pictures, which can then be uploaded to "You've Got Pictures" to order prints and to share with others. For larger projects, consider stock photography. For video and stills, the new breed of digital-video equipment provides a source of digital pictures as well.

Even though digital imaging has changed photography in many ways, considerations of light, subject, and composition apply to both film and digital photography. In the next chapter, you can brush up on some of the guidelines for taking good pictures and find out how they apply when you use a digital camera.

TAKING GREAT PICTURES

A QUICK LOOK

What kind of camera you use doesn't really matter. Photography is all about your eye, not your lens. Whatever camera you have, learn how to use all of its features. And don't get a camera that's so fancy you can't take the pictures you really want to take.

Taking a digital picture doesn't cost much, so feel free to experiment. Try new perspectives, look for new visual patterns, and take more casual people shots. And because potential photographs are everywhere, you can find inspiration just about anywhere you look.

Capturing everything that's going on in a scene can be fun, but what do you want people to focus on? What's important in the scene? Many photographers divide a picture into a grid of three evenly spaced horizontal and vertical lines. Wherever the lines intersect is often a good place for your subject. For people subjects, try to minimize distractions. For landscape subjects, try to provide a sense of scale by including something in the foreground.

Lighting can be the trickiest part of picture taking. A lack of light inside is why people use flashes; too much light is why pictures shot in bright light don't always come out very well. Sometimes it's better to take photographs on a cloudy day and to use a fill flash when you can't avoid photographing in bright sun.

Chapter 3

Taking Great Pictures

A big misconception is that digital photography is somehow better than traditional, film-based photography. That's just not true — so don't chuck your film camera for a new-fangled one quite yet. The fact is, you don't need expensive gear or even digital gear to take excellent pictures. Look at photographs by Ansel Adams or Robert Capa if you have any doubts about what can be done with film — and black-and-white film, at that.

You can use a beat-up old camera or even a disposable one. A good camera can be a big help, particularly in difficult or unusual lighting conditions, if you know how to use it. Many people never take advantage of even the basic technology they have at hand. So if you want to take consistently good pictures, the best advice is to use what your camera already has to offer. It's your eye that matters, after all, not the fancy or not-so-fancy or hopelessly confusing features on your camera.

Digital cameras differ from traditional cameras in many ways, some of which affect *how* you go about taking good pictures. Most important, digital cameras use computer memory instead of film. Since memory can quickly fill up, you need to start thinking of your pictures one at a time, deleting from your camera's memory the pictures you don't want. (Check your camera's manual to find out how. Most likely, you probably use the built-in viewer on the back of the camera to see and delete pictures in memory.) Composing pictures one at a time is, in any case, a key to taking good pictures.

Never Leave Home without It — Your Camera, That Is

Keep your camera handy and ready at all times. Great photos are often a matter of luck, and you increase your chances of getting lucky if you have the camera with you. If you have more than one camera, you may want to keep the most portable one in your purse, backpack, or car for unexpected moments. Fortunately, digital cameras are smaller and lighter than the clunkier traditional single-lens reflex (SLR) cameras, which have heavy bodies and bulky lenses.

With digital cameras, you don't use film, and memory is *reusable*. So when you find a great subject, take several pictures of it and delete the pictures that don't cut it. If you're an avid photographer, you may want to carry an extra memory card so you can take additional photos without taking the time of reviewing and comparing the pictures you've taken.

Tip

If you're using a traditional camera, always have an extra roll of film handy. And regardless of whether you're using a traditional or digital camera, always carry extra batteries in your camera bag.

3

Taking Great Pictures

See Actively

Look for inspiration everywhere you go. Examine the photos around you, in magazines, ads, and the newspaper. Consider how each picture was taken and how you would have composed the picture. For that matter, practice composing pictures even when you don't have your camera handy. Some photographers recommend carrying around a card with a cutout designed to represent the shape and size of your camera's viewfinder, so you practice your composition anywhere.

Taking Care of Your Camera

Whether you have a very expensive digital camera or a less expensive or older traditional camera, the rules are the same for maintaining your camera's life and keeping it working like new. Here are a few tips to help you take care of any camera.

▶ Keep the camera's body and lenses as clean and dry as possible.

▶ Avoid temperature extremes; don't take a cold camera indoors or otherwise warm it rapidly — you can damage it with internal condensation.

▶ Salt is bad for cameras, and obviously sand is not great either, so take particular care at the beach. If you have a single-lens reflex (SLR) camera, keep a clear filter over your lens to protect that expensive glass. All digital cameras are delicate and expensive to repair, so take special care when using them in sandy and wet conditions.

Tip

Don't buy a camera you're afraid to take anywhere — you're better off with a less expensive model that you're comfortable taking everywhere. The key may be to buy a camera that fits your needs and temperament. For example, if you often take pictures in rugged conditions, you're probably better off with a sturdy old (perhaps used) camera rather than a slick modern one full of delicate electronics.

Relax

For the best pictures of most subjects, concentrate on holding the camera as steady as you can. Common sense goes a long way here, but here are a few pointers:

▶ **Make sure that your body (posture) and hands (grip) are as comfortable as possible so you don't have to hurry a shot.** Improvise a tripod; *be* a tripod. Find something to rest your elbows on. Use whatever is handy to steady your body, arms, and camera — lean on a fence, lie on the ground, or use the partially open car window, with the engine turned off.

▶ **Hold your breath when you press the shutter release.** Squeeze the shutter release smoothly; don't rush or punch it. Especially with digital cameras, practice squeezing the shutter until you get a sense of the amount of touch required to activate it.

▶ **Use a tripod with a cable release or self-timer to make sure that you're steady.** If you don't want to carry a big tripod, buy a miniature one — some great tiny plastic folding ones are available. You may also want to get a Velcro strap to attach the tripod to a branch or pole.

▶ **Always take a second look before you click the shutter.** Scan the whole frame to look for potential distractions.

The Rule of Thirds

A general principal of composition, called the Rule of Thirds (see Figure 3-1), suggests that it's pleasing to the eye to break up the frame into thirds, either horizontally or vertically. The butterfly shown in Figure 3-2 is not centered, but shown off-center in such a way as to enhance the lines and suggested movement in the subject itself. (This area is highly subjective, and the shot could have been composed with a different focus.) Practice placing your subject roughly on one of these imaginary lines that divide up the frame — or at the intersection of lines dividing the frame horizontally and vertically.

Tip

With image-editing software, you can tighten compositions by *cropping out* (removing) extraneous material, replicating the effect of a rule-of-thirds composition even if it's not what you had in mind when you took the picture!

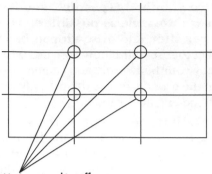

Consider positioning your subject off-center
on one of the points where the grid lines intersect.

Figure 3-1. The Rule of Thirds.

Figure 3-2. The blurred background highlights this off-center subject.

Focusing on Your Subject

Get close, especially when taking people pictures. When composing your pictures, trim away the clutter (which is called *cropping*). Clutter is not a pejorative term; it's just a way of referring to anything that's not your subject. Although editing software makes it simple to correct for many compositional problems (see Chapter 9 for details), why not start with a better picture, focused on the important subject and without the distractions? That way, you start with more "information" (in digital photography, more pixels) about your subject. If you're using editing software, the more information you start with, the more you can cut away without reducing quality. Figure 3-3 shows the difference in two pictures with successively reduced background clutter.

These marks show where part of the picture was removed.

Figure 3-3. Removing and blurring the background can result in a stronger composition that better highlights your subject.

Don't forget the rule of thirds when you frame your subjects. Just because a subject is the central focus doesn't mean it has to be in the center of the picture. Keep it off-centered, imagining the grid shown in Figure 3-1, with each set of intersecting lines a possible place for the subject.

Watching the Background

The tip to watch the background when composing your shots is the reverse of the advice to make your subject the most important part of your picture. You can easily end up with all sorts of distracting elements in the background of photographs, including things that appear to stick ridiculously out

Because digital pictures are inexpensive to take, try out new ways of seeing things and composing snapshots. For example, why not take a picture of *most* of a face?

If you're planning to pose, consider moving your subject into a neutral location so that there's nothing distracting in the background.

3

Taking Great Pictures

of people's heads, because you're concentrating on the subject in the foreground. Use plain and neutral backgrounds when possible or at least backgrounds that don't compete with your subject (see Figure 3-4). Finding neutral backgrounds is surprisingly difficult in many situations, especially at home. So if you're planning to take pictures, think ahead about where you can place the subject to limit such distractions — consider photographing your kitty in a big empty bathtub, for example.

Figure 3-4. Nothing in the background competes with this subject.

In Chapter 10, you find out how making the background blurry keeps the viewer's eye focused on the subject. Adding blur can compensate for the fact that many digital cameras don't give you control over which parts of your pictures are in focus and which parts are not (something called *depth of field*). Figure 3-5 shows the usefulness of blur, as does Figure 3-2.

Figure 3-5. The blurred background and strong contrast make for a dramatic, subject-focused, off-center picture.

Choosing the Best Angle

Sometimes it makes perfect sense to position yourself at your subject's level before taking the picture. In the case of children, for example, you want to crouch down to their eye level, instead of (as in real life) towering over them. When you're on their level, children are more comfortable and thus more natural in your photographs.

For inanimate subjects, you needn't take every photo at your eye level. Get close to that wall and capture its forbidding height by photographing it from the base, aiming your camera toward the sky. Squat, kneel, lie down, climb up a ladder. Find the predominant line of the image you want to photograph and take the picture either vertically or horizontally, as appropriate. For a pair of winding railroad tracks glinting in the sun, consider a horizontal shot, where the viewers' eyes are drawn from the left of the scene all the way to the right. For a pair of converging tracks on which you are standing, consider a vertical shot, holding the camera parallel to the ground. Try other ways, other lines, of leading into and out of the picture. Figure 3-6 illustrates ways of emphasizing line and angle.

Tip

Get wet, get dirty! Try taking photos you'd normally shoot straight on from above or below or from the back. The key to finding the best angle is experimentation.

Figure 3-6. The camera is on its side, emphasizing the strong vertical direction. It's close to the slide's surface to emphasize the child's experience. The photo is enhanced by the striking reflection.

Composing the Big Picture

Picture takers have a strong tendency to capture a dramatic landscape or other views with a shot showing the entire far-away scene presented as one big background, with nothing in the foreground. The problem with such an approach is that instead of capturing the dramatic experience that prompted the picture in the first place, you can often diminish its impact. Old camera or new, the straight-ahead, horizontal shot, with the subject at a uniform distance, is a good way to strip away some of the scene's intrinsic interest. With a digital camera, so few pixels are devoted to each part of a faraway scene that it may appear as a color blob. (The higher the resolution and steadier the camera, the more justice you'll do to the scene.) That's where framing, as shown in Figure 3-7, can come in handy.

Figure 3-7. A fresh view of the Washington Monument at cherry blossom time, with the foreground framing and reflecting the subject.

The blurry runner or biker in the foreground or the lovers holding hands provides a foreground as well as background, a sense of scale, and a human touch. Adding people to a scene is also one of the easiest ways to give viewers an idea of how big that tree is or how far it is up that cliff. Try shooting through a tree or bush or fence, even if it's blurry. Just about everyone has taken a picture that uses trees or branches to frame the distant mountain. Try other ways of framing. Surround the subject with a background of different contrast, color, or texture, for example.

Tip

Because of the amount of detail in trees, they're hard to photograph effectively with a digital camera. It's a case of too much information, too few pixels. Simpler and more solid forms often do better as subjects or backgrounds in pictures taken with digital cameras.

Seeing Differently

If you take pictures when you travel or during big events, consider shots other than that standard waterfall, monument, or church. Hey, that's what postcards are for, and it's usually hard to top a postcard's quality (or impersonality). If you want to try something different, start by looking around, wherever you are.

▶ Consider the small-scale shots — leaves, bugs, a cute baby's face, swaying grass, patterns of parked cars, and so on.

▶ Capture the unusual patterns often overlooked in a normal scene by looking for a visual pattern or getting close (see Figure 3-8). Creative picture-taking activities can even be a good way to encourage kids to notice things they would have ignored. Look for repeating patterns in landscapes as well as in grains of sand.

▶ Remember that flowers are photogenic not only at their peak, but also when they bud, dry, and wither. Industrial scenes can make for wild (if not necessarily beautiful) photos — the same with urban decay, parking lots, and shopping malls. Because we're stuck in these places much of the time, why not try to take a good picture there? With digital cameras, taking pictures is inexpensive. With image-editing software (explored in Chapter 10), you can further enhance your images with filters and other tools.

Note

Keep in mind that taking pictures of the ferns and rocks and the trail will help you remember that special time and give others a more complete sense of the place you were trying to capture.

Find It Online

Two Web sites highlighted in Appendix A provide examples of using photographs for documentary purposes: DoubleTake online (based on *DoubleTake* magazine) and Journal E. Documentary photography often has artistic value and serves a variety of educational and community purposes.

Considering Weather and Light

Pictures are made of light, so get used to gauging the light in your scene and try to shoot when the lighting is best. Generally what people consider the best weather conditions — clear bright blue skies — are the worst for taking pictures. Bright light tends to be more contrasty (sharp differences between highlights and shadows) than film can handle and puts harsh shadows in people's eyes. Plan ahead so you can be ready to shoot early and late in the day in these conditions. If you must shoot in harsh light or other bad conditions, such as very gray cloudy days, take it as a challenge; ask yourself "How can I work with this intense contrast to produce a good picture?"

Figure 3-8. A fallen-down Vermont barn, shot to emphasize the pattern of timbers and shadows.

Bright snow and sand scenes can baffle the built-in exposure meter in your digital or point-and-shoot camera, as can backgrounds that are brighter than your subject. Take a picture of a black labrador retriever on a bright day, and you're likely to get a black, underexposed blob because your camera averaged the lighting and didn't give the dog even light to get properly exposed. Figure 3-9 shows a backlit scene in which the face and sandcastle are correctly compensated.

Tip

AOL's PhotoCam has a setting available on its menu called W. Balance (white balance). With the white-balance setting, you first select the setting that best describes the current lighting condition (the PhotoCam choices are *daylight, shady, lamp, fluorescent,* and *auto*). The camera then attempts to calculate the best exposure for the whites in the image, figuring out the rest of the colors in relation to the whites. You may want to experiment with white balance before relying on it for important shots. *And don't use flash when you use white balance.*

Figure 3-9. Backlit scenes are not necessarily a disaster; fill flash rescued this one.

Tip

Learn how to use the different flash modes that your camera offers. That way if you find yourself in the midst of a forest with multicolored mushrooms everywhere, you'll know how to capture them. See Chapter 7 for more about flash.

This *back lighting* tends to mess things up because light is so unevenly distributed; everything is lit up but your subject. Many digital cameras offer something called *fill flash,* which you can use to lighten up deep shadows when you shoot a picture into the sun (or when your subject is otherwise lost in shadow). It may seem to make sense to photograph with your back toward the sun, but your subjects (people and animals at least!) will probably be uncomfortable.

Some of the most interesting pictures are taken in the worst weather. The next time you get a hard rain, grab your camera and umbrella and get out there. Try to capture the bouncing drops and running water. Likewise, snow blurring a scene can be much more interesting and uncommon than a photograph of the same scene after the snow stops.

Peopling Your Pictures

Photographing people is complicated, half psychology and half photography, and most photographers either love or hate shooting people. Here are a few general suggestions about photographing people:

▶ Try to capture people doing activities that they're comfortable and natural doing.

▶ Which is better: posed shots (see Figure 3-10) or candid shots (see Figure 3-11)? Neither; both can work if you pay attention to the purpose, subject, and setting.

▶ Use simple backgrounds.

▶ Avoid distractions in the picture; it's the subject who counts, unless the distractions provide some essential context that makes sense of what the subject is doing.

▶ Try to get the subjects' faces turned toward the light, rather than the shadow. If your camera has fill flash, use it to battle contrasty light and unwanted shadows.

▶ For unposed shots, wait a while before taking the picture. Sometimes I like to keep my other eye open to see everything that's going on and get a better sense of the whole picture. When the moment is right, taking multiple shots in succession can increase your chances of getting a good result.

Figure 3-10. A posed portrait that seems natural because the subject is comfortable.

Though candid shots can produce more interesting pictures, posing your favorite person — if he or she is not averse to the whole idea of being photographed — can be fun and imaginative, even if it's a bit contrived and you don't have fancy lights and gear. Use your imagination, try natural light, halogen desk lamps, whatever. Taking digital pictures is so inexpensive that you can continually experiment in ways like this.

Figure 3-11. Caught in the act — an unposed storyteller.

Experimenting with Motion

Trying to capture the exact moment a seagull's mouth opens to catch a flying french fry is fun and exciting, but it's not necessary to freeze motion in every single picture. After all, your goal is probably to get your viewer's attention and capture your experience, not to make an exact record of reality. Figure 3-12 shows a picture (of joggers) in which nothing is in focus, but the subject is still very clear. A dog bounding through a staid scene, appearing blurry in a slow-shutter-speed picture, may convey the experience of motion better than any freeze-frame effect. Similarly, long-exposure night shots — those streaks of light that cars, airplanes, and stars create across the frame — are fun to take. (Warning: Photographing stars requires patience, a warm coat, and a good tripod.)

Figure 3-12. Why does everything have to be sharp? Relative sharpness can create a strong effect, as with these joggers.

Definition

Panning is a method of picture-taking in which you move the camera to capture a wide horizon, complex setting, or moving subject, taking several shots in succession. With a digital camera, you can capture a wide horizon in this way, and then use image-editing software to stitch several images into one, usually long image.

One good method for taking action shots is to *pan* with the movement — that is, position yourself and your camera so that you can pivot your trunk to follow the marathon runners or cheetahs or whatever you're photographing. As the subject swings by, follow it with your camera, taking several pictures in progression to increase the chances that one of them captures the experience. With a digital camera, panning is *required* to take a series of shots that you can use to create a panoramic view of a horizontally oriented landscape. With editing software, you then take the individual shots and "stitch" them together to form a long panoramic picture.

Summary

This chapter very briefly reviewed some of the guidelines that photographers tend to follow. Because a photographer's goal is to take pictures that really say something or capture something special, straying from these guidelines can usually be justified for the sake of the goals. One of the best things about digital cameras is that you can be much more flexible in how and when you take pictures, so don't be afraid to experiment. Photos are everywhere in life, and so are pictures that could be taken.

Part II provides a complete reference to AOL's "You've Got Pictures": its features, its possibilities, and the many ways it can help you acquire, store, and share your digital pictures.

 Find It Online

Panoramic views are a much-loved trick of traditional photographers when they have to capture vast landscapes. The Library of Congress has created a digital collection of panoramic photographs as part of its American Memory Collection (`lcweb2.loc.gov/ammem/pnhtml/pnhome.html`). Panoguide (`www.panoguide.com`) shows you how to make your own panoramas out of digital pictures.

GETTING AND STORING
YOUR PICTURES ONLINE

A QUICK LOOK

Visit AOL Keyword: **Photo Developer** to find a place to drop off your film or to look for the address of a retailer who can develop your pictures by mail. In either case, you get your prints (as usual), and you also get your pictures delivered directly to your AOL account.

After your film is processed and available online, you can click the "You've Got Pictures" button on the Welcome screen to view your photos.

"You've Got Pictures" provides each AOL screen name unlimited online space for digital pictures. Find out how to manage your rolls and individual pictures to make the most of your space.

"You've Got Pictures" is where you keep your digital pictures online; your computer is where you keep and use them offline. When you see a photo you want to save to your computer, select the check box beside the picture and then click the Download Pictures button. If you already have digital pictures — from a scanner or a digital camera, for example — you can quickly upload them to "You've Got Pictures" for online storage and sharing.

Chapter 4

Getting and Storing Your Pictures Online

IN THIS CHAPTER

Getting your rolls developed

Having your pictures delivered online with "You've Got Pictures"

Viewing and saving your rolls and pictures

Downloading pictures from "You've Got Pictures"

Uploading pictures to "You've Got Pictures"

Downloading premium-quality files

Q & A

Q: Do I have to use a special camera to get my photos online with "You've Got Pictures"?

A: The best part about "You've Got Pictures" is that no special equipment or film is required. All you need is a regular camera (35mm, APS Advanced Photo System, or disposable camera), a computer, AOL, and a roll of film, and you're all set to get your pictures online!

Thanks to AOL's "You've Got Pictures" service, you don't have to buy a digital camera or scanner to get your pictures in digital form. All you need is a regular 35mm or APS (Advantix) camera, or even one of those inexpensive disposable cameras. When you take in your film to be developed, ask for "You've Got Pictures." Not only do you get your prints as usual, but your pictures are online in 48 hours. One-hour photo developers will post your pictures in a matter of hours.

Only AOL 5.0 gives you full access to everything "You've Got Pictures" has to offer. If you haven't yet installed AOL 5.0, visit AOL Keyword: **Upgrade** to learn about and obtain the newest software.

Finding a PhotoNet Dealer

Nearly 40,000 dealers participate in "You've Got Pictures" through their association with Kodak. The next time you take in your film to be developed, look for the "You've Got Pictures" option on the film processing bag or go to AOL Keyword: **Photo Developer** (see Figure 4-1).

Figure 4-1. Look for these logos on the film-processing bag.

Why not let your mouse do the walking, though? "You've Got Pictures" maintains a complete list of participating dealers at AOL Keyword: **Photo Developer**, or you can click the handy blue hyperlink on the "You've Got Pictures" main page (AOL Keyword: **You've Got Pictures**). Clicking this link takes you to the Photo Developer Dealer Locator, shown in Figure 4-2.

Cross-Reference

See Chapter 5 for ideas for sharing the pictures you collect at "You've Got Pictures."

Q & A

Q: Do I have to use a certain type or brand of film?

A: "You've Got Pictures" processes any brand of 35mm color print film, single-use cameras, and APS (Advanced Photo System) film.

Q & A

Q: Is "You've Got Pictures" available only to AOL members?

A: "You've Got Pictures" is an exclusive service for AOL members using AOL 4.0 or higher for Windows and Macintosh. "You've Got Pictures" is currently available only in the United States. Even so, you can share your digital pictures with anyone in the world who has access to the Internet. After the pictures are online, you can share them with anyone who has an Internet e-mail address, including non-AOL members. Both AOL members and non-members can download pictures and order picture gifts.

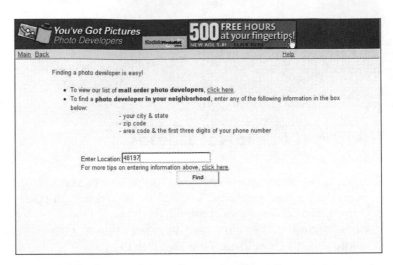

Figure 4-2. The Photo Developer Dealer Locator. In the text box, type your zip code, or your city and state, or your area code and first three digits of your phone number; then click the Find button.

With nearly 40,000 dealers on that list, AOL makes it easy to find photo developers in your own backyard. Just enter your city and state, or zip code, or your area code and the first three digits of your phone number in the Enter Location text box, click the Find button, and you receive a listing of "You've Got Pictures" dealers in your area. If your area has more than 20 participating dealers, click the Next button at the bottom of the list to see more listings (up to 100 in all). Regardless of whether your search turns up 100 dealers or none at all, you'll find a new Enter Location box at the bottom of the page, which makes it easy to try again.

AOL also provides a listing of mail-order photo labs that participate in "You've Got Pictures." Just look for the Click Here link on the Photo Developer Dealer Locator page.

Choosing a Photo Lab

Here are a few points to consider when choosing a photo processor:

▶ **Convenience.** AOL's photo dealers list makes finding a nearby dealer very easy. If no dealers are in your area or your search comes up empty, see the "Improving Your Search Results" sidebar. On the page listing the photo retailers in your neighborhood, or the empty page if there are no nearby retailers, click the Mail Order Photo Developers link for alternative, mail-in services such as Mystic Color Lab and York Photo.

▶ **Price.** Although the recommended price for "You've Got Pictures" is $5.99 per roll, dealers can and do charge more or less for the service. Some charge different rates depending on the number of exposures on the roll, while others charge a flat rate. Some require that you also order prints of a certain size or quality.

▶ **Range of services.** Most photo labs process only 35mm or Advantix print films and disposable cameras. Some labs offer additional services, including scans of 35mm slides, existing 35mm negatives, or even copies of old prints. If you need these extra services, it pays to make a few phone calls.

Dropping Off Your Film

You can drop off your film at most major supermarkets and large drugstores, or mail it in to many of the popular mail-order photofinishers.

Whenever you drop off your film, ask for the "You've Got Pictures" service, and check the AOL check box on the film processing envelope, shown in Figure 4-3. Then write in your AOL screen name; otherwise, the processor won't know where to send your digital pictures when they're finished. Your AOL account can have up to seven screen names, and you can send your pictures to nearly any screen name you choose. The exception? Screen names with Parental Controls set to Kids Only or Young Teens cannot access "You've Got Pictures."

Q & A

Q: How do I know which photo developers are participating "You've Got Pictures" dealers?

A: You can find a participating retailer by using AOL Keyword: **Photo Developer**. Just enter your city and state, or your zip code, or your area code and the first three digits of your phone number, and you receive a complete list of developers in your area.

Q & A

Q: Is the cost of "You've Got Pictures" added to my AOL account?

A: No. Because the cost of having your film uploaded to your AOL account via "You've Got Pictures" is added to the price of your film processing, you pay your retailer for your online pictures as part of the bill for developing the negatives and making the prints. Your film is then uploaded to "You've Got Pictures."

Some one-hour photo labs can do all the developing right on the premises — they have scanning equipment that sends the digital images straight to "You've Got Pictures." Bring in your film, return in one hour for your prints and negatives, and your digital pictures may be online before you get home!

Screen names with Parental Controls set to Kids Only or Young Teens cannot access "You've Got Pictures."

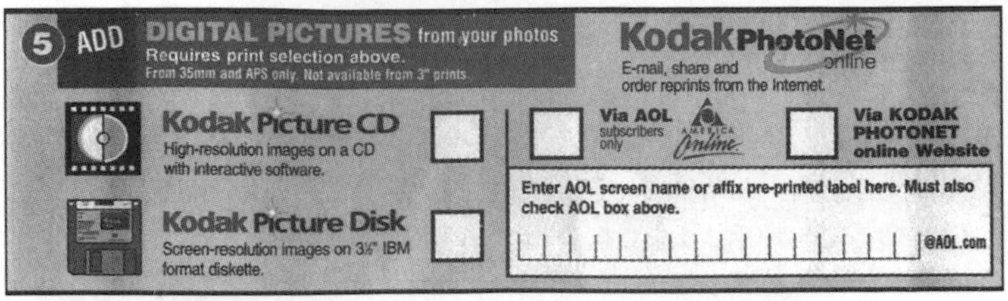

Figure 4-3. The Digital Pictures section of Rite Aid's photo processing envelope.

Don't worry if you'd rather not share your favorite screen name with the store clerk. You can preserve the privacy of your screen name by using a new screen name created just for the purpose of sharing pictures or by not supplying a screen name at all. As you'll see in the next section, you can access your pictures by using the Roll ID and Owner's Key, which you receive when you pick up your prints from the store.

Making Sure Your Photos Arrive Online

AOL has a safeguard to ensure that your online pictures don't show up in someone else's account. When AOL receives your pictures, the screen name you supplied to the photo dealer is compared to your AOL account information. If your screen name doesn't match the name and telephone number in AOL's account records, you will not hear "You've got pictures" (although you can access your pictures an alternate way).

Here are a few ways to ensure that your photos do reach you:

▶ Before you bring in your film to be developed, go to AOL Keyword: **Billing**, click the Change Your Name or Address link, and update your account information (only screen names with Master rights can access and change billing info).

▶ Be sure that the name, phone number, and screen name you give to the photo lab match the information you supplied to AOL Billing.

▶ Double-check all the information you supplied. All you have to do now is wait!

Picking Up Your Pictures Online

Waiting was sometimes the hardest part of traditional (film) photography. Many questions plague you between taking your pictures and getting the prints. Did the camera work? Are the exposures good? What about that wonderful sunset over the water or those precious shots of your retriever chasing the ducks?

Developing film used to mean dashing down to your favorite photo processor and dropping off your film. And waiting. "You've Got Pictures" can save you all this waiting around because picking up your (digital) pictures is just about as easy as getting your e-mail. Just sign on to America Online, go to "You've Got Pictures," and with a couple of clicks (see the "Viewing Your Pictures" section for details), you're looking at your pictures! Just to make sure, AOL also sends you e-mail notification that your pictures have arrived. If you use a mail-order lab, you have to wait for the U.S. Mail to do its work before you receive your prints, but you may receive your pictures online before your prints even arrive.

Right below the mailbox icon on your AOL Welcome screen is the "You've Got Pictures" icon, which now has a colorful little picture emerging from that film cannister, as shown in Figure 4-4.

Q & A

Q: How do I know when my pictures are online?

A: When the pictures are delivered to your AOL account, you receive an e-mail message from the screen name `AOL YouveGotPics`, indicating how to access your pictures. In addition, if you have AOL 5.0 for Windows, the "You've Got Pictures" icon on the main AOL Welcome screen changes from an empty film canister to one with a piece of film coming out of it, and a familiar voice announces "You've got pictures!" Click the icon or use AOL Keyword: **Pictures** to view your new roll.

Q & A

Q: How long does it take to get my pictures delivered online?

A: After you drop off your film, your pictures should be uploaded and online within 48 hours. If you drop off your roll at a participating one-hour photo lab, your pictures may be online in a matter of hours.

"You've Got Pictures" icon

Figure 4-4. If your digital pictures have arrived, you hear "Welcome! You've got pictures!" when you sign on.

Viewing Your Pictures

Viewing your pictures online is the equivalent of tearing open the envelope containing your brand-new prints. First, you have to sign on to AOL with the screen name you gave to the photo lab. After you're connected to AOL, click the "You've Got Pictures" icon on the AOL Welcome screen (see Figure 4-4), or use *any* of the following AOL keywords to access "You've Got Pictures":

▶ **YGP**

▶ **You've Got Pictures**

▶ **Pictures**

Near the top of the "You've Got Pictures" page, shown in Figure 4-5, you find four *tabs* (which are sort of like the index tabs in a notebook): New Rolls, Saved Pictures, My Albums, and Buddy Albums. For now, focus on the New Rolls tab. If it isn't already selected, click the New Rolls tab to display the New Rolls page. If you have a roll (or rolls) waiting for you, the New Rolls page displays automatically.

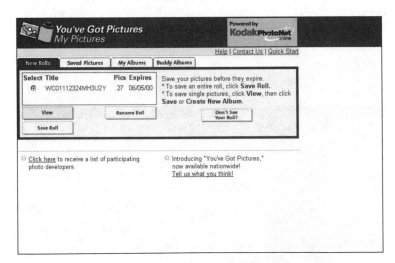

Figure 4-5. The "You've Got Pictures" main page, showing a new roll of pictures.

Every new roll of pictures that you receive is stored at "You've Got Pictures" for 30 days. Listed next to each roll is a title, the number of exposures, and the expiration date of that roll. Any images that you don't save (see "Managing Your Digital Pictures," later in this chapter) by the end of that 30-day period are deleted, just as old e-mail is deleted from your online mailbox.

Viewing a Roll

Right below the list of new rolls are four buttons — View, Rename Roll, Don't See Your Roll, and Save Roll. The first thing you want to do is view your new pictures. To do so, make sure to click inside the circle (so that it's selected) next to the roll you want to view and click View. Within moments the Roll Viewer page opens, displaying every image on the roll, as shown in Figure 4-6. If you have more than one roll of film, you can select and view any roll to see the individual digital pictures.

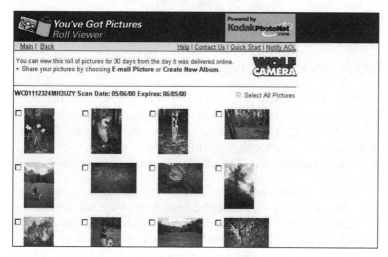

Figure 4-6. The Roll Viewer page displays every photo on your roll. Click a picture to see a larger image.

The images you see, often called *thumbnails*, are pretty small (otherwise they wouldn't all fit on one page). Click one of the images to see a larger version of the picture (see Figure 4-7). As an alternative, you can select the check box alongside a picture and then click the View Full Picture button at the bottom of the Roll Viewer page.

Q & A

Q: How long are my new rolls of pictures available to me on AOL?

A: Your new rolls remain in the New Rolls area of the My Pictures page for 30 days from the day they are delivered to your AOL account. As expiration nears, you receive two e-mail reminders letting you know that your rolls are about to expire. When your pictures expire, they are deleted from the system. Be sure to save the pictures you want to keep as soon as possible.

Tip

If your pictures have been deleted from "You've Got Pictures" and you have the prints, you can scan them and upload them to "You've Got Pictures." That way, you can have specific pictures online, whenever you want. You can find uploading procedures later in this chapter and scanning instructions in Chapter 8.

Click either of these buttons with your mouse to go back to the Roll Viewer page.

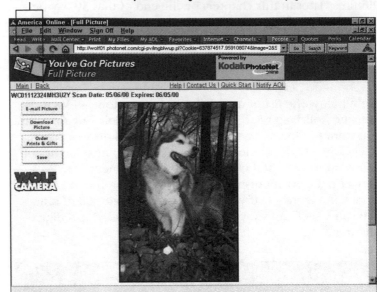

Figure 4-7. The larger version of one of the thumbnail images shown in Figure 4-6.

Ah, that's better! Now you can really see what's going on. Notice the Next Picture and Previous Picture buttons below that picture, and the thumbnail (small-sized) preview of those other pictures. Click either button to move through your roll, displaying a larger-sized image of each photo as you go.

If you'd rather not step through the roll one shot after another, like a slide show, click the Back link at the top left of the Full Picture page or click the Back button on the navigation bar. You skip right back to the Roll Viewer page, where you can select a different picture to view up close.

Renaming a Roll

Tip

The original roll ID and owner's key don't change. If you just got back ten rolls of digital photos following your vacation, Rename is a very handy feature.

After you have a good look at a roll, you will probably want to change its title from WC01112324MH3U2Y (or whatever random number the photo processor dishes out) to something more descriptive. If you're not already there, open the New Rolls page (see Figure 4-5), click a radio button to select the roll you want to rename, and click the Rename Roll button. This opens the Rename Roll page.

The roll name that you choose can contain 20 characters, including letters, numbers, spaces, and common punctuation marks. The name change is only for your convenience.

"You've Got Pictures" — But Still Missing a Roll?

There's nothing worse than thinking your pictures have been lost, which is why "You've Got Pictures" has a button especially for people who can't find their pictures. On the New Rolls page, click the Don't See Your Roll button, which opens the page shown in Figure 4-8.

You've Got Pictures

Help | Contact Us

You can retrieve a roll of pictures not listed under **New Rolls**.
* Enter the **Roll ID** and the **Owner's Key** below.
* Click **OK**.

Roll ID: WC01112324MG3T4W

Owner's Key: F4F44

Tips
* Your Roll ID and Owner's Key are located on the claim card inside the envelope containing your prints.
* If you do not have your prints, please pick up your prints and negatives from your photo developer.
* If a claim card was not included with your prints, and you have the envelope or the customer receipt, click here for Customer Service.

[Ok]   [Cancel]

Figure 4-8. Retrieve missing rolls on the Don't See Your Roll page.

Every roll of film scanned by "You've Got Pictures" gets a unique Roll ID and an Owner's Key, both of which are printed on a card that comes inside the envelope containing your prints. Just type them into the appropriate boxes in the Don't See Your Roll page and click the OK button at the bottom of the page.

On this page, you can also retrieve rolls that were sent to a different screen name, (for example, if a family member wants to give you ownership of the pictures). Don't use this feature if all you want to do is share your pictures with someone else. There are better ways to do that, as you see in Chapter 5.

Caution

If you use the Roll ID and Owner's Key to retrieve pictures that were saved under another screen name or another person's account, that roll disappears from the other screen name's New Rolls list.

Cross-Reference

For more on sharing pictures, see Chapter 5.

4

Getting and Storing Your Pictures Online

Your pictures may not have arrived in your New Rolls window for several reasons:

▶ You gave the photo lab a different screen name. Look at the envelope from the photo lab. It should show the screen name that was used for "You've Got Pictures." Switch to the screen name you gave to the lab and see if your pictures are there.

▶ There was a typographical error in your screen name, or you misspelled your screen name. If you see a typo or misspelling, use the Roll ID and Owner's Key to retrieve your photos.

▶ The name or telephone number you gave to the photo lab doesn't match your AOL account information and screen name(s). This security measure prevents the wrong person from accidentally receiving your photos, but may also prevent you from accessing your photos. Go to AOL Keyword: **Billing**, click the Change Your Name or Address link, and type in your current information. *Note:* Only Master screen names can change AOL Billing information.

Q: How can I keep my pictures from expiring in 30 days?

A: To save your pictures before they expire, store them online on your Saved Pictures tab. AOL provides its members with free storage space for pictures, and once they are stored online, your pictures don't expire — unless you delete them from your Saved Pictures space. You can also download them to your hard drive or to a floppy disk.

What happens if you didn't get a card or other document containing a Roll ID and Owner's Key? Make sure that you requested "You've Got Pictures." Double-check the processing envelope to find out whether you checked the option and the lab charged you for that service. If you're sure that you should have pictures, go to the Don't See Your Roll page and look for the tip that says, "If a claim card was not included with your prints, or if you need further assistance, click here for Customer Service." This takes you to the Customer Service Roll Assistance page, shown in Figure 4-9, which helps you find your missing pictures.

You've probably noticed a few more buttons along the bottom of the Roll Viewer page and down the left side of the Full Picture page: E-Mail Picture, Create New Album, Save, Download Picture, and Order Prints & Gifts. We discuss these options later in this chapter and in Chapter 5.

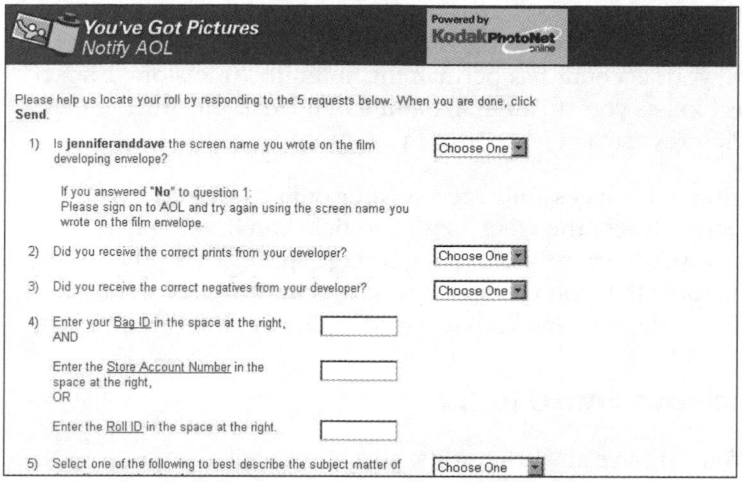

You've Got Pictures
Notify AOL

Powered by
Kodak PhotoNet online

Please help us locate your roll by responding to the 5 requests below. When you are done, click **Send**.

1) Is **jenniferanddave** the screen name you wrote on the film developing envelope?   [Choose One ▼]

   If you answered "**No**" to question 1:
   Please sign on to AOL and try again using the screen name you wrote on the film envelope.

2) Did you receive the correct prints from your developer?   [Choose One ▼]

3) Did you receive the correct negatives from your developer?   [Choose One ▼]

4) Enter your <u>Bag ID</u> in the space at the right, AND   [   ]

   Enter the <u>Store Account Number</u> in the space at the right, OR   [   ]

   Enter the <u>Roll ID</u> in the space at the right.   [   ]

5) Select one of the following to best describe the subject matter of   [Choose One ▼]

Figure 4-9. AOL helps you find your missing roll of pictures.

Managing Your Digital Pictures

After you successfully receive your pictures, the clock begins to tick. You have 30 days of free online storage for your new roll(s). After 30 days, the pictures that you've chosen to save remain online until you delete them yourself; all unsaved digital pictures are deleted. You have to decide whether you want to save some or all of those pictures, or let them disappear from your account. Or you can download the pictures to your PC and save them for as long as you want.

Saving Individual Pictures

When all the pictures in a roll are displayed in the Roll Viewer (shown in Figure 4-6), you can save one or more pictures by selecting the check box next to any picture and then clicking the Save button at the bottom of the page. Or, to save all the pictures on your roll, select the Select All Pictures radio button before clicking Save.

Q & A

Q: I'm trying to purchase merchandise, but AOL won't let me. What's going on?

A: Premium Services access must be "turned on" for a particular screen name in order for someone using the screen name to purchase any gift items, prints, or Premium Offer downloads. To enable this feature, you need to be signed on to a Master Account. Then go to AOL Keyword: **Parental Controls**, click Set Parental Controls, and in the drop-down list, select the screen name for which you want to add Premium privileges. Scroll to the last Custom Control and set it to Allow Premium Services.

Your digital pictures are saved (stored) online. You get 30 days free rent with every roll you process, and *every screen name* on your account has permanent, unlimited free storage space as long as you are an AOL member and visit the "You've Got Pictures" area at least once in a 6-month period.

After you successfully receive your online photos at "You've Got Pictures," the clock begins to tick. You have 30 days to save your new roll(s) to your storage space. After 30 days, the pictures that you've chosen to save remain online until you delete them yourself; all unsaved digital pictures are deleted.

Saving Entire Rolls

You can save an entire roll with a few clicks of your mouse, if you have enough online storage space for all those pictures. Just follow these steps:

1. Click the New Rolls tab on the "You've Got Pictures" main window.
2. Select the roll that you want to save by clicking Select (adjacent to that roll).
3. Click the Save Roll button toward the bottom of that screen. A new window appears, asking whether you're sure you want to save the roll.
4. Click OK or Cancel, depending on your needs.

If you don't have enough storage space for all the pictures on the roll, "You've Got Pictures" allows you to purchase more storage space. After your roll has been saved, you find all the pictures under the Saved Pictures tab.

Downloading Pictures to Your Computer

If "You've Got Pictures" is such a useful way to collect your digital pictures, why would you want to download them to your own computer? Here are a few reasons:

▶ To edit them with image-editing software such as MGI PhotoSuite (see Chapters 9 and 10 for a full discussion).

▶ To use your digital pictures in Web pages (see Chapter 13).

▶ To use your digital pictures in photo activities for work or home, including greeting cards, family trees, newsletters, and invitations (see Chapters 12 and 14).

▶ To free up storage space in "You've Got Pictures."

Downloading without Pain

When you download files of any type, you copy them to your computer. In doing this, you are *not* removing them from the source from which they are downloaded. "You've Got Pictures" lets you download one or several pictures at a time; you can even download an entire roll. Follow these steps to download digital pictures:

1. Go to AOL Keyword: **Pictures**.

2. If you have previously saved the pictures, click the Saved Pictures tab, shown in Figure 4-5.

   If the pictures are part of a new roll, click the New Roll tab, select the roll you want to view, and click the View button. From there, you can see a set of small pictures from which to select.

3. Find the picture you want to download and select the check box next to it. You can download more than one picture at a time by selecting more than one check box. Or you can click the Select All Pictures radio button in the upper-right corner of the window to select all the pictures.

4. Click the Download Pictures button at the bottom of the page.

Q & A

Q: If I ever need to delete my current screen name or cancel my AOL account, can I keep my pictures?

A: If you plan to delete a screen name that contains saved pictures or albums, simply create an album that includes all the pictures you want to keep (up to 100, including pictures drawn from Buddy Albums, as explained in Chapter 5) and share it with another screen name on your account. Then, sign on with the new screen name and be sure to save the album before you delete your old screen name. To keep your pictures offline, you can download them in one big file (or several smaller files), as explained in Chapter 8. Once a screen name has been deleted, other albums you have created will be lost, and those with whom you have shared Buddy Albums will no longer have access.

The more often you download digital pictures from "You've Got Pictures," the more you'll appreciate a *broadband* (high-speed) Internet connection. As a matter of fact, AOL is creating entire new types of multimedia content designed to take advantage of broadband. For more information about broadband, visit AOL Keyword: **AOL Plus**.

Q: Is it possible to download several pictures or a whole roll at once?

A: Yes, when viewing the roll you want to download, select a group of pictures by clicking inside the check box next to the pictures you want. Or select the entire roll by selecting the Select All Pictures radio button. Then click the Download Pictures button, select the download option, click OK, and all the pictures you have selected are downloaded at once, in one big file. "You've Got Pictures" assigns each picture a unique number. After the download is complete, you can give your pictures useful names and copy them to different folders on your hard drive.

5. On the next page (shown in Figure 4-10), select one of these resolutions:

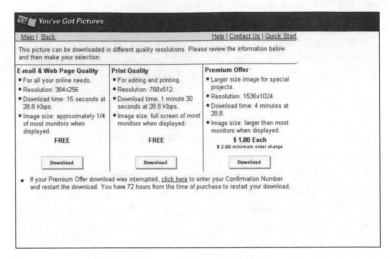

Figure 4-10. When downloading a picture, you have a choice of two free downloads, and a third, premium download. The pictures vary in resolution.

- **E-mail & Web Page Quality:** Select this resolution if you'll be using your digital picture as an e-mail attachment or on a Web page.

- **Print Quality:** Select this resolution if you want to print the picture or edit it with graphics software.

- **Premium Offer:** This is the highest resolution, appropriate for those important pictures and special projects. See the Premium Offer information on the page for more info about this option. Skip ahead to the "Purchasing the Highest-Quality Digital Pictures" section for information about special orders.

6. If you select the Premium Quality resolution, you can skip the remainder of these steps. If you select the E-mail and Web Page Quality option or the Print Quality option, click the Download Pictures button in the page that appears.

7. In the File Download dialog box, shown in Figure 4-11, make sure that the Save This Program to Disk radio button is selected and then click OK.

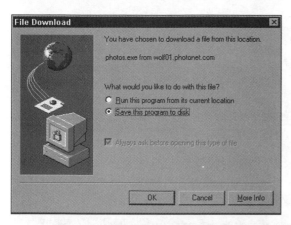

Figure 4-11. You see this dialog box when you begin the downloading process.

8. In the Save As dialog box (shown in Figure 4-12), indicate where you want the pictures to be saved.

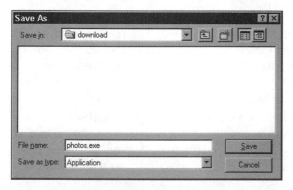

Figure 4-12. Here you indicate where you want to download your picture(s).

While the picture downloads, the Windows Download dialog box tracks its progress. When the download is done, the dialog box reads Download Complete, as shown in Figure 4-13. Do *not* put a check in the Close This Dialog Box When Download Completes check box.

Note

Keep in mind that with high resolutions, the picture is larger, the download time is longer, and the print quality is better.

Caution

When you download pictures, "You've Got Pictures" downloads them by default to America Online's Download folder. It's usually fine to accept that choice in the Save As dialog box. However, "You've Got Pictures" saves *all* downloaded pictures as a file called photos.exe (on the Mac, the file is called photos.sit). Because every picture you save in the Download folder has the same name, the second photos.exe file that you download replaces the first one, the third replaces the second, and so on. Therefore, don't download digital pictures until you've extracted pictures from the previous photos.exe! After you've extracted pictures from photos.exe, the individual picture files have their own names and can be stored in any folder, so you don't have to worry about accidentally replacing them with new pictures.

4

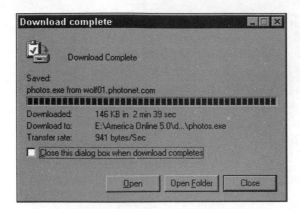

Figure 4-13. The digital picture(s) have been successfully downloaded. Click the Open Folder button to continue.

Before you can view the pictures you downloaded, you need to extract the pictures from the file you just downloaded by following these steps:

1. Click the Open Folder button (see Figure 4-13) in the Download Complete dialog box. You now see the contents of the America Online 5.0/Download folder (or the folder in which you chose to save your downloaded pictures). The file, photos.exe, is highlighted.

2. Double-click the downloaded file. The progress of "extracting" your pictures from photos.exe is shown in a small text window with a black background. During the process, the file or files containing your digital picture(s) are listed. The names of the picture files have weird numbers, so you may want to make a note of these numbers. For each picture being extracted, you'll see a line that reads

   Inflating: /.X67N_001.jpg

   In place of X67N_001.jpg and X67N_002.jpg, and so on, you'll see the names of the files with *your* pictures.

3. Your digital pictures can now be viewed! Scroll through the Download folder to find your file. See Figure 4-14.

Figure 4-14. A computer file with a digital picture, ready to be viewed (for example, 3t4w_013.jpg).

4. Double-click the file to view it. A default image-viewing application such as Windows Paint Shop Pro then opens. Or, from AOL, select the file using File⇨Open or File⇨Open Picture Gallery.

   Windows 98 associates every major file type (JPG in this case) with a specific application. Double-click a JPG file, and the associated application program opens, displaying the file. To change the way Windows handles associations and to see your pictures in the program of your choice, you may want to look at Chapter 9.

Renaming and Copying Your Downloaded Pictures

To view your pictures, choose File⇨Open Picture Gallery from the AOL toolbar. Navigate to the folder that contains the downloaded pictures and click the Open Gallery button to see your images.

The first thing you'll notice about a downloaded digital picture is the weird file name, something ugly like ZHUW_007.jpg, or worse. Such numbers are useless because they have no relationship to the content of your picture.

Q: I downloaded my pictures to my computer, but I can't find them. Where did they go?

A: Most often, pictures are automatically downloaded to your America Online Download folder and are, by default, called photos.exe. If they aren't there, try searching your computer by using your computer's Find or Search tool. After you locate the pictures, note the folder name. Then choose File⇨ AOL Picture Gallery from the AOL toolbar and navigate to the folder that holds your pictures. After you open the file in the AOL Picture Gallery, your pictures appear as a series of numbers. Double-click a picture to view it. The Picture Gallery is discussed in Chapters 8 and 10.

4

Getting and Storing Your Pictures Online

Q & A

Q: Can I download my pictures to a floppy disk?

A: Yes, but you first need to download your pictures to your hard drive and then copy them to your disk. After you have downloaded and extracted your picture(s), insert the disk into the floppy (A:) drive. In Windows Explorer, right-click the file that contains the picture you want to copy to your disk and choose Copy. Still in Explorer, navigate to your floppy drive, right-click the A: drive designator, and choose Paste. The picture is then copied onto the floppy disk. Repeat this process for each picture.

Tip

Choose Cut instead of Copy if you want to remove the file from the folder into which it was downloaded and avoid cluttering up your hard drive.

To rename a picture you've just downloaded, follow these steps:

1. Find the folder that contains the file you want to rename (which is probably the Download folder) and then right-click the file you want to rename.

2. Choose Rename from the context menu that appears.

3. Type in a new filename for the picture but don't change the file type (the .JPG part). You may want to rename your files with AOL Picture Gallery open, so you can quickly match the filename to what's in the actual picture.

Next, you need to copy your pictures to the folder in which you'll be storing and using them. (For more about creating, arranging, and naming folders, see Chapter 8.) To copy picture files from the folder into which they were download to another folder, follow these steps:

1. Open Windows Explorer and display the folder into which you want to copy the downloaded pictures.

2. Double-click the Download folder or whatever folder you used to download from "You've Got Pictures."

3. For a single picture, just click it once to select it. For more than one picture, hold down the Ctrl key and click each picture you want to copy. For many pictures in a row, hold Shift and click the first and last pictures in the sequence. When you're done, right-click and choose Copy.

4. Switch to the folder you selected in Step 1. Then right-click the folder and choose Paste. Your pictures are then copied into the folder.

Purchasing the Highest-Quality Digital Pictures

When you have your digital pictures delivered online, they're available in several different versions, as described in "Downloading without Pain." The Premium Service from

"You've Got Pictures" lets you download high-resolution, print-quality versions of any digital picture. To use this service, the image must have a sufficiently high resolution (you'll be told if it doesn't!). Digital pictures you upload from your computer may lack this minimal resolution. See "Uploading Pictures to 'You've Got Pictures.'"

To order a high-resolution file, simply follow the procedures in "Downloading without Pain." In Step 5, click the button in the Premium Offer section. You then see the window shown in Figure 4-15. The window shows what you have selected to download, how many pictures you are downloading, and the unit cost and total costs. Each row displays a single item in your "You've Got Pictures" shopping cart; an item can consist of more than one digital picture.

In this window, you can complete your order, change or cancel it, or continue shopping in the "You've Got Pictures" store. This way, you can batch your orders and avoid multiple mailings.

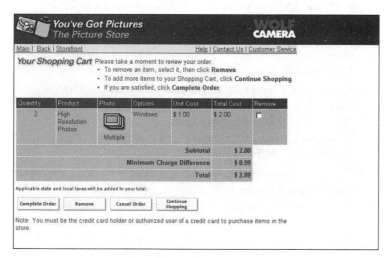

Figure 4-15. Downloading a high-quality image.

Here are your options at this point:

▶ **Complete your order.** Click the Complete Order button to enter the information shown in Figure 4-16: your credit card type, number, and expiration date, along with your full name.

Note

Downloading high-resolution images incurs a minimum charge of $3.00, and each image that you download costs $1.00. If you select fewer than three pictures, you see a number in the Minimum Charge Difference box, which reports the difference between the number of pictures you selected and the $3.00 minimum. It makes sense to download at least three pictures per order. If you do order more than three pictures, the Total Cost reflects the number of pictures in the order times $1.00 per picture.

Tip

AOL Quick Checkout is a service provided throughout Shop@AOL (AOL Keyword: **Shop@AOL**), an online shopping mall featuring hundreds of AOL-certified vendors. When you register for Quick Checkout, the credit card and billing info you provide is saved for use the next time you're at a participating Quick Checkout merchant (such as "You've Got Pictures"). You won't have to provide all the details again, and your checkout will be that much faster. Visit AOL Keyword: **Quick Checkout** to learn more and to sign up.

4

Getting and Storing Your Pictures Online

Figure 4-16. Type your credit card information here.

Q & A

Q: Can I download pictures as many times as I want?

A: Both the E-mail & Web Page Quality and the Print Quality downloads are free, and you can download as many pictures, as many times, as you want. However, if you choose the Premium Offer, downloads cost $1.00 per picture, with a minimum of $3.00 per order.

Click Next, and you come to a page where you supply your address and other billing information. Clicking Next brings up the final page, in which you confirm the details of your order: what you're ordering, how much it costs, how you're paying, and your billing information.

Click Next to see a final summary of your purchase details. Click Continue to process the order. A final page shows that your order has been completed. Click OK to acknowledge the message and continue working and playing at "You've Got Pictures."

▶ **Remove an item.** To remove an item without canceling the whole order, select the Remove check box (click inside the box) and then click the Remove button. If you have several items in your shopping cart, removing one item leaves the others untouched. Removing all of the items in your shopping cart amounts to the same thing as canceling your order.

▶ **Cancel your order.** Click the Cancel Order button if you don't want to buy anything. After clicking Cancel, you'll be asked to confirm the cancellation.

▶ **Continue shopping.** Click this button to pay a visit to the "You've Got Pictures" store, where you can buy a mouse pad, T-shirt, or other items with the digital picture of your choosing (see Chapter 6 for more about the goodies available here). After visiting the store and perhaps purchasing an item, you can return to the Premium Offer area by clicking the browser's Back button repeatedly.

Uploading Pictures to "You've Got Pictures"

From time to time, you may want to *upload* digital pictures to "You've Got Pictures" in order to share them with others by e-mail or as part of an online album. (Uploading means *copying* a file from your computer to an Internet-connected computer.) Uploading stores your images online at "You've Got Pictures", along with your other saved pictures. Anything you can do with pictures processed by a "You've Got Pictures" photo processor and stored on "You've Got Pictures" can be done with any pictures you upload from your computer. You can

▶ Share them with others using the "You've Got Pictures" e-mail and albums (see Chapter 5)

▶ Use them in products such as coffee mugs and the like (see Chapter 6)

Here's how the uploading process works:

1. Go to AOL Keyword: **Pictures**.

   • Click the Upload button on the main page or from the Saved Pictures or My Album tab.

   • To upload a picture to your collection of up to 50 stored pictures on "You've Got Pictures," click the Saved Pictures tab and then click Upload Picture.

   • To upload a digital picture to a specific album (a collection of digital pictures you can maintain at "You've Got Pictures"), click the My Albums tab, select the radio button to the left of the album into which you want to import the picture, and click Upload Picture. Albums are discussed in Chapter 5.

Q & A

Q: I have digital pictures on my hard drive. Can I upload them and create albums?

A: Yes. You can upload your digital photos to "You've Got Pictures" and organize them into albums, share them with your friends and family, and order prints and gifts from them. You can find the Upload button in both the Saved Pictures and My Albums areas, and on the main page at AOL AOL Keyword: **Pictures**.

Any picture stored on your computer's hard drive, a disk, a CD, or even a scanner can be easily added to your albums by using the Upload feature. Each uploaded picture fills one available picture space in your Saved Pictures area. You can use the uploaded picture just like you use all of your other stored pictures, including adding it to an album, sharing it in e-mail, or having it printed on a T-shirt or mug. Chapter 8 goes into more detail about scanning.

Note

You can upload only one picture at a time to "You've Got Pictures," but you can download several at a time.

4

Getting and Storing Your Pictures Online

2. Follow the instructions on the screen: Preview the picture before uploading it and then click Upload Picture to upload it.

"You've Got Pictures" can display pictures in several popular graphics file formats, including JPG (or JPEG), GIF, and BMP. "You've Got Pictures" recommends that your images have a resolution of at least 640 x 480 if you intend to order picture merchandise with those images. See Chapter 6 for more information on "You've Got Pictures" merchandise.

Q & A

Q: How safe is it to share albums, and can anyone, other than those I designate, access my pictures?

A: The "You've Got Pictures" service is a confidentially secure space, just like AOL e-mail. Only those people you specify on your Shared List (see Chapter 5) can access your pictures, allowing you to safely share your albums with those you know and trust. However, be aware that the people with whom you share your album can also download your pictures to their own "You've Got Pictures" space as well as share them with their friends and family.

Safety Considerations

America Online has a well-deserved reputation for providing a safe and secure online environment, and "You've Got Pictures" has been made safe for minors. "You've Got Pictures" provides a thorough discussion of online safety and security issues in its Help area, which can be reached by clicking the Help link on any "You've Got Pictures" page, or by using AOL Keyword: **You've Got Pictures Help**. There's no room here to duplicate all that information, so be sure to visit "You've Got Pictures" Help very soon, especially if you have children.

Understanding AOL's Terms of Service

"You've Got Pictures" is covered by AOL's Terms of Service (TOS), which governs members' conduct on AOL. "You've Got Pictures" has its own set of rules regarding the special conditions that can arise when using and exchanging digital pictures. In addition to the usual prohibitions of sexually explicit, obscene, and defamatory material, "You've Got Pictures" has rules regarding issues such as soliciting business and infringing copyright.

Keeping Kids Safe at "You've Got Pictures"

"You've Got Pictures" is integrated with AOL's Parental Controls, a special feature that allows you to protect your children from unsolicited, inappropriate images and to prevent them from ordering services without your permission. For more about Parental Controls, see Chapter 12. Also, read the

Safety & Security page in the "You've Got Pictures" Help area. Here are a few points to keep in mind when setting Parental Controls:

▶ Kids Only and Young Teens screen names do not have access to AOL Keyword: **Pictures**.

▶ Screen names in the Mature Teen category have full access to "You've Got Pictures" but cannot purchase additional storage space. The only way a Mature Teen can purchase additional space is to have his or her Parental Controls set (by the adult master account holder) to allow for Premium Subscriptions.

Visit AOL Keywords: **Parental Controls** and **Community Watch** to learn of the many ways you can protect your children online.

Secure Commerce

AOL makes online commerce safe, easy, and reliable. "You've Got Pictures" is part of AOL's Certified Merchants program, which gurantees the safety of your credit card information and sets stringent standards for customer support and accountability to consumers.

Privacy

AOL matches the screen name that you provide to "You've Got Pictures" with your address and telephone number. This security measure ensures that a simple error doesn't send your pictures to the wrong person.

Q & A

Q: Can my computer get a virus from using "You've Got Pictures"?

A: The most common way to contract a computer virus is by downloading an infected file that is attached to an e-mail. "You've Got Pictures" **never** sends e-mail with attached files. When you share an album, it is delivered directly to the recipient's "You've Got Pictures" space, and although a notification e-mail is sent from the screen name AOL BuddyPics, the album is not included as an attachment. There are also no risks associated with the official "You've Got Pictures" Web site when downloading your pictures from your own My Pictures area. To be safe, you should always go to AOL Keyword: **Pictures** to view your online photos and albums.

Keeping Track of Your Saved Pictures

Saved pictures occupy online storage space, and you'll probably want to know what pictures you have online on the Saved Pictures page. You can review how many pictures you're storing and where you're storing them — in albums or as individual pictures.

Q: If I delete pictures from my Saved Pictures space, will they be deleted from my albums, too?

A: Yes, the pictures in all of your albums are really copies of the pictures in your Saved Pictures space. If a picture is deleted from Saved Pictures, then any copies of that picture are deleted from all albums in which it resides.

The only way to preserve the full quality of your pictures is to store them online, or pay for Premium Offer quality downloads at $1 per picture.

You may want to make some choices about which pictures to keep online, but you do have some alternatives. You can:

▶ Download pictures to your hard drive before you delete them.

▶ Store them on one of your other screen names. To do so, sign onto AOL with that other screen name (if you're already online, choose Sign Off⇨Switch Screen Name). Go to AOL Keyword: **Pictures**, and use the Roll ID and Owner's Key you received with your prints.

▶ Share your pictures with a friend or relative who has an AOL account, as described in the next chapter. When you share your pictures with friends and relatives, they can save them online on their accounts. After your pictures have been saved elsewhere, you can delete them from your own account.

Summary

This chapter only scratches the surface of what you can do with "You've Got Pictures." So far, you've found out how to get your pictures online. But what good are pictures if you can't share them? In the next chapter, you'll find out how to share your pictures with anyone online.

A QUICK LOOK

Chapter 5

Sharing Your Digital Pictures

Taking pictures is one thing, and developing pictures is another, but how many of us would bother at all if we couldn't share those pictures with our friends and families? In Chapter 4, you found out how to use "You've Got Pictures" to put your conventional pictures online. Now it's time to share them!

Ways to Share Your Pictures

Whether you're a proud parent showing off your toddler's antics, or a shutterbug bursting to show your latest, greatest pictures to the world, "You've Got Pictures" adds a whole new dimension to the act of sharing. You can stuff your pictures in an e-mail "envelope," pass around electronic photo albums, emblazon gift items with your images, and display your pictures in electronic photo galleries. Here's a brief overview of what you can do:

▶ **E-mail.** This is the easiest way to pass around your digital pictures. "You've Got Pictures" has its own, easy-to-use system for e-mailing individual pictures, and AOL's regular e-mail features make sending your own pictures a snap. If you send e-mail to AOL members, you can include the pictures in the body of the e-mail. You can find detailed procedures for using e-mail to share pictures later in this chapter.

▶ **Albums.** Why send individual pictures when you can assemble photo albums that nearly anyone with Internet access can display? With "You've Got Pictures" albums, you can organize and share your favorite moments with one person, or dozens. You can learn more about albums later in this chapter.

▶ **On AOL.** America Online offers members many ways to share their pictures with each other. You can upload your image files to libraries, enter your pictures in contests, and share them in online galleries. Some of the many online communities where you can share your pictures are featured toward the end of this chapter.

▶ **Products based on digital pictures.** "You've Got Pictures" can take your digital photos and turn them into quality prints and enlargements, and put them on mugs, sweatshirts, and teddy bears, to add a whole new dimension to gift giving. You can find out about gift-giving options in Chapter 6.

Caution

All pictures that you share via AOL are subject to AOL's Terms of Service (TOS). It's a good idea to look over the rules regarding shared pictures at AOL Keyword: **TOS** and to read the "You've Got Pictures" Guidelines in the "You've Got Pictures" Help area.

▶ **The Web.** If want to share your photos with an even bigger audience, you may prefer to put them on a Web page. Let "You've Got Pictures" do the processing, and add the results to your home page. Visit Chapter 13 to learn the ins and outs of sharing your pictures with (potentially) the global audience of people with access to the Web.

Sharing a Picture via E-Mail

Like using a toothbrush or a telephone, writing and sending e-mail messages has become a fairly routine part of life for many, many people. Did you know that an e-mail message can carry more than a simple text message? It can hand-deliver your pictures, too. E-mail is available throughout AOL: It's built into "You've Got Pictures," it's integral to the AOL service (note the AOL toolbar's Read and Write buttons), and it's even available on the Web at www.aol.com/aolmail. It will be available, too, in the next version of the Netscape browser.

Sending E-Mail from "You've Got Pictures"

Life doesn't get simpler than this. Go to "You've Got Pictures" (AOL Keyword: **Pictures**), select the picture you want to e-mail, supply the necessary e-mail address or addresses, type in a brief message, and "You've Got Pictures" does the rest, free of charge. When your recipients belong to AOL, they receive a message with an *embedded* picture — the picture appears within the message itself — so they don't have to download the picture (see Figure 5-1).

If some of the receipients are not AOL members, they receive e-mail messages containing a *link* (Web address) and an attached file. The recipients can choose to download the picture or click the link to visit the Buddy Picture Web page created for this purpose.

5

Sharing Your Digital Pictures

Figure 5-1. AOL members see the picture right in the e-mail.

Caution

Recipients can download, save, share, and order gifts (at their expense) based on the pictures you send. So be sure you're sending your pictures to people who won't share them with the world — unless you want them to!

Here's how you share a digital picture using "You've Got Pictures":

1. At AOL Keyword: **Pictures** ("You've Got Pictures"), view the picture(s) you want to send. You can send any picture that's on the New Roll, Saved Pictures, My Albums, or Buddy Albums tabs. For now, click the Saved Pictures tab. (I discuss My Albums and Buddy Albums later in the chapter.)

2. Find the picture you want to send and select the check box next to the picture, as shown in Figure 5-2.

Note

These steps apply to New Rolls, My Albums, and Buddy Albums.

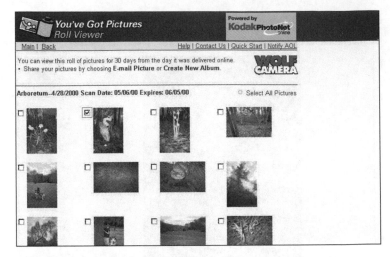

Figure 5-2. Select a saved picture by placing a check in the box next to it.

3. Click the E-Mail Picture button at the top or bottom of the Saved Pictures page to open the E-Mail Picture page, shown in Figure 5-3.

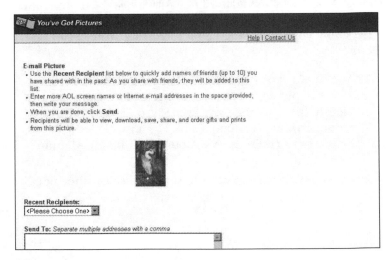

Figure 5-3. The top portion of the E-Mail Picture page.

5

Sharing Your Digital Pictures

4. Enter the addresses of any recipients. You can select an address two ways:

- If you've recently sent digital pictures to the address, select that address from the Recent Recipients drop-down list, shown in Figure 5-3. Select the Add All Names option to send the picture to every name on that list.

- If an e-mail address isn't in the Recent Recipients list, just type it into the Send To box. Use the screen name of AOL members (for example, JenniferAndDave) or type the full Internet e-mail address of non-members (for example, YGPuser@passporter.com).

  If you're sending the picture to several people, separate their addresses with a comma. The new names that you enter are automatically added to the Recent Recipients list for future use.

5. Type your message in the Message box.

6. When everything is set to go, click the Send button.

If your recipient(s) are AOL members using AOL 4.0 or higher, the picture is automatically displayed in the e-mail message they receive, as long as their Parental Controls settings allow pictures in mail and file attachments (see the "Parental Controls and Safety" sidebar for details). Messages sent to non-AOL e-mail addresses contain a linked Internet address so that the receipients can click to view the picture at the "You've Got Pictures" Web site. The picture is also attached, if the recipient wants to download it.

Tip

If you'll be e-mailing photos to many of the people on the Recent Recipients list, select the Add All Names option and then delete any addresses you don't want to use in the Send To box.

Parental Controls and Safety

Not everyone can view e-mail containing embedded pictures of the kind sent by You've Got Mail. AOL provides Parental Controls so that parents can protect their young ones (and themselves) from viewing pictures from strangers. These controls allow parents of minors to set their screen names to one of several age categories. Children whose screen names are set to Kids Only or Young Teens cannot receive e-mail containing pictures or attached files. For more on setting Parental Controls, see Chapter 12. AOL Keyword: **Parental Controls** has advice for protecting your family online.

Parental Controls includes a Custom Controls feature so that e-mail with pictures or attached files can be blocked from any screen name, not just screen names set to Young Teens or Kids Only.

When adult AOL members receive e-mail with pictures or attached files, AOL posts a warning message to inform them of the possible dangers of pictures or files sent by strangers. If you do not receive such a warning, it means that at some point you chose not to receive it. You can reinstate the warning, though. Choose My AOL⇨ Preferences⇨Graphics from the AOL toolbar and select the Notify Before Opening Mail Containing Pictures check box.

"You've Got Pictures" e-mail does have its limitations. Your message text is contained within one block, displayed right below the picture, if you send the picture to another AOL member. Also, you can't format your text or change the font, and if you normally use a signature line in your e-mail, it won't appear in your "You've Got Pictures" mail. Furthermore, each e-mail message can contain only one picture, so if you try to send more than one picture, "You've Got Pictures" tells you to send a Buddy Album instead. (You can find out more about albums later in the "Creating and Viewing Albums" section.)

Another limitiation is that when a recipient receives your e-mail, it comes from a screen name called AOL BuddyPics (if you send the picture to an AOL member) or an e-mail address called AOLYou'veGotPics@aol.com (if you're sending it to an Internet address). Therefore, the recipient can't easily reply to the message. If you'd prefer to have your own e-mail address displayed in the From line, you have to compose your own e-mail as discussed in the next section.

Inserting Pictures into AOL E-Mail Messages

AOL members can compose an AOL e-mail message with digital pictures embedded right in the body of the message. Unlike the e-mail created by "You've Got Pictures," your regular AOL e-mail can contain more than one image, the message can conclude with a signature, and you have many creative options for making great-looking messages. With just a little practice, you can even create attractive greeting cards. Figure 5-4 shows a message with an embedded picture.

Q: Can I e-mail more than one picture without creating an album?

A: Yes. If you're using AOL version 5.0, you can send pictures via e-mail two ways. First, you can download your pictures to your hard drive and then attach several at once to a single e-mail by clicking the Attachments button in the bottom-left corner of the Write Mail window. Several pictures attached to a message are automatically *zipped* into a single file. Alternatively, you can embed a group of pictures directly in the e-mail by clicking the camera icon on the e-mail toolbar.

Because many members are cautious about opening messages with embedded pictures or attachments, you may want to consider creating a Buddy Album as a safe alternative and informing your recipients in the subject line that you're sending digital pictures.

Figure 5-4. Kippi the Wonder Dog takes a trip through cyberspace.

First, you must have the digital picture somewhere on your computer's hard drive or on another drive accessible by your computer. If the picture you want is online at "You've Got Pictures," download it at E-Mail & Web Page quality (see

Chapter 4 for details). The images download quickly from "You've Got Pictures." Likewise, they'll download quickly and automatically when the recipient opens the message.

To insert a picture into an AOL e-mail message, follow these steps:

1. Click the Write icon on the AOL toolbar to open a Write Mail window (shown in Figure 5-5).

2. Enter your e-mail message. It's a good idea to start writing your e-mail message before you insert the picture because it's easier to position your picture(s) when there is some text in the message box.

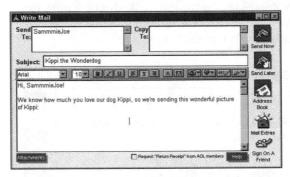

Figure 5-5. The AOL Write Mail window (Windows 95/98).

3. Click the Insert a Picture button on the Write Mail toolbar (refer to Figure 5-5 — it looks like a camera). And from the drop-down list that appears, select Insert a Picture.

4. In the Open dialog box, navigate to the folder containing your picture, select your picture, and click the Open button. Repeat Steps 2 and 3 to insert additional pictures, if you want.

AOL's File⇨Open command has a Preview Picture option. Click any picture file listed in the dialog box to take a peek at that image.

After inserting a picture in an AOL e-mail message, you can use all the usual text-editing techniques, including copy, paste, cut, and delete. You can even highlight the image with your mouse and apply text formatting options to center the image on the page, or to align left or align right.

You can add many pictures to the page, and if you use the numerous text formatting tools provided by AOL, your e-mail can look like a greeting card or even a magazine layout. Select a background color to set the mood for your e-mail, select an attractive font, center and change the size of the text to create titles and headlines, and so on. The possibilities are endless!

Using the Picture Gallery to Insert Photos in E-Mail

Another tool for inserting pictures in an AOL e-mail message is the AOL Picture Gallery, which displays every picture in a single folder on your hard drive, as shown in Figure 5-6. With the Picture Gallery opened, you can drag a picture into an open Write Mail window (click the picture, move it, and release the mouse button). Or, you can first click the picture to modify it before inserting it in a message. Chapters 8 and 10 go into more detail about the Picture Gallery.

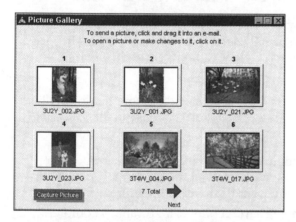

Figure 5-6. The AOL Picture Gallery displays the picture files on your hard drive.

Follow these steps to use the Picture Gallery to insert a photo in an e-mail message:

1. Open the Picture Gallery by choosing File⇨Open Picture Gallery from the menu bar.

2. In the Open Picture Gallery dialog box, select the folder containing the pictures you want to view and click Open Gallery.

3. Single-click a displayed picture to open it in AOL's built-in image Picture Gallery editor, which you can use to rotate, crop, and resize the photo as well as adjust the contrast and brightness. See Chapters 8 and 10 for more about the Picture Gallery.

4. When you're done editing the image, you can save the result, and then drag the picture into a message in a Write Mail window. Or you can just click the handy Insert in Email button.

AOL Mail Extras

AOL Mail Extras is a collection of pictures, clip art, effects, and other digital images you can insert in your AOL e-mail. The collection makes it easy to jazz up a simple e-mail message. Just click the Mail Extras button in any Write Mail window.

Attaching Digital Pictures to AOL Mail

Yet another way to share photos via e-mail is to *attach* them to an e-mail message. An attached file is not part of the message itself, but the recipient can download the file if he or she wants to see it.

AOL e-mail allows you to *attach* one or more files of any kind to an e-mail. Attaching photos makes sense in the following situations:

▶ You're sending e-mail to Internet recipients. Because they can't view *inserted* pictures, you must *attach* pictures that you want to share with them.

▶ You're sending several photos and want to compress the size of the photos for quicker transfer.

▶ You know that your recipient intends to download the picture but has no need to view it at the same time he or she reads the message.

To attach one or more photos to an AOL e-mail, follow these steps:

1. Download the photos that you want to send from "You've Got Pictures" or from your scanner or digital camera. Chapter 8 has much more information about downloading images.

2. Open the AOL software and click the Write icon on the toolbar. A new, blank Write Mail window opens for you.

Q: How do I attach pictures to an e-mail message?

A: You first need to download your picture(s) to your computer. Then click the Write icon on the AOL toolbar, click the Attachments button, and click the Attach button. Navigate to the folder with the picture and double-click its name to add it to the list. To add more than one picture, repeat this process and click OK when you're finished. Your pictures are now attached to the e-mail.

3. Fill in the recipient's screen name or e-mail address, a descriptive subject line, and a message explaining the photo(s) you're sending (refer to Figure 5-5).

4. Click the Attachments button in the lower left-hand corner of the Write Mail window. The Attachments window appears, as shown in Figure 5-7.

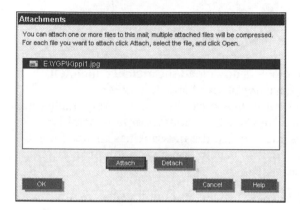

Figure 5-7. The Attachments window lists files you're attaching.

5. Click the Attach button in the Attachments window.

6. In the Attach dialog box that appears, find and select the first photo file you want to attach and then click Open. The dialog box disappears, and your first photo file is listed in the Attachments window (refer to Figure 5-7).

7. Repeat Steps 5 and 6 to add more files, if you want.

8. After you've selected the last picture, click OK in the Attachments window. Your Write Mail window now shows the name of the *first* file that you attached next to the Attachments button, along with a new icon (two floppy disks). You can review your attached files by clicking the Attachments button again.

9. When you're ready to send the message, click the Send Now button to send your e-mail and any attached file. If you attached more than one file, AOL compresses the files. A File Transfer dialog box appears (see Figure 5-8).

Tip

The File Transfer dialog box appears every time you send or receive a file attachment via e-mail. If you're sending a large file or a set of files or have completed your online business for the day, you may want to select the Sign Off After Transfer check box in the File Transfer dialog box. Selecting this option means that AOL will sign off when it's finished sending the file(s). Alternatively, you can click the Send Later button and use Auto AOL to send your e-mail at another time. Choose Mail Center⇨Set Up Automatic AOL from the toolbar to configure Auto AOL.

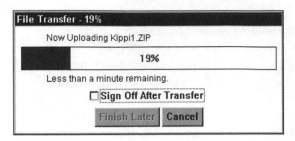

Figure 5-8. Watch your e-mail's progress as it sends your attached file(s).

How do your recipients download the attached file? AOL members who have *not* blocked attached files at AOL Keyword: **Mail Controls** receive the e-mail in their mailboxes as usual. Whether they're AOL members or non-members, their mailboxes indicate that the message has an attachment by displaying an icon — usually some variation of an envelope with a floppy disk attached to it

Here's how to download an attachment if you're an AOL member:

1. Open the e-mail that contains the attached file.

2. Click the Download Now button in the lower-left corner of the e-mail. If an E-Mail Attachment Warning appears, read it carefully and click Yes if you want to continue.

3. Select a good location for the file on your computer and click the Save button (see Figure 5-9).

Caution

Never download attached files from individuals you do not know or from anyone claiming to be an AOL employee or "You've Got Pictures" employee. Neither AOL nor "You've Got Pictures" will e-mail attached files to an AOL member.

Note

By default, AOL selects the America Online/Download folder on your computer's hard drive to save files you download from the Internet and from your e-mail. You can choose any folder to be the receptacle of your downloaded files, however. Just choose MyFiles⇨Download Manager and click the Download Preferences button.

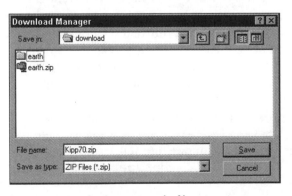

Figure 5-9. Decide where to save the file on your computer.

AOL displays a progress thermometer as the file down-loads. If the estimated download time is longer than you want to wait, you can click the Finish Later button. Keep in mind, however, that you can do many other things while the file downloads.

4. If the attached file is a common graphic file (and con-tains a single picture instead of several zipped pic-tures), AOL displays the image as it downloads.

If the file you downloaded was compressed (for example, the file name ends in .ZIP or .SIT), you need to decompress the file before you can view it. You can do this by using AOL's Download Manager. To decompress a file you've already down-loaded using AOL, follow these steps:

1. Choose My Files⇨Download Manager from the toolbar. Click the Show Files Downloaded button to see a list of files you've downloaded, as shown in Figure 5-10.

Tip

If your file ends in .SIT, it was compressed on a Macintosh computer. You can locate and download a de-compression program such as StuffIt (which is available for Windows) at AOL Keyword: **Download Center**.

Definition

Compressing files is an effi-cient way of sending a few files at once — rather than sending several e-mail mes-sages, each with one file. When you decompress the file, individual items are ex-tracted, or pulled out.

Tip

If the file you downloaded and decompressed contains a number of images, you may prefer to choose File⇨Open Gallery from the menu bar and navigate to the folder where your downloaded files are located. This command displays all the images in a particular folder as small pic-tures (thumbnails), making it easier to find and open the specific image you want.

Figure 5-10. A handy-dandy list of files you've downloaded.

2. After you have located and selected the file you want to decompress, click the file and then click the Decompress button. A window appears, showing the progress of the decompression. When the decompres-sion is complete, you see a File Transfer Status window, which shows the number of items extracted from the file. To locate downloaded files, click Show Files Downloaded, select the file that you just unzipped, and click Locate.

3. Choose File⇨Open from the menu bar, find the files you just downloaded, and open them. Most image files will open and display in AOL, including files you've downloaded from "You've Got Pictures."

E-Mail That Picture . . . from the Web

Did you know that you can read your AOL e-mail and send messages on the Web — without using the AOL software? Your messages can even include attached digital pictures. Why would you want to do this? Say you're using someone else's computer, or you're on the road and don't have access to your AOL software. You can now use *any* Internet connection to check your e-mail; just visit the AOL Mail site at www.aol.com/aolmail. If you want to send a digital picture via that site, you have to have the picture file with you — on a floppy, for instance.

Follow these steps to e-mail a picture from the Web:

1. Go to www.aol.com/aolmail and click the button to indicate that you want to *read* your mail.

2. On the next page, type in your AOL screen name and password and then click the Enter AOL Mail button. After correctly entering this information, a page appears, asking you to confirm your desire to use AOL Mail.

3. Click the Please Click Here to Complete the Sign-In Process button to continue. A page displaying your e-mail messages in your AOL mailbox comes up. If you want to read a message, click the link for that message.

4. To send a message, click the Write icon at the top of the window. A new page comes up, which looks very much like the Write Mail window shown in Figure 5-5.

5. Fill in the standard information (addresses of any recipients, a subject, and your message), just as you do in the AOL Write Mail window.

6. Click the Attachment button, find the picture you want to include (on your hard drive or elsewhere), and click the Attach button. Click OK when you are done attaching pictures.

7. When you're ready to send your message, click the Send button. For both AOL and non-AOL recipients, the picture is available as an attachment to the e-mail message.

Sharing Collections of Pictures (Albums)

Picture this: Your child is just learning to walk, and you've been snap-happy, taking plenty of digital pictures of her first steps. Naturally, you want to share your photos with friends and family members. You could print them out on that new inkjet printer, of course, and give copies to everyone likely to be interested, or even e-mail your favorite shots to family and friends who live elsewhere. But prints and e-mailed photos may take more time and money than you're willing to invest. There's a better way to share a collection of photos with others: Put them in online *albums* and send them to anyone who has Internet access!

Albums are a fun, easy way to organize your favorite photos and share them with others. Photos in online albums can consist of up to 100 photos, which can be gathered from

- ▶ Your saved pictures in "You've Got Pictures," new rolls, and current albums
- ▶ Your Buddy Albums (that is, albums that others have shared with you)
- ▶ Pictures uploaded from your own computer

After you've chosen the photos for your album, you can personalize the album presentation with background colors, descriptions, and captions. When your album is ready, you can share it with specific individuals.

Creating and Viewing Albums

If you want to make an album composed of many pictures from the same roll of film, the easiest way to create a new album is to visit AOL Keyword: **Pictures** and view a roll of pictures. If you want to create an album made of your favorite pictures from several rolls, begin in the Saved Pictures area. Viewing photos in either the New Rolls or Saved Pictures tab, follow these steps to make an album:

1. Select the photos you want to display in the album by selecting the check box to the left of each photo, as shown in Figure 5-11.

Many home graphics programs, such as Print Shop, PhotoSuite, and PhotoDeluxe, make it easy to create attractively formatted collections of albums, but they do not always provide direct ways of sharing them online. Some, like PhotoSuite, create Web pages based on albums. Using AOL Hometown, you can easily make those pages available on the Web (see Chapter 13 for details). These programs and their albums are mentioned in Chapter 8.

If you don't have any rolls, saved pictures, or Buddy Albums, consider uploading a picture. To do this, click the My Albums tab, click the Upload Picture button, and follow the directions for uploading, as explained in Chapter 4.

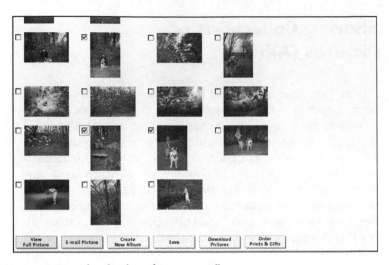

Figure 5-11. Select the photos for your new album.

2. Click the Create New Album button at the bottom of the window. "You've Got Pictures" displays the photos you selected for your new album, along with a default title (your screen name and the current date), and the amount of space used and the amount of space available.

3. From here, you have three choices:

   • Customize your album (to make it more attractive for others)

   • Save your album (to stop for now or to keep the album as is — if you're making the album for yourself, to organize your pictures)

   • Cancel

   For now, click the Save button — you can return to customize it later.

4. Next, you're prompted to agree to the "You've Got Pictures" terms — once you do, your new album is created.

You can take a look at your new album by clicking the View button. As shown in Figure 5-12, your default title is displayed at the top, followed by your photos, and then an array of options along the bottom.

Q: I put an album in my Favorite Places folder, but when I click it to see my pictures, it won't work. What's going on?

A: You can't use the Favorite Places feature with "You've Got Pictures." This ensures that only the people to whom you send Buddy Albums or place on your Shared List can see your photos.

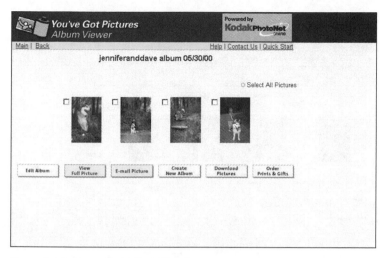

Figure 5-12. A new album, fresh from the computer.

Look a bit drab? The next section shows how to add some piz-zazz to your album with customization!

Customizing and Editing an Album

After you've created an album, you can customize it with a title, captions, a specific layout, and even a matching back-ground. To begin customization, go to AOL Keyword: **Pictures**. Click the My Albums tab, select the album you want to customize, and click Edit. You now have several customiza-tion options (as shown at the bottom of Figure 5-13):

▶ **Add Pictures.** This button returns you to the main "You've Got Pictures" page where you can access your rolls, saved pictures, and Buddy Albums. To add a pic-ture from one of these sources, click the appropriate button, select the photo(s) you want to add to your al-bum, and click OK. Your album is shown again, this time with your new pictures included. Note that if the picture hasn't already been saved, each picture you add to an album must be saved in one of the 50 storage spaces provided for each screen name.

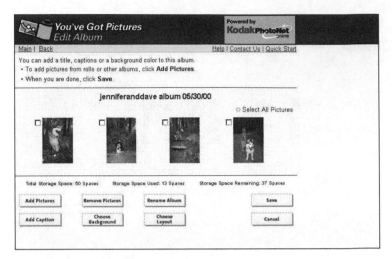

Figure 5-13. Customizing your album. Use the buttons at the bottom of the page to alter the layout, change the color, and add a caption.

If you want the pictures in your album to display in a particular order, add each picture individually in the order you prefer. Each new picture is added to the end of the list of photos in your album.

If you sign off before you're able to save any changes to your album, your modifications will be lost. To prevent this from happening, save your changes frequently by clicking the Save button.

▶ **Remove Pictures.** Select the pictures in your album that you want to remove, click the Remove Pictures button, and confirm the removal. Your album redisplays without the selected pictures. Don't worry; removing pictures from an album does *not* remove them from "You've Got Pictures."

▶ **Rename Album.** Click this button to type in a new name of up to 32 characters, plus a description of up to 60 characters, and then click OK. If you're creating an album for archival purposes, be sure to include the date or season. If you're planning to share your album with others, be sure to give it a name and description that adequately characterize it.

▶ **Add Caption.** If you want to add captions to any photos, click the Add Caption button. The first photo in your album appears, along with space in which to type a caption of up to 32 characters. You can then click the Previous Picture and Next Picture buttons on the caption page (shown in Figure 5-14) to move to subsequent photos and add captions to them. If you prefer to add a caption to a specific picture, select it in the album before clicking Add Caption.

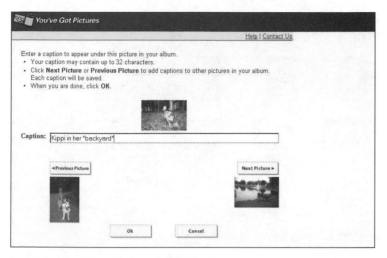

Figure 5-14. Adding captions to the album's photos.

▶ **Choose Background.** Click this button to choose from different-colored backgrounds. Select a color you like and click OK. At the time of writing, ten different colors are available. Avoid black and red, because they can make it very difficult to read the captions.

▶ **Choose Layout.** Clicking this button lets you choose how many photos are displayed per line: one, two, or four (default). Choose *one* for the largest possible picture display, *two* for medium sized pictures, and *four* for the smallest pictures. Click OK to save your changes.

Be sure to save your album when you're finished customizing it. After saving it, you have the option to view your album so you can see how others will see it (see Figure 5-15).

Tip

You can edit any album you create at any time. Just display the album and click the Edit Album button to see the list of customization options.

Q: I want to share my albums with friends who aren't members of AOL. Is that possible?

A: Yes, you can share your favorite pictures or albums with anyone who uses e-mail, even non-AOL members. Non-members receive an e-mail instructing them to go to pictures.aol.com and enter their username and password, which are included in the e-mail. After viewing the pictures, non-members can download the pictures as well as order picture gifts and prints.

Q: Can I share as many albums as I want?

A: You can share as many albums as you want, and each album can be shared with as many as 100 people. If you want to share an album with more than 100 people, simply create an identical album and begin a new list of screen names.

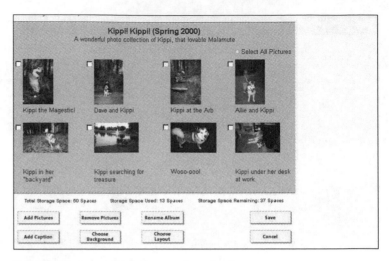

Figure 5-15. A customized album, ready to share!

Sharing an Album

Now that you've got a snazzy album filled with your favorite photos, show it off! To share an album, click the My Albums tab, select the album you want to share, and click Share. A new page appears, where you can indicate who should receive your album (see Figure 5-16).

Figure 5-16. Type the e-mail address of each person who should receive your album.

To add a name to the list of folks who can access your album, type each individual's exact e-mail address in the top field and click the Add Name button. If your recipient is an AOL member, you do not need to type `@aol.com` after that person's screen name. All other e-mail address do require the @ symbol and domain name, however.

Each time you click the Add Name button, the page updates, and the receipient's e-mail address is added to the list on the right. Continue typing e-mail addresses and clicking Add Name until all recipients appear in the list. You can add up to 100 names to your list. If you need to remove a recipient, select that person's name in the list and click Remove Name.

After your list is complete, click the OK button to save your list and share your album. "You've Got Pictures" sends an e-mail to each recipient on your list announcing the availability of the new album. The message comes from the screen name `AOL BuddyPics` (if the recipients are AOL members) or `AOLYou'veGotPics@aol.com` (if they are not AOL members). The message contains directions on how to access the shared album. For AOL recipients, the shared album now appears in their list of Buddy Albums (albums *shared by* someone else) at AOL Keyword: **Pictures**.

After sending the message, a confirmation page displays the address of each person who can access the album. Your album has now been added to their list of Buddy Albums.

If you later decide you don't want one of your recipients to view an album, you can remove that person's name from the list. Just click the My Albums tab, select the album, click the Share button, select that person's address in the list, and click the Remove Name button. Recipients who are removed from an album access list no longer see the album under their Buddy Albums tab in "You've Got Pictures." They can continue to view the album only if they saved it as their own.

Receiving Buddy Albums

When someone sends *you* an album, you receive an e-mail from `AOL BuddyPics`. The "You've Got Pictures" icon on the Welcome screen will say "You've Got Pictures," indicating that new pictures have arrived.

Tip

If you've shared albums before, the names of past recipients may appear in the Recent Recipients drop-down list. Select a name from this menu to add that person's name to your list.

Caution

If you receive an e-mail from a screen name other than `AOL BuddyPics`, indicating that someone has sent you an album, don't believe it. Only `AOL BuddyPics` notifies you of new albums.

Q & A

Q: A friend sent me an album, and I viewed it. But now it's gone. Where did it go?

A: Buddy Albums do not expire, but the friend who sent the album may have either removed your name from his or her Shared List or deleted the album altogether. Check with the person who shared the album with you. To make sure you don't lose the Buddy Album, you can always save it in your My Albums tab, if you have adequate storage space.

Tip

If you want to save photos but don't want to use the storage space on your screen name, send the photos in a Buddy Album to another one of your screen names. Then switch screen names, view the new Buddy Album, and save the photos under that screen name. When you return to the original screen name, you can delete the pictures to free up space.

Caution

When you share an album with others, they can download your photos just as easily as you can. Keep this in mind when you're deciding what pictures to share and with whom you share them. If you don't want others to use your pictures in their own work, ask them not to!

To access an album that someone has shared with you, go to AOL Keyword: **You've Got Pictures**, click the Buddy Albums tab, select the new album, and click the View button. Shared albums offer many familiar options: view full picture, e-mail picture, create new album, download pictures, and order prints and gifts.

A new option is to save the Buddy Album, which stores the photos in your own storage space. Save a Buddy Album only if you really want *all* the pictures in the album saved in the space allocated to your screen name. If you don't save the album, the photos remain accessible as long as the person who shared the album with you retains them. If you really like a particular photo, you may want to go ahead and save it in your own storage space.

Managing Albums

If you enjoy the albums feature, it's a good idea to learn how to manage your albums and expand their potential. Here are some tips for making the most of your albums:

▶ **Develop a naming system.** Names may include an initial (to indicate who took the pictures), the date or season, and the subject. If you use abbreviations consistently, you'll be able to identify your various albums at a glance. Chapter 8 explores the practical subject of file naming.

▶ **Use albums as an organizational tool for your saved photos.** Add the photos you want to save to your albums in small groupings, giving the albums appropriate names. This may help you when it's time to clean house and free up more storage space. Again, Chapter 8 discusses using albums as an organizational tool.

▶ **Remember that any changes you make to an album are visible by all who have access to it.** You can use this to your advantage by adding new pictures to an album and letting others know that the album has been updated. Of course, if you delete photos from an album, these photos will also be inaccessible to others unless they've already saved them.

▶ **To add a personal touch to your album, use the Upload Picture feature to include a personalized image in the album.** Try using your favorite graphics program to create an image with an introductory note, captioned photo, or fancy title (see Figure 5-17).

Q & A

Q: Each time I update my photo album, do I need to notify people that they can look for new updates or are they automatically notified?

A: If you make any changes to an existing album currently being shared, your recipients automatically see those changes the next time they access the album. However, if you want to alert them to those changes, you can either send them an e-mail from your screen name, or you can remove all the names from your Share Roster list and create a new list, which will generate an e-mail notification from "You've Got Pictures."

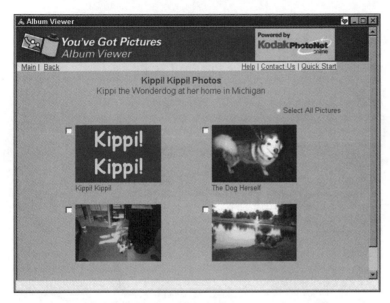

Figure 5-17. An album with a personalized image.

▶ **If you need to delete an album, click the My Albums tab, select the album you want to delete, and click the Delete button.** After you confirm the deletion, your album is removed and inaccessible to you and anyone with whom you shared it. Note, however, that deleting an album does not delete the photos within it; you delete individual pictures in the Saved Pictures area.

Places to Share Pictures

You've just taken an amazing shot of Cal Ripken at the moment he hit that 11th-inning home run. You already showed it off to your friends and family by e-mail or in an album. Now you want to show it off to the world! Where can you go to share pictures with others who enjoy good pictures? You'll

Q: How can I edit my pictures?

A: "You've Got Pictures" does not yet have an online editing tool. However, if you're using AOL version 5.0, you can download your photos onto your computer and use AOL's Picture Gallery to edit them any way you want. Just choose File⇨Open Picture Gallery and navigate to the picture you want to edit. After you have edited your picture, you can use the Upload feature to place it back into your Saved Pictures space. For more complete control of your images, you need to use image-editing software, as described in Chapters 9 and 10.

Soon, the community area will be just one click away from the main "You've Got Pictures" page.

find a wide variety of forums on AOL and the Internet where you can upload or otherwise submit your photo to share with others.

The "You've Got Pictures" Community Area

The "You've Got Pictures" community leaders host an area where you can submit your favorite photos. Your photo may even be chosen for the picture of the week! Regular contests are sponsored through the Picture This newsletter, too. To reach the community area, shown in Figure 5-18, go to AOL Keyword: **You've Got Pictures Help**, click the Customer Service link, and click the Message Board link.

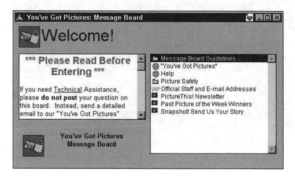

Figure 5-18. Share your photos with the "You've Got Pictures" community!

Pet of the Day

The perfect place to submit your favorite pet photo is the Pet of the Day area (AOL Keyword: **Pet of the Day**), shown in Figure 5-19. Click the Nominate Your Pet Here link to learn how to send in your pet's photo and story.

Figure 5-19. What better way to show off your pet to the world? Note: Cat's eyes are subject to red eye, too! See Chapter 10 on red eye.

Love@AOL Photo Personals

If you're more interested in showing off your pretty face than your pet's, try Love@AOL's Photo Personals (AOL Keyword: **Photo Personals**). You can create a personal profile and include a photo of yourself with it! Click the Create a Personal button to learn how to create your personal profile and upload a photo for it.

Family Photo Contest

Submit that great photo of your family in the Family Photo Contest (AOL Keyword: **Family Photo Contest**), sponsored by Kodak and ritzcamera.com. Contests are held regularly and often revolve around holidays such as Father's Day and special events.

Garden Gallery

Want to share your photo of a prized rose? Visit AOL Keyword: **Garden Gallery** to upload a photo and share it with other nature lovers (see Figure 5-20). Members can even vote on their favorite photos here.

Q & A

Q: Can I use my pictures on my homepage? On Love@AOL? On eBay?

A: Yes, you can use your pictures in all kinds of applications including photo personals, classifieds, Web pages, and auction sites such as eBay. You start by downloading the picture to your hard drive. Then you upload it to the online area you want. Or you can capture the URL by right-clicking on the Full View of the picture you want, choosing Properties, and copying the address (URL). You can paste this address into the eBay field that asks for the URL or address of the picture you want to use. Bear in mind, though, that unless you save your picture, it will disappear from "You've Got Pictures" after 30 days.

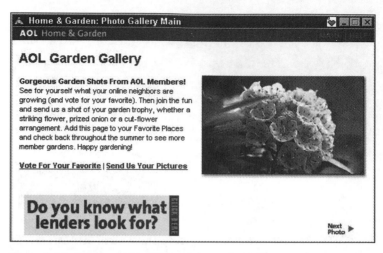

Figure 5-20. Share your plant pictures in the Garden Gallery.

Image Exchange

Photographers will enjoy the Image Exchange, an artist's community with thousands of images. Upload your photography to the Member Showcase, where up to 8 million people can ooh and ahh over your masterpiece. Use AOL Keyword: **Image Exchange**.

Photo Libraries

Libraries where you can upload photos abound on AOL. Here are some favorites:

▶ The Grandstand (AOL Keyword: **Grandstand**) offers file libraries for all your favorite sports. For instance, the Motor Sports forum (AOL Keyword: **GS Auto**), part of Grandstand, has a Motor Sports library where you can upload your race-car photos and view others' photos.

▶ The Independent Traveler (AOL Keyword: **Traveler**) offers several libraries where you can upload your best vacation photos.

▶ The Graphic Arts Community (AOL Keyword: **Graphics**) lets you upload photos to the Graphics Arts Libraries for others to search and download. Read the Upload Guidelines carefully.

Find It Online

The Picture This! weekly newsletter, delivered via e-mail, keeps you informed of goings-on in the "You've Got Pictures" world, including places to post your pictures. At AOL Keyword: **You've Got Pictures Help**, click the Customer Service link, and then click the Message Boards link. In addition to message boards, you can find information about the newsletter, an archive of newsletters, and links to Snapshot!, the newsletter's picture of the week.

Summary

Perhaps the clearest way in which digital pictures differ from photographic prints is the ease with which you can share them. With digital pictures, the tools for sharing are at your fingertips, from the e-mail built right into "You've Got Pictures," to AOL's many types of e-mail, to the "You've Got Pictures" tools for assembling and sharing groups of pictures, or albums. Many online areas on AOL give you the chance to share pictures with other members who share a particular interest.

Sharing is one of the friendliest things you can do, especially when it comes to giving gifts. In the next chapter, we discuss ways you can create gifts with your digital pictures.

GIVING YOUR
PICTURES AS GIFTS

A QUICK LOOK

Chapter 6

Giving Your Pictures as Gifts

IN THIS CHAPTER

Turning digital pictures into gifts

Ordering prints and Picture CDs

Emblazoning your pictures on coffee mugs, mouse pads, prints, T-shirts, and teddy bears

Adding pictures to greeting cards

Other places where you can get your digital pictures turned into gifts and useful business items

D igital photography involves more than putting pictures on a computer screen. With "You've Got Pictures," you can share your virtual pictures by turning them into real gifts.

Everyday Uses of Digital Pictures

What would life be like without photos? You'd have no baby pictures to show off, no vacation snapshots to make your co-workers envious, and no wedding photographs to show everyone who couldn't be at the event. Shopping would be a guessing game without product photos, and global news would lack immediacy without on-the-spot coverage. Photographs are woven into the very fabric of our lives.

You may be surprised at all the things you can do with digital pictures. To give you an idea of the possibilities, here's a partial list of traditional and creative uses for digital pictures:

▶ **For showing off:** Send pictures of your new baby or puppy by e-mail to your family.

▶ **For consulting:** Share a picture of the new dress you bought with your friend across the country.

▶ **For documenting:** Record your child's progress or your garden's growth and then store the pictures for later.

▶ **For archiving:** Store pictures of valuable household items in "You've Got Pictures" for insurance purposes.

▶ **For communicating:** Share a picture of your latest project with your co-workers.

▶ **For copying:** Make a virtually unlimited number of digital copies of your photos without additional cost or hassle.

▶ **For editing:** Crop out the old boyfriend by downloading your pictures and modifying them in image editing software.

▶ **For decorating:** Place the photo of your new car on your computer as desktop *wallpaper* (background).

▶ **For creating:** Make a mug with a photo of your own "mugshot" on it. Keep it for yourself or give it as a gift!

The uses for digital photos are endless. Gift giving is one of the more popular uses, and certainly one of the easier uses, thanks to the power of digital photos and the services by online vendors. In fact, you can order photo gifts online directly through "You've Got Pictures."

"You've Got Pictures" makes ordering gifts easy. Just look for the Order Prints & Gifts button when you view pictures in the New Rolls, Saved Pictures, or albums tabs, and start selecting your options in the "You've Got Pictures" Picture Store, shown in Figure 6-1.

Q & A

Q: Is gift ordering available only to AOL members?

A: No. Non-AOL members can also order picture gifts featuring the photographs that they've received from AOL members. Non-AOL members who receive a Buddy Album notification can go to `pictures.aol.com` and sign in using their username and password. From there, they select the picture they want to use and click the Order Prints & Gifts button.

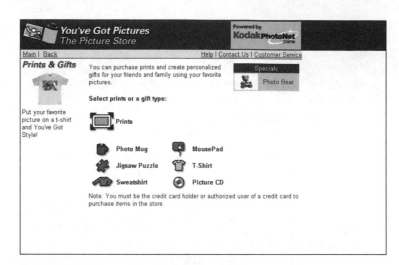

Figure 6-1. The Picture Store offers prints and much more.

For Those Wired Grandparents . . .

Grandparents just love to get pictures of their grandchildren, and they love to share those pictures with their friends and relatives, too. If grandma and grandpa happen to be online, send them Buddy Albums with the latest pictures of your young 'uns. They'll be able to order all the prints and gifts they want without even needing the negatives.

Ordering Prints and Picture CDs

Whether they're carefully mounted in a frame on top of the piano or taped to the refrigerator door, photographic prints make a great gift for you or anyone else in your life. And anyone with whom you've shared your pictures by e-mail or album (see Chapter 5) can also order prints and gifts from "You've Got Pictures."

You can order prints in three sizes: 4 x 6 inches (the traditional jumbo snapshot size) for $0.49 each, 5 x 7 inches for $1.49 each, and 8 x 10 inches for $4.49 each (all prices are subject to change). The minimum charge is $3.00, so you'll want to order more than one of the smaller-sized prints. The benefits of online ordering include:

▶ Convenience

▶ Availability of the service to the people with whom you share your pictures

Here's how you and your buddies can order prints:

1. While viewing pictures on any tab (New Rolls, Saved Pictures, My Albums, or Buddy Albums), click the Order Prints & Gifts button to go to the Picture Store.

2. Click the Prints button.

3. At the top of the Order Prints page, shown in Figure 6-2, select a print size (4 x 6, 5 x 7, or 8 x 10) and then indicate which picture(s) you want to have printed. Alongside each image in the album is a text box in which you can indicate the quantity of prints you want of each image.

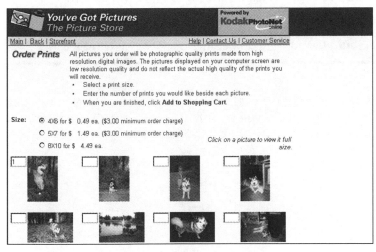

Figure 6-2. Select the picture(s) you want to have printed.

To order prints in other sizes or from other albums, you have to make those selections later in the ordering process.

4. When you've finished selecting pictures from this album, click the Add to Shopping Cart button at the bottom of the page. If you'd rather select prints from another album, click the Choose Another Album button at the bottom of the page (any selections you made in the current album will be ignored).

Can I Crop?

Currently, you cannot crop or otherwise modify the images stored by "You've Got Pictures" unless you first download the images, edit them in a graphics program, and upload them to "You've Got Pictures."

If you want to maintain the same high resolution of the original scan when you order your prints, you have to download the Premium Offer high-quality file (which currently costs $1 per image) and retain that resolution throughout the image-editing process. You can learn the ins and outs of image editing in Chapters 9 and 10. Alternatively, you can acquire high-resolution digital pictures with a digital camera. First download the pictures to your PC, and then upload them to "You've Got Pictures."

When you click the Add to Shopping Cart button, you see a list of all the prints you've ordered so far as well as a thumbnail image of each, as shown in Figure 6-3.

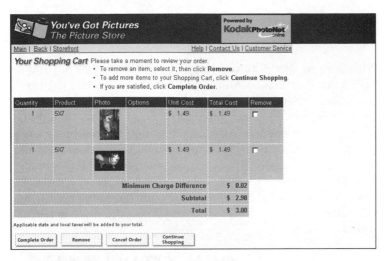

Figure 6-3. The shopping cart displays your selections.

You can remove photos from the shopping cart, continue shopping, cancel your order, or, when you're finished, click the Complete Order button. If you want more prints, click the Continue Shopping button to return to the Picture Store (refer to Figure 6-1). From there, you can order more prints or prints of other sizes, or any number of other gifts.

Cross-Reference

You can find out how to purchase and download high-resolution copies of your digital picture files in Chapter 4.

Print Quality

"You've Got Pictures" prints your photos on high-quality photographic paper. However, the overall quality of the image depends on many factors, including the resolution of the original image (in pixels) and the size of the print you order. Pictures processed by "You've Got Pictures" are stored at a resolution of 1536 x 1024 pixels. To most casual observers, this resolution provides very good results at 4 x 6 and 5 x 7 inches, and acceptable results at 8 x 10 inches. If you upload digital pictures created at a lower resolution (such as 768 x 512), or use the free, middle-grade download from "You've Got Pictures," larger prints will likely be less satisfactory.

Picture CDs

With "You've Got Pictures," you can copy up to 100 of your digital images on a CD. Although "You've Got Pictures" gives you unlimited space for pictures, you can also include pictures shared with you by other people in the form of Buddy Albums, which are discussed in Chapter 5. Picture CDs can be an easy, though not free, way to store your digital pictures and favorite photo collections. By offering an alternative to online storage, Picture CDs help you create room on "You've Got Pictures" for new and uploaded pictures. Putting your pictures on a CD also enables you to take them with you on the road or when you visit people.

You can use these pictures in all the ways you use downloaded pictures: embed them in e-mail, in home and school projects, on Web pages, and so on. Chapters 12–14 explore these uses of downloaded digital pictures.

For instructions on ordering Picture CDs, see "How to Order from 'You've Got Pictures,'" later in this chapter. The only difference between ordering Picture CDs and other non-print products is that you can use up to 100 pictures on a Picture CD but only one picture on coffee mugs, teddy bears, and other products.

Choosing Photo Gifts

Would you rather have a plain, boring mug or one with a photo of your new house on it? A store-bought sweatshirt or one with a picture of your mom? Thanks to Photo Gifts at "You've Got Pictures," you can personalize mugs, puzzles, mouse pads, T-shirts, sweatshirts, and more.

Photo gifts are an ideal way to showcase that favorite photo in a manner that's both practical and personal. You can make a gift for yourself or send it to a friend, family member, or co-worker. In fact, a photo gift may be just the thing for someone who has everything.

Photo gifts are normally shipped within five business days following receipt of your order, but if it will take longer than five days, you're notified by e-mail and given an opportunity to cancel your order. Gifts are shipped U.S. First Class Mail and should arrive within 7 to 14 days after you place your order.

As with prints, you can order gifts directly from "You've Got Pictures" by clicking the Order Prints & Gifts button when you're viewing a picture. If you select the check box adjacent to a single picture before you click the Order Prints & Gifts button, that image is automatically selected for your gift. If you click more than one image (or none at all), you later have the choice of any image in that album. Once again, you see the Picture Store window (refer to Figure 6-1), where you can select from the following gift items, each described in the next pages:

► Photo mugs
► Mouse pads
► Puzzles
► Special gifts
► Clothing

Photo Mugs

Birthday or holiday coming up? Treat someone to a dishwasher-safe, ceramic mug personalized with a photo. To place the order, you don't have to leave your computer or break the bank. Mugs come in two sizes: 11 ounce and 15 ounce.

Mouse Pads

Stumped for a gift idea for your staff or coworkers? How about a mouse pad with your company's building or logo on it? Or maybe a favorite nature picture would be a better choice to reduce their 9-to-5 stress. The "You've Got Pictures" mouse pad has the traditional non-slip rubber backing and cloth top. Prices vary.

Tip

Order a mug with a photo of each member of your family or office staff. The photo on the mug will help each person identify his or her mug. It may also encourage folks to clean out their own mugs!

Jigsaw Puzzles

Speaking of puzzles, why not send a loved-one a surprise jigsaw puzzle? What's the surprise? When it's put together, the puzzle turns out to be a picture of someone special in that person's life. This puzzle won't challenge jigsaw-puzzle fanatics. It measures 10½ x 15 inches and only has 80 pieces, but there's still lots of room for friendly fun.

Special Gifts

If that special person in your life isn't the type who would wear a photo T-shirt or sweatshirt, perhaps she'll appreciate a special gift, such as a teddy bear wearing a photo T-shirt! This is a great Valentine's Day item and makes an especially cute gift for a baby's room — a very special way to display a newborn's portrait.

Clothing

Photo T-shirts and sweatshirts are very versatile gift items. From proud grandparents sporting their newest grandchild to a project leader looking to build team spirit, anyone can think of a way to customize a T-shirt. Your picture is printed on the front of a cotton T-shirt or on a sweatshirt for about $25. You have your choice of fabric colors, and shirts are available in seven sizes, from children's small to adult extra-large.

How to Order from "You've Got Pictures"

To order a photo gift, follow these simple steps:

1. Locate the photo you want to use at AOL Keyword: **Pictures**.
2. Select the check box next to the desired photo. If you select more than one, you'll be asked to reselect just one photo later in the process.
3. Click the Order Prints & Gifts button.
4. On the next page that appears, click the icon of the item on which you want your photo to appear. Another new page displays the selected product, a thumbnail-sized version of the selected photo, and size and quantity options, as shown in Figure 6-4.

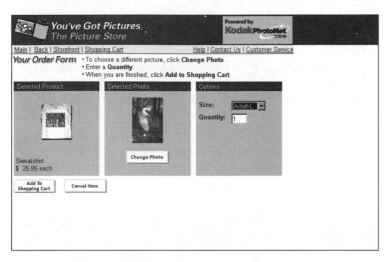

Figure 6-4. Ordering a sweatshirt? Choose your options here.

5. Click the Change Photo button to select another image, select any other options you want, and click the Add to Shopping Cart button. Yet another page appears, displaying the contents of your shopping cart (see Figure 6-5).

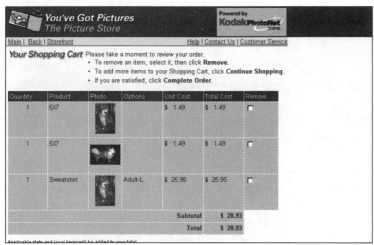

Figure 6-5. Your shopping cart summarizes your order.

Q & A

Q: Is it safe to use my charge card for making purchases online in the Picture Store?

A: Shopping online is reliable, safe, and secure. AOL is committed to providing members with the most advanced, up-to-date security technology by incorporating a secure browser that scrambles any information that you provide. Since the inception of AOL's Guarantee in October 1996, AOL has never received a report of a credit card that was compromised during a shopping transaction with Certified Merchants on AOL.

Tip

If you have not already signed up for AOL Quick Checkout (which speeds up your online purchases), you see a notice on the page asking for your billing information that says `We're sorry. AOL Quick Checkout is only available to AOL members.` Click the Help button to learn more about Quick Checkout or click the OK button to proceed with your purchase. The "Completing the Transaction" section, later in this chapter, has more details about Quick Checkout.

6. Review your order. To remove something (or everything) from your shopping cart, select the Remove check box adjacent to that item and click the Remove button. You can then click the Continue Shopping button or the Cancel Order button, or if you're ready to pay for your purchases, click the Complete Order button.

7. On the next page, shown in Figure 6-6, enter your billing and shipping information and then click the Continue button. The next page summarizes your order information.

![You've Got Pictures – The Picture Store billing and shipping information form, powered by Kodak PhotoNet online. Navigation links: Main | Back | Storefront | Shopping Cart   Help | Contact Us | Customer Service. Text reads: "Instead of using AOL Quick Checkout, please enter your billing and shipping information below." "Please enter your billing information exactly as it appears on your credit card statement, then click Continue." Your Billing Information with fields for Name, Address, City, State (Select a State), Zip, Country: USA, Day Phone. Your Credit Card Information with Credit Card Type options: MasterCard, Visa, Discover, American Express; Account Number.]

Figure 6-6. Enter your billing and shipping information.

8. Click the Change button if you need to make any changes, or click the Continue button. You're still free to click the Cancel button if you've changed your mind about your order.

9. The next page presents you with your order confirmation number. It doesn't hurt to *write it down* or print it out. You will also receive an e-mail containing your confirmation number and detailed help instructions.

Completing the Transaction

AOL goes to great lengths to make your online shopping experience simple and safe. All transactions are encrypted and secure if you're using AOL 3.0 and higher software and if you're using the browser supplied with that software. If, by some small chance, you do fall victim to credit card fraud, AOL provides coverage for your loss. You must report the fraud to your credit card company, and AOL will then pay up to an additional $50 for any remaining liability for the unauthorized charges.

AOL Quick Checkout

To speed up your online purchasing, you may want to sign up for AOL Quick Checkout, which securely stores information for up to ten of your credit cards, your address, and the addresses of those to whom you frequently send gifts. Then when you make a purchase at "You've Got Pictures" or at any other online merchant participating in Quick Checkout, you'll finish in record time. Visit AOL Keyword: **Quick Checkout** to find out more.

Because your "You've Got Pictures" purchases are customized, your return privileges are limited. Obviously, you're covered if your order is damaged or if there is a discrepancy in your order (check your order carefully when you receive it). You can also receive a full refund if your order is not 100 percent free from defects in materials and workmanship. Be sure to save the original packing materials and file your claim within 30 days of receipt.

When you're in the "You've Got Pictures" store, you'll find handy hyperlinks at the top of each page for Help, Contact Us, and Customer Service. Review these areas before you place your first order. You'll feel much better about the entire process.

Caution

Never give your credit card information or password to unauthorized persons contacting you via e-mail or Instant Message. These requests are always fraudulent. AOL will never ask you for this information — ever.

Note

Neither AOL nor its affiliates will ever ask you for your credit card number (except during initial AOL registration or when you're actually making a purchase online).

Sending Photo Greeting Cards

American Greetings (AOL Keyword: **AG**) operates a huge on-line service site offering free and low-priced online greeting cards (the kind that are sent via e-mail and viewed in a Web browser). Now when you send an online greeting, you can upload your own picture to accompany the card. Depending on the occasion, you may want to send a picture of yourself, a picture of your newborn baby, or a picture of your new home so folks will recognize it when they come to your housewarming party.

Follow these steps to send a photo greeting card:

1. Download a picture to your hard drive (if it's not already there); see Chapter 4 for details on downloading. The image file must be less than 50K (kilobytes) in size, so you should download an E-Mail & Web Page Quality image; higher-quality downloads are too large.

2. Go to AOL Keyword: **AG**.

3. In the Online Greetings area, select an online greeting card and fill in the Personalize Your Greeting form, along with your choice of font and font color. You can also choose the date on which you want the card delivered.

4. In the Add a Photo section at the bottom of the page for your chosen card, click the Browse button and then select the picture file of your choice from your hard drive. You're then asked to verify that you own the right to use the photo and to agree to American Greetings' Terms of Service.

5. Click the Send Your Greeting button. Your recipient will receive an e-mail invitation to view the card on the Web. When viewing the card, that person sees a big View My Photo button alongside the regular greeting card.

Tip

American Greeting's online greetings are also available whenever you write an AOL e-mail message (click Write on the AOL toolbar). In the Write Mail window, the new Greetings button, which used to be called Mail Extras, offers choices of pictures, drawings, and sounds to use in your messages. Click Greetings for the American Greetings Web page. There, you can select an online greeting, which will be sent independently of your e-mail message.

Other Sources of Photo Goodies

Many Web sites would love to sell you goods emblazoned with your digital pictures. Among the biggest is pix.com (www.pix.com), which offers picture stationery, pendants, watches, post-it notes, and even "100% edible" cookies, "guaranteed to start stories." For a more business-oriented spin, try iprint (www.iprint.com).

Photofinisher Wolf Camera, a participating "You've Got Pictures" photo dealer, offers a variety of gifts at its Web site www.wolfcamera.com. In addition to products similar to those offered by "You've Got Pictures," you can order tote bags, aprons, neckties, hats, photo albums, and buttons, all decorated with your digital pictures.

In addition to the wide choice of goodies, Wolf can produce photo enlargements from digital files up to 12 x 18 inches. On the downside, Wolf recommends a print resolution of 1164 x 1528 pixels to produce a good 12-x-18-inch print! P.A.W.S. also requires that you download and install a separate program (PC and Mac versions are available) to use the service.

By the time this book appears on shelves, the picture products and services planned by Kinko's and liveprint.com should be available. Home and business users can find a wide range of useful products, beginning with staples such as stationery and cards. AOL is working with Kinko's to make these products readily available and affordable to AOL members.

Summary

In this chapter, you found out about many possible uses of digital pictures, from stationery and mouse pads to T-shirts and toys, for sending photo-based gifts. If you require professional quality and service for business or gift-giving purposes, you'll definitely want to turn to a service such as "You've Got Pictures," liveprint.com, or iprint. All you have to do is provide the picture (and the charge, of course); the companies create the object and send it off, nicely wrapped.

CHOOSING THE RIGHT DIGITAL EQUIPMENT

A QUICK LOOK

Chapter 7

Choosing the Right Digital Equipment

Getting digital pictures is just the start. After you've gathered your pictures in AOL's "You've Got Pictures" area, saved them as online albums, and shared them with family and friends, you can start downloading and actively using your pictures. On your PC, you can enhance, organize, and print pictures, and you can start creating cards, newsletters, T-shirts, and visually exciting reports for school and work. For all these basic activities, from organizing digital pictures on your hard drive to using them at home and work, you may eventually need to buy some extra gear.

If you're not in the market to buy new equipment now, knowing what's out there is a good idea, if only to know what's possible with your growing collection of digital pictures. Prices are dropping while choice and quality are improving. And as computer products go, this stuff is fun. Plus, these products are bewildering enough in purpose and variety to need a guide. That's the purpose of this chapter.

In this chapter, I discuss essential digital equipment, including digital cameras and scanners. I also discuss computer-storage devices, which are becoming increasingly important as you begin taking part in the digital world.

Choosing a Digital Camera

Digital cameras take pictures just like old-fashioned cameras, but instead of negatives and prints, they produce computer files. These cameras are selling — and changing — fast. Prices range widely from around $100 to thousands of dollars for professional models. Figures 7-1 and 7-2 show AOL's digital camera, the PhotoCam.

Figure 7-1. AOL's PhotoCam (front view).

Only the most expensive digital cameras approach the quality of the photographs produced with the best traditional cameras, but digital cameras more than make up for this shortcoming with their convenience and speed. No film processing is necessary — just download and view.

 Cross-Reference

Chapter 11 is devoted to the other major type of equipment: the wonderful world of printers (inkjets, lasers, and photo-printers).

7

Choosing the Right Digital Equipment

Note

If you'll be using digital pictures on a Web site or in e-mail, you don't need the same levels of resolution required in old-fashioned snapshots, because a monitor can display only so many pixels at a time.

Figure 7-2. AOL's PhotoCam (back view). The viewer lets you see the image before you capture it. After the picture is taken, you can view it and, if necessary, delete it from your camera's memory in order to make room for additional pictures. You can also use the viewer to display the menus providing control of the many features.

Considering Digital Camera Resolution

Digital cameras measure pictures in pixels per *image* (not pixels per *inch*). A *megapixel camera,* for example, records more than a million pixels per digital picture, for example 1024 pixels (the picture's length) by 768 pixels (the picture's width).

What's a Pixel?

A *pixel* (or *picture element*) is an imperceptibly tiny square, a fraction of an inch on each side, carrying a single color and tone. Put together thousands of pixels, and, to the mind's eye, you see a picture of an acorn or a child's face, not just a bunch of small colored squares. The goal of digital cameras and other graphics products is to gently fool the mind into seeing a picture of your cat, your kid, your dad, or whatever it happens to be, exactly as you meant it to be when you took the picture.

What's an Interpolated Pixel?

Interpolated pixels are "transitional" pixels (between existing ones) created by a camera's software to give the appearance of continuous color and tone. Unlike a real pixel, an interpolated pixel doesn't carry real information about your subject's color and tone. When shopping for digital cameras and other devices, it's important to make sure that you're getting real pixels and not *interpolated* pixels.

Many digital cameras let you adjust the pixel resolution, giving you a choice of high- and low-pixel pictures. The more pixels, the more information your pictures can contain and the bigger your files get.

Determining Picture Quality

Some cameras, like the AOL PhotoCam, let you adjust the picture quality, which is something different from resolution. *Quality* refers to the amount of compression applied to the files containing your pictures. Compression takes large files and makes them smaller (in kilobytes) by consolidating identical and similar pixels into blocks. In general, you gain information and get higher quality when you choose the Fine quality setting (or whatever a particular camera calls it — if it offers the capability).

Remember, then, that resolution alone does not determine quality. The following are other important factors to consider when evaluating a camera's picture quality:

> ▶ **The amount of compression.** Less compression makes for better quality.
> ▶ **Optics.** There's no substitute for a good lens.
> ▶ **Good paper.** Good paper makes a surprisingly big difference in the quality of your images if you'll be creating printouts.

How Digital Cameras Differ from Traditional Cameras

Here's what makes a digital camera different from an old-fashioned, film camera:

> ▶ Digital cameras produce no negatives. Instead, your digital pictures are available as files that can be stored on computers, modified by software, and transferred over networks.

A *card* is a rectangular electronic circuit board that goes inside your computer and supports computer capabilities such as sound, networking, and video. In this case, a memory card is simply the thing that gives your camera memory — a device not much bigger than a stick of chewing gum — on which you can store digital pictures until you've transferred them to your computer. *Removable* cards can be easily upgraded to cards with more memory, hence room for more pictures. All digital-camera cards have reusable memory, which means that you can use them again and again. Some cards can be placed in an adapter and inserted in a PC's A drive, where the pictures can be quickly accessed.

▶ Most digital cameras can take pictures at several different resolutions. The higher the resolution, the fewer photos it takes to fill a digital camera's memory. Memory? That leads to the next point.

▶ Picture files are stored on reusable *memory cards,* which can usually be removed and upgraded.

▶ Digital camera memory fills up, like a drive on your computer fills up. To take additional pictures, old pictures must be either deleted from the camera's memory or copied to your computer for storage on your hard drive or other storage device. Because you're not using rolls of film, you need to manage your pictures one at a time by deleting shots that didn't come out quite right and copying as many pictures as possible to your PC as often as possible.

▶ Just about all digital cameras have a small viewer based on a technology called liquid crystal display; you'll see the impressive-sounding acronym *LCD* all over the place. These viewers let you see what your picture will look like before you take it. After you take a photo, digital cameras let you view and delete the photo by using the same viewer in order to help you manage the images in your digital camera's memory.

▶ Just about all digital cameras these days come with software for editing and organizing your digital pictures. The AOL PhotoCam, for example, currently comes with a version of MGI PhotoSuite. Other software you'll see includes Adobe PhotoDeluxe and Adobe Photoshop LE.

How Digital Cameras Work

Traditional cameras record images on film, which is coated with a light-sensitive chemical. To retrieve the recorded image, the film must first be developed (creating negatives) and then printed (creating paper prints).

Digital cameras work differently. Like traditional cameras, the picture-taking process starts when you click the shutter button, briefly admitting light into the camera. That's about as far as the similarity goes. Digital camera images are recorded not on film, but on a light-sensitive electronic gadget called a *charge-coupled device* (CCD). The CCD itself does not record the image in the way film does. Instead, the CCD converts light into a series of electrical charges that are transmitted to the camera's electronic memory, where they are stored.

Thus, a digital camera, like a computer, has memory. If you're going to use digital pictures, the amount of memory determines how many pictures your camera can hold. In memory, an image's color information is saved as tiny square blocks of color called *picture elements* or *pixels*. A camera with a high resolution (a million pixels per picture, for example) is not necessarily better than a camera with lower resolution if your goal is to create something online — such as photo albums or Web pages.

To transfer digital pictures from the camera's memory to your PC requires a cable or card. (These options are discussed in more detail in Chapter 8.) Most cameras offer both options. After pictures are in your PC, they can be viewed, edited, and copied to "You've Got Pictures."

Understanding Flash Units

Just about all digital cameras come with a built-in flash unit, usually with several flash settings. AOL's PhotoCam, for example, has automatic flash and fill flash, both of which can be turned off by using the menu on the LCD viewer on the back of the camera. What do you need? When do you use which one?

> ▶ *Automatic flash* creates a generally dispersed flash whenever the built-in light meter estimates that light is insufficient to "expose" the image sensor (CCD). Indoors, you'll appreciate automatic flash because the CCD's low sensitivity (see the Note icon in the margin) requires that indoor shots be lit by a flash to create a reasonably good exposure. In higher-end cameras with adjustable aperture settings, you can compensate for low lighting by letting in more light by lowering the F stop or letting in light for longer by lowering the shutter speed, or both.
>
> Automatic flash can be turned off. You would want to turn it off for bright outdoor scenes without people or other close-in subjects and for any scene when a

Note

In traditional, film-based terms, a film's sensitivity to light is measured by its ASA (now ISO) number. ISO 100 film is appropriate for bright, outdoor shots. ISO 400 film is appropriate for scenes that are less well-lit. Digital cameras typically have an ISO/ASA of around 100, meaning you'll often require a flash to fully expose a picture.

7

Choosing the Right
Digital Equipment

natural shadow itself is of interest. Shadows are often the most interesting part of any scene, adding an extra dimension to the form of your subject.

▶ *Fill flash* is a flash that makes sense for outdoor use. In bright outdoor shots, of people in particular, faces can be underexposed (dark) because the camera, confused by the extreme brightness of the overall sunny scene, did not adequately let in enough light to expose the face. Fill flash brightens facial features that would otherwise be cloaked in dark shadow.

▶ In some cameras you'll see a *red-eye flash* option. To prevent a reddish reflection from the normal flash bouncing off the subject's iris, red-eye flash is a kind of warning flash that happens before the normal (automatic or fill) flash. Red-eye flash desensitizes the eye, so that the real flash does not create the "red-eye" effect. Experts doubt the usefulness of the red-eye flash. Whatever the case, image-editing software gives you a relatively simple way of removing the red-eye effect altogether. See Chapter 9 for more information about the red-eye effect.

Find It Online

At AOL Keyword: **Personalogic**, click Digital Cameras for a complete digital-camera buying guide. Buying guides are also available from the opening screen of AOL's Computing Channel. You will find a set of questions and answers, a price-comparison guide, a set of product reviews, and more.

What to Look For in a Digital Camera

The cost of a digital camera depends in good part on the resolution that it is capable of capturing. Currently, you can buy digital cameras that are capable of capturing 3 million pixels per image. Resolution alone buys you very little if your purposes are primarily to create digital pictures for online use, where much lower resolutions suffice. For prints, the more pixels, the better.

Here are the main factors to consider and questions to ask when shopping for a digital camera:

▶ **Amount of memory.** Memory directly determines how many digital pictures can be stored in the camera at various resolutions. Having removable memory cards means that you can carry around extra memory cards that you can use in case you fill up one card with good shots and don't have a computer around. See the nearby sidebar, "Memory: CompactFlash versus SmartMedia."

Memory: CompactFlash versus SmartMedia

Digital cameras offer two major types of memory: CompactFlash and SmartMedia. Whatever camera you decide to buy will support one technology or the other.

CompactFlash is supported by major brands, such as Nikon, Canon, and HP. AOL's PhotoCam comes with a CompactFlash card. A benefit of CompactFlash is that you can buy cards with more memory (up to 160MB, currently) than you'll find with the other major type of camera memory, SmartMedia.

SmartMedia has the advantage of offering lower-priced cards and an adapter for your memory card that fits directly into your computer's A drive. Drop your card in the adapter, slide the adapter into the drive, and you can upload your pictures much faster than you can via cable. CompactFlash adapters require an additional piece of hardware: a special card reader, such as the SanDisk (less than $100), which plugs into your computer's parallel or USB port (the plugs on your computer).

▶ **Download method.** All cameras come equipped with a plug and a cable. Attach the cable into the camera's receptacle at one end and a PC's serial or USB port at the other end, open the camera's software on the computer, and you're ready to let the software manage the downloading for you. AOL's PhotoCam comes with a serial cable, as shown in Figure 7-3; to order a USB cable, go to AOL Keyword: **Camera Shop**.

You'll need an adapter in order to use the card in an A drive or directly in the USB port. Using a removable memory card and adapter is a faster method of downloading than using a cable to transfer files.

▶ **Quality of the lens.** Just as in traditional cameras, lens quality is important. Unfortunately, you may not have much of a choice of lenses in digital cameras unless you are willing to purchase a more expensive camera.

Note

Downloading specifics depend on the digital camera and the supporting software. (All cameras come with some software for downloading and managing pictures.) See your camera's documentation for the details.

Tip

When shopping for a digital camera, make sure that the camera's memory can be removed and make sure that you are getting brand-name software (such as PhotoDeluxe, PhotoShop, PhotoSuite, and the like) to manage the downloading and editing process.

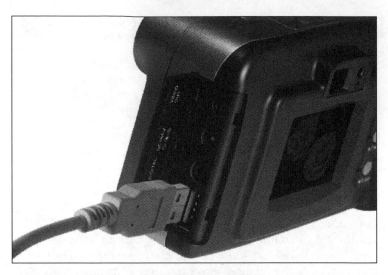

Figure 7-3. AOL's PhotoCam. This figure shows a USB cable; the other end is plugged into a USB plug on the back of a computer. To use the standard serial cable, use the round camera plug just above the one shown here.

▶ **Amount of lag time.** *Lag time* refers to (1) the time between pressing the shutter and capturing the image and (2) the time from one exposure to the next. The longer the lag, the less suitable the camera is for action shots. If you're a photo enthusiast waiting for the perfect moment to do a shot, you want your camera to be as responsive as you are (which means that you want a short lag time).

▶ **Availability of a video-out feature.** Video-out features let you connect a digital camera to a TV or other video device. Displaying digital pictures on a TV means that people without a computer can enjoy them, and larger groups of people can enjoy the equivalent of an old-fashioned slide show.

▶ **Availability of video and audio modes.** You use these modes to record video clips (as AVI files) and audio clips (as WAV files) as well as digital pictures. Only higher-end digital cameras — and good digital-video cameras — offer these enhancements.

▶ **Weight, size, look, and feel.** Don't underrate basic usability features such as whether the camera is easy to grip, the controls are legible and conveniently located, and so on. You may want to try out digital cameras in a photo shop before making your purchase decision.

▶ **AC adapter.** You can use these to run the camera from household electricity instead of running down those AA batteries. For indoor use, you may want to use the adapter when transferring pictures via cable to your PC. This item is standard equipment, but make sure that it's there just the same.

Is There a Downside to Digital Cameras?

Shopping for a digital camera differs from shopping for a traditional film camera, particularly if you're used to a single-lens reflex (SLR) camera, with all those fancy settings and detachable lenses. Currently, you won't find some traditional SLR features in digital cameras unless you are a professional photographer prepared to spend a thousand dollars or more. For instance, your choices may be limited in a couple of ways:

▶ **Aperture settings:** These settings, also called *f-stop settings,* refer to how much light is let in when you click the shutter. A high f-stop (such as f/16) has a small aperture and is appropriate for a bright scene. A low f-stop (such as f/2.8) results in more light being let in and can be used in low-light situations. In determining aperture, you're also determining *depth of field* — how much of the picture is in focus. Depth of field is one of the best ways to highlight your subject and prevent foreground and background items from distracting from the subject. For those higher f-stops (f/11 or f/16), just about everything is in focus, and your subject can get lost. For lower f-stops, you can effectively place just the subject in focus.

Most digital cameras come with a fixed f-stop, but the cameras with adjustable apertures are coming down in price.

▶ **Shutter speeds:** Shutter speeds, like aperture settings, are usually fixed in digital cameras. A camera's shutter speed determines how long light is let in when the shutter is clicked. A fast shutter speed ($\frac{1}{250}$ of a second or shorter) lets you freeze action; a longer shutter speed ($\frac{1}{30}$ of a second) can cause blur but can also result in some interesting effects.

▶ **Film choices:** In traditional film photography, you can match the type of film to the needs of setting, subject, and available light. For bright days, you can use ISO (formerly ASA) 100; for darker days, ISO 400. Digital cameras currently lack this flexibility, giving you the equivalent of around ISO 100, which is best suited for the brightest lighting.

▶ **Through-the-lens viewing:** Through-the-lens (TTL) viewing means that the image you see through the viewfinder is the same image that will hit the film when you click the button and open the shutter. You won't find through-the-lens (TTL) viewing in many digital cameras under $1,000, as you do in some traditional cameras. Digital cameras, like point-and-shoot cameras, generally use a *parallax system,* which means that what you see through the viewfinder differs slightly from what the film (or memory) will record. The difference is greater when you're doing close-ups. The LCD viewer on the back of just about all digital cameras provides a more reliable view than does the viewfinder, but neither the LCD viewer nor the viewfinder will perfectly represent the content of the resulting picture.

Partly because the viewing and photographing systems are detached in digital cameras, you'll see some unusual camera designs, such as the Nikon Coolpix, which has a lens that swivels around the camera body, making it easy, for example, to photograph things at floor level.

▶ **Batteries:** Digital cameras usually run on AA batteries, but some cameras run on fancier nickel-based batteries. Batteries must power the camera's viewer, its focus mechanism, and its flash. Extra batteries are to digital cameras what extra film is to film cameras.

Choosing a Scanner

A scanner is like a copy machine except that instead of creating a paper copy it makes a digital copy, or *file,* that can be manipulated by software, inserted into e-mail messages, and used in a hundred ways. (See Part IV for some of these ideas!)

Good color scanners, once expensive, are today available for less than $100 — and are quite easy to use. Better yet, many of these inexpensive scanners offer several related hardware functions, serving for example as fax and copy machines.

Types of Scanners

Two types of scanners are available for home use, sheet-fed scanners (sometimes called personal document scanners) and flatbed scanners. Figure 7-4 shows a flatbed scanner.

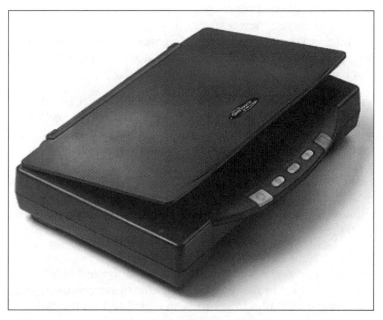

Figure 7-4. The Visioneer One-Touch 8100 flatbed scanner. Use the flatbed scanner when you will be scanning images of different sizes and shapes (appropriate for old photographs).

Sheet-fed scanners are usually better for scanning documents or multiple items of the same size, and they generally take up less desk space. Flatbeds are better for heavy graphics use and for stiff or fragile documents. A flatbed scanner tends to be more versatile than a sheet-fed scanner.

What to Consider When Shopping for a Scanner

When choosing a scanner, the key factors are scanner resolution, speed, ease of use, and sophistication of the accompanying software. Scanners are becoming commodities: You can count on the presence of certain features, so your choice is simplified to factors like price, appearance, packaging, bundled software, and ease of use.

Scanners use two types of resolution. The *optical resolution* is the actual number of pixels per square inch you see on your monitor when you view a scanned image. *Interpolated resolution* refers to the technology that creates the appearance of more pixels per inch by creating intermediary values between adjacent pixels.

Resolution is a key factor when choosing a scanner, but don't confuse a vendor's resolution claims with the reality. *Optical* (or *native*) *resolution* is the physical number of dots per square inch you see on your monitor when you view a scanned image. *Interpolated resolution* describes improved resolution based on a scanner's ability to perform sophisticated tricks by using software to improve resolution. An actual resolution of 300 dpi can have an interpolated resolution of almost 5,000 dpi. Optical resolution values tend to be fairly objective; interpolated values should be taken with a grain of salt.

Some low-end scanners offer optical resolution of "only" around 300 dpi, but this is satisfactory for on-screen uses, such as creating digital pictures for use in e-mail and on the Web. Many others — a step up in cost — offer 600 dpi or better resolution; these are more suitable for printing pictures.

Considering All-in-One Devices

A new breed of multifunction hardware can scan your pictures and also perform a host of services all related to printing services. Samsung, for example, makes an all-purpose machine for around $299 that does color printing, 300-x-300-pixel color scanning, and color copying, while also providing fax support. The great benefit of such machines is that, by combining so many major functions in one machine, they take up much less desktop space. On the other hand, some of the functions (like scanning and printing) may not provide as

Tip

The system memory of your computer — RAM — is critically important in scanning performance. Most scanners require a computer with16MB, and 32MB is preferred. As always, when it comes to memory, the more the better. Even with more memory (I use a PC with 128MB), scanning an image can cause other computer tasks to crawl to a stop.

many features as you would find in a single-purpose device costing less than the multi-purpose device. If you need a little of each function, a multipurpose, all-in-one device (such as the one shown in Figure 7-5) might make sense. If you have heavy-duty needs for printing or scanning, consider a higher-octane device.

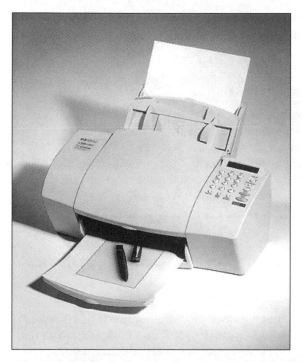

Figure 7-5. Multifunction hardware does it all. Requiring little desktop space, such machines scan, print, copy, and fax.

Scanner Shopping Tips

Here are some considerations to keep in mind when shopping for a scanner:

▶ Consider what you'll be scanning. Will items be mostly the same size? Will you be scanning many sheets at once? Is a scanner that produces 8½-x-11-inch images sufficient? Then get a sheet-fed scanner.

Continued

Scanner Shopping Tips (continued)

▶ Do you need to be able to scan bound documents, or irregular, large, or fragile documents? Then consider a flatbed scanner.

▶ Consider how much space on your desk your printer will require. Flatbeds take up more space, but many people also consider them more versatile.

▶ If you're shopping at a store, try out the equipment so that you can compare speed and resolution, particularly optical resolution.

▶ Consider ease of use. What exactly must you do to create a quick scan? Can you control the scanner from the hardware *and* from the scanner's software? Visioneer has brought one-touch simplicity to its scanners, and you should expect simple access to all important features in any scanner you buy.

Understanding Your Storage Options

Tip

If you're in the market for a new PC and plan to make heavy use of digital pictures, graphics software, and a scanner, buy as much RAM as your budget permits (at least 64MB, but aim for 128MB) and as large a hard drive as you can afford. A portable disk drive or recordable CD can be used to keep any hard drive from becoming stuffed with files.

Are you going to store many digital images on your computer? Remember that digital pictures can be hundreds of kilobytes. Relatively low-resolution images (30K and under), such as the "You've Got Pictures" screen downloads or other digital pictures meant for on-screen use, eat up less storage space than high-resolution images. If you'll be doing anything with digital video, your storage needs can really soar. Merely editing ten minutes of video by using Avid Cinema, popular video-editing software, for example, requires 700MB of *hard drive* space (RAM often uses hard drive space while working with large files). Storing that ten minutes of video will set you back many megabytes as well.

Floppies

Floppy disks — the popular 3½-inch-square disks that aren't really floppy — hold about 1.4MB of computer files. That may sound like a lot, but a Web-quality picture weighs in at about

50K (384 x 256 pixels). A digital picture suitable for printing at a small size is about 100K (768 x 512 pixels), while the premium-quality picture (1536 x 1024 pixels) is over 200K. It takes only five or six high-quality JPG images to fill a floppy, though from one to two dozen lower-resolution JPGs could fit on the same disk. Take the large files produced by a program like Adobe Photoshop, and a single file can exceed the limits of a floppy. For the same reason, digital cameras (such as the Sony Mavica) that use floppy disks directly inside the camera offer tremendous convenience. On the downside, the Mavica quickly runs out of space when the camera is being used to take high-resolution images.

Hard Drives

Filling up 1 gigabyte of hard drive space (just over 1,000MB) doesn't take long if you store photos, have a number of graphics programs, and create projects, such as banners, calendars, albums, family trees, family newsletters, birthday cards, and the like. If you are buying a new computer, get as many gigabytes as you can afford; the frustration of running out of space combined with the cost of adding a drive later more than make up for the up-front investment in a big hard drive. You'd be amazed how fast the biggest drives can get clogged with software files. Then, if you are running out of space on your existing drive, you might consider adding a portable disk drive so that you can create archives and free up space.

Portable Disk Drives

You probably won't use individual digital pictures very often, so why keep them all on your hard drive? Those 3½-inch floppies are of little use for storing anything but small or low-resolution graphics because they can store only 1.4MB. (A single digital-picture project, or a short video file, can exceed this size.) Who wants to store hundreds of floppies?

Welcome to the world of the high-capacity portable disk drive, an elegant cross between a floppy (in size and portability) and a hard drive (in the sheer amount of data it can hold). Archive disks hold from 100MB up to 1 gigabyte or more, compared to about 1.4MB on today's typical floppy. These super-disks are widely accepted — just about any service

Tip

At AOL Keyword: **Software**, you can find many programs to *compress* your digital pictures — *reduce* them in size and bundle several of them up into a single compressed file. Click the Shareware tab, open the Utilities & Tools folder, and check out the current listing of File Utilities for many useful compression programs. A favorite of many is called WinZip. In the past, I have squeezed more than 50 digital images totaling almost 10MB into a single compressed file that could fit on a 3½-inch disk (1.4MB).

7

Choosing the Right
Digital Equipment

bureau (full-service copy shop, such as Kinko's) can accept them — making it easy to transport data from place to place. Drives are fairly inexpensive, starting at about $100, with disks running about $10 each.

The Iomega Zip drive, which uses 100MB cartridges, was the first popular drive of this type; many computers now come with Iomega or other portable disk drives. These drives are also quite fast, so you don't necessarily have to move the files to your hard drive to work with them. Currently, 250MB and from 1- to 2-gigabyte disks (and drives) are available, too. Figure 7-6 shows a 250MB Iomega Zip drive and disk.

Which to buy: CD-R or CD-RW? You may face this decision when you buy a new computer or buy an external drive. Experts prefer the CD-Rs for two reasons. The disks are cheaper (around $1 rather than around $8), and they last longer (a century or so, rather than three decades or so). *Burning CDs* (recording your digital pictures or digital anything on CDs) lets you unclutter your hard drive, while also creating a collection that you can share with others.

Figure 7-6. An external Iomega Zip drive and 250MB disk.

Writable CDs

These popular drives, standard issue on many new consumer PCs, are beginning to replace today's read-only CD-ROM drives, the kind you use to install software and play music while working at your PC. The new writable CD drives let you save your own files on a CD.

You may encounter two types of writable CD drives. Writing, by the way, is computer jargon for saving; writing files to a CD just means saving them on it.

Today's popular DVD drives can play DVD movies, of course, but they can also play earlier CDs. In the near future, software that no longer fits on a CD will be delivered on a DVD disc. Ask your dealer for details about the compatibility of specific drives and specific types of discs.

▶ CD-R (the R stands for *recordable*) drives allow you to write (save) to any disk just *once,* making them a valuable and affordable tool for archiving your files. You can read (use) them as often as you want, just as you can re-use music CDs as often as you want.

▶ The more expensive CD-RW *(rewritable)* drives let you save files — any files, including digital pictures, many times.

Both types of drives can read earlier CD-ROMs and play music. CDs are more universally used than any of the other removable media (other than 3½-inch disks), a significant issue if you need to physically take data elsewhere, such as to a graphics shop, printer, or collaborator.

Both kinds of writable CD drives use optical storage, which experts consider a safer bet for the long-term storage of digital pictures than the magnetic media used in most other drives. On the other hand, writable drives can be slow, making them better for archiving but less suitable for day-to-day use.

Summary

Some day, sooner than you may think, you may want a digital camera. The reason lies in the many conveniences, from portability to savings in film and processing. Or you may feel the need for a scanner to start digitizing a lifetime's worth of snapshots. And if your digital picture collection starts to grow (which it will), you may want to look into a larger hard drive, a high-capacity portable disk drive, or a writable CD drive, or all of these media, the next time you buy a PC. This chapter has tried to spell out your options in making these key choices. Although the individual products change rapidly, the features to watch for tend to be relatively stable.

The next chapter looks into ways of keeping track of a collection of digital pictures on your computer.

A QUICK LOOK

Chapter 8

Managing Your Digital Pictures

T he "You've Got Pictures" service is perfect for getting digital pictures when you use a traditional film camera and want to share your pictures quickly and inexpensively with others. This chapter takes a close look at the *other* important place you can store your digital pictures: your own computer.

This chapter examines three related topics:

▶ Acquiring digital pictures via scanners and digital cameras

▶ Storing all your digital pictures on your own system

▶ Using software to manage your collection of digital pictures

You may remember from Chapter 2 that you can store digital pictures online using "You've Got Pictures." Even with unlimited storage space, sooner or later you may want to download part of your collection to your hard drive.

Downloading is just the start. Without a good way of organizing the digital pictures on your computer, you will simply not be able to use them. All the time and investment you've put into making digital pictures will have been a big waste. It would be like keeping all your old snapshots in a series of un-ordered stacks in various places around the house (sound familiar?).

 Cross-Reference

The next few pages look at downloading pictures from digital cameras and scanners. Chapter 4 has the details you need to download pictures from "You've Got Pictures."

Downloading Digital Pictures from a Scanner

The only difference between a scanner and a photocopy machine is that the result of scanning something is an electronic file, not a piece of paper. You start by scanning a piece of paper, such as a photographic print; you wind up with a file containing a digital picture.

Here's an example of how to scan a photographic print and save the digital picture on your PC. After the digital picture is on your PC, the digital picture can be

▶ Uploaded to "You've Got Pictures" and shared by e-mail (see Chapter 5)

▶ Edited or used in a photo project (such as the ones described in Chapters 12 and 14)

▶ Uploaded to AOL Hometown and used on a Web page (see Chapter 13)

What do you need in order to scan? The activity of scanning takes advantage of a handy but little-used feature built right into AOL's Picture Gallery that lets you organize pictures and do simple edits (File⇨Open Picture Gallery). Of course, you'll need a scanner, and you must have installed the software that came with your scanner. If you have a digital camera and have installed its software, you can often use its software to initiate a scan and manage the resulting file.

To scan and save an image to your computer, follow these basic steps. In this example, I use the simple and relatively inexpensive PaperPort OneTouch scanner, which has its own software (also called PaperPort). Your scanner may have different names for things, but the steps won't vary too much from scanner to scanner.

1. Log on to AOL. From AOL's Edit menu, select Capture Picture to bring up the Capture Picture window. Figure 8-1 shows the Capture Picture window. (You'll only see this option if you have a scanner and have installed its software.)

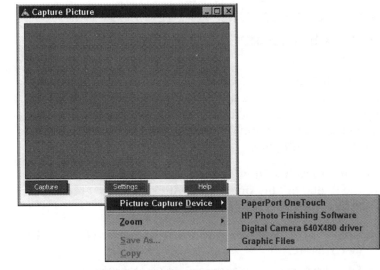

You may be tempted to scan at a higher resolution, but don't forget that for online use (Web and e-mail), 72 x 72 pixels per inch is plenty. To set the scan's resolution, click Advanced Settings (shown in Figure 8-2). Chapter 9 goes deeper into the delights of resolution.

Figure 8-1. The Capture Picture window, which presents a choice of different programs you can use to download a digital picture from a scanner or digital camera.

All the major graphics programs I mention in Chapter 9 enable you to initiate a scan from within the software. Refer to your user's manual for more information about how this option works on your scanner.

2. Choose Settings⇨Picture Capture Device and select the scanner software you wish to use to create the scanned image. AOL provides a menu of likely programs, making your job easier.

3. Position the image you want to scan (such as a photographic print) on your scanner; then click the Capture button in the Capture Pictures window (refer to Figure 8-1) to start the scanning process.

Your scanner may take a moment to warm up. When it does, you'll see the scanner software's window, where you can specify how you want to do the scan — in

Chapter 8 ▲ Managing Your Digital Pictures   153

black and white or color, with high or less-high quality, with greater or lesser contrast, at a certain size, and so on. See Figure 8-2 to see the choices offered by PaperPort Scan Manager software.

4. To perform the scan, just click Scan. The process (and button names) will likely be similar in your software.

   The scan may take a few minutes if you selected high-quality color and are scanning a large image; or the scan can take considerably less time if you chose to scan a lower-resolution, smaller, grayscale print. You'll know that the scan is done when the scanner stops and the software's progress indicators indicate that the job has been completed.

5. After the scan has been completed, choose File⇨Save and complete the process by saving the scanned file with a specific name, file type, and folder location. See "Managing Digital Pictures on Your PC," later in this chapter, for some tips on ways to name and organize digital pictures.

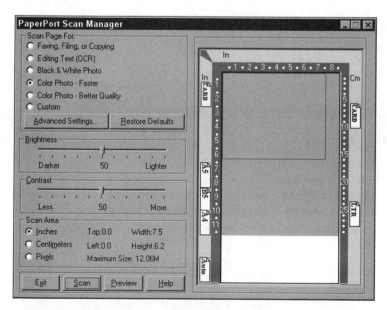

Figure 8-2. The software that came with an older model of the Visioneer OneTouch scanner.

8

Managing Your Digital Pictures

Unless you have a specific need, save the scanned image as a JPG file, the most common type of graphic file used on the World Wide Web. Figure 8-3 shows a digital picture that was created from a photographic print.

Figure 8-3. Part of a scanned image. For the origins of the image, see this book's Quick Start.

Downloading Pictures from a Digital Camera

Generalizing about downloading digital pictures from a digital camera to your PC is difficult. Not that the process is hard. Far from it. It's just that the specific downloading process varies by digital camera and editing software, and most cameras offer a choice of downloading methods.

Note

When you *download* a file, you're merely *copying* it. The original stays put and is not moved.

You can download pictures from a digital camera to your PC in three different ways. Some cameras may give you a choice of downloading methods. The AOL PhotoCam, for example, lets you download your pictures from the camera to your computer by using a cable that links the camera to your computer. You can also use a separately purchased adapter that goes into your PC's A drive. To download pictures, simply insert the PhotoCam's removable CompactFlash memory card into the adapter. You control the process from the camera's software, which you installed when you got your camera.

Here are the three ways you can transfer pictures:

▶ **Capture pictures directly onto a floppy (3½-inch) disk.** When the disk is full, remove the disk from the camera and place it in your PC, where you can transfer the images directly to your PC. Currently, the Sony Mavica is one of the few digital cameras offering built-in floppy support. Instead of buying expensive memory cards, you just carry around a box of disks in your camera holder. This method does not support gigantic megapixel files, but can't be beat for normal pictures of average size (under 100K).

▶ **Let your PC read the camera's memory card directly.** Some memory cards can be placed in a special adapter and inserted into either the A drive or an inexpensive reading device. (See Chapter 7.) The beauty of removable cards is that you can remove them and buy larger amounts of additional memory — an option not available if you're using an otherwise convenient floppy disk, as with the Sony Mavica.

Some digital cameras (like the newer Sony CyberShot) have memory *sticks,* which record pictures as well as sound and come with adapters enabling them to be used in a PC's A drive.

▶ **Use a serial or USB cable.** Most cameras use a serial cable (cord) attached to the camera on one end and connected to a PC's serial port (on the back of a PC) on the other end. More and more cameras come with Universal Serial Bus (USB) cables that can be plugged into a newer kind of port (called a Universal Serial Bus) on the back of a computer. (Refer to Chapter 7.) USB connections are becoming standard issue on new PCs.

Regardless of cable type, transferring pictures by cable can take a while (see the next section for an example of the process and the time involved), but the procedure is pretty simple: Attach the cable, turn on the camera, open the camera's software on the computer, and pull the pictures in by using the software. All digital cameras come with graphics software that is useful for downloading, managing, and (to some extent) editing digital pictures.

Tip

Whatever the method you choose for downloading and uploading pictures, doing so as often as possible ensures you'll have enough memory to take new pictures. Because digital cameras have no film, you can't just go to the drug-store for film whenever you want to take more pictures. Get in the habit of managing pictures by deleting the ones you don't want and frequently downloading the rest.

Cross-Reference

Digital cameras use two major types of memory: CompactFlash and SmartMedia. See Chapter 7 for information about these types of memory.

Transferring Pictures from a Digital Camera to Your PC: An Example

Here's an example of how easy it is to download digital picture files from a digital camera (the Hewlett-Packard C20) using a serial cable. I've chosen to use this camera as an example because this older digital camera (one of the first megapixel cameras) is still perfectly usable, and the basic principles haven't changed during several years of continuous refinement. The point to remember is that although digital cameras are computers in some ways, such cameras are primarily creative tools that don't rely on an operating system or big software applications; they rely on you.

After you attach the cable between the camera and computer, open the sliding door covering the camera's lens to start the downloading process. This simple action causes the HP software to open automatically and download previews *(thumbnails)* of the pictures on the HP 20C CompactFlash memory card. The pictures are displayed in the software's main window. *At this point in the process, the pictures themselves have not been downloaded, just the thumbnails.*

The thumbnail versions of the pictures do not yet have filenames, and the actual digital-picture files are still on the camera's memory card. In the HP PhotoSmart software, you now follow these steps:

1. Click the Save button to indicate your intention to save the files, which are only now automatically given filenames (corresponding to the date recorded for the pictures; the date, in turn, can be set using the camera's built-in menu).

2. Next, click the Save/Export button (see Figure 8-4) and indicate where to save the files (choose the disk icon, representing your hard disk, in this example).

3. Select a folder in which you want to save the downloaded files. The full files are now downloaded and saved to the selected folder. A progress meter records the process, which can take 1 to 2 minutes per image depending on resolution and processor speed, among other factors (see Figure 8-4).

Click this button to indicate where on your PC the images will be saved.

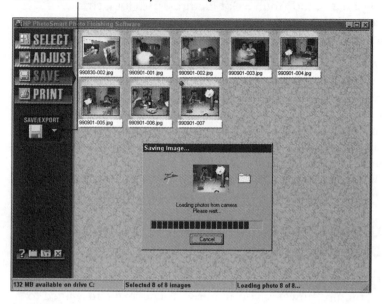

Figure 8-4. Using HP PhotoSmart.

Managing Digital Pictures on Your PC

After you start using "You've Got Pictures," scanning old photos, taking new digital photos with a digital camera, creating Web pages, and turning the kids loose with programs like Kai's SuperGoo, your hard drive is going to start filling up with a myriad of files, some very large, scattered across a dozen folders. You'll first realize that you're getting flooded when you can't find a favorite digital picture for use in a home or work project.

Finding those pictures is a lot harder than searching for documents consisting only of words, because you may have more than one version of the same image. Have you ever taken a dozen shots of the same beach, fountain, or baby on one roll of film? Worse, two or three rolls during the same weekend? Adding to the potential confusion is the fact that digital

cameras automatically assign numbers to digital pictures (usually a date), and "You've Got Pictures" uses long strings of random-seeming numbers to identify both rolls and downloaded pictures.

Whether you're getting your pictures on your computer using "You've Got Pictures," or with a digital camera or scanner, you will want to rename those pictures as soon as they're downloaded to your PC so that you can identify them in terms that make sense to you. More than that, you need to use some consistent naming scheme to retrieve that certain digital picture in the future. Short and sweet: To keep track of your digital pictures, you need to make a slight effort to get organized. The next few pages introduce some ideas and tools for doing so.

Using AOL Picture Gallery to Manage Your Digital Pictures

Chances are, you won't be completely satisfied with your digital picture, however you acquired it. The image may need to be *cropped* (have extraneous parts of the picture trimmed away), it may need to be rotated or resized, and so on. To help out with these basic tasks, AOL provides Picture Gallery. Chapter 10 provides more details about *editing* with Picture Gallery, but for now I introduce the tool and indicate how you can use it to view your pictures, folder by folder.

To open a digital picture in the AOL Picture Gallery, follow these steps:

1. Sign onto AOL and choose File⇨Open Picture Gallery. The Open Picture Gallery box appears.

2. Select the folder on your hard drive (or other disk) that contains the pictures you want to view. Because Picture Gallery displays only GIF files, JPG files, and BMP files, you're only able to open a folder containing at least one.

   Any images in the selected folder now appear six at a time in the Picture Gallery window, shown in Figure 8-5. If the folder has more than six digital pictures, click the Next arrow to see additional images.

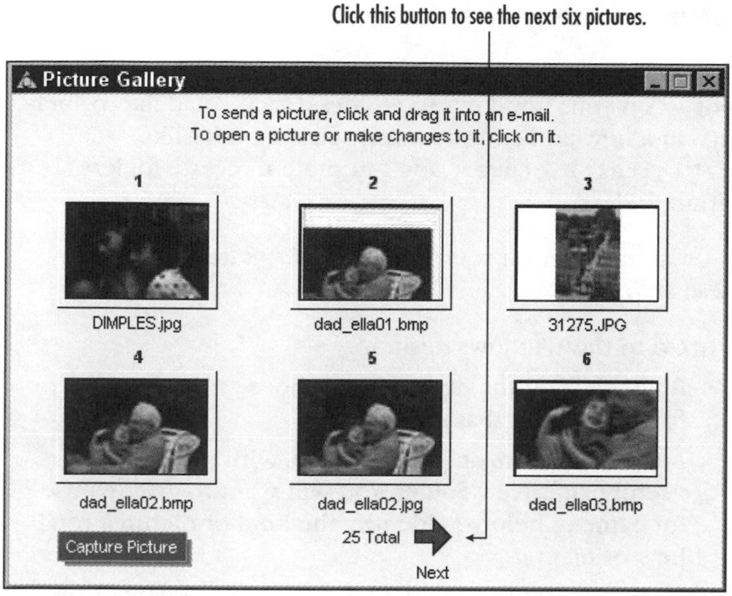

Click this button to see the next six pictures.

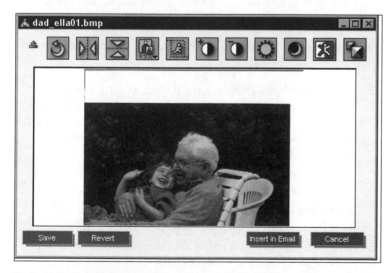

Figure 8-5. The AOL Picture Gallery displaying the figures in a folder. Click a picture to edit it.

3. To edit a scanned picture, click the image, which will now appear in its own window (see Figure 8-6). See Chapter 10 for more information on editing images with Picture Gallery.

Figure 8-6. Use AOL Picture Gallery to view any image and do some basic editing.

8

Managing Your Digital Pictures

Suppose you've already downloaded digital pictures attached to e-mail messages. Where are those pictures now? They may be in your America Online 5.0/Download folder or in a few random spots on your hard drive — in folders whose names and locations you may have lost track of. There's nothing easier than losing track of photos and folders, after all. Before things get out of hand, consider creating a folder, or a structure of folders, for all your pictures. You can't do all those fun photo projects if you don't know where you've kept your files!

Use whatever type of organization you'd like. One personal setup, used by a friend of mine, is shown in Figure 8-7. Sometimes, a chronological manner makes the most sense, as when you're tracking a child's development. You might set up a folder for each year, or even for each season, if you plan to create an ongoing collection. You can create folders by subject (such as Family or Vacation) or by photographic theme (such as Portraits or Landscapes), or both.

Taking Charge of Your Folders

Create a new set of folders for your pictures in a handy spot — on your Windows 95/98 desktop if you'd like, or perhaps in a new and conspicuously named folder like C:/Digital Pictures. Don't hesitate to create folders within folders.

To create a folder on your Windows 95/98 desktop, follow these steps:

1. Go to the Windows desktop.
2. Right-click on the desktop and choose New⇨Folder from the menu that appears.

   A folder appears on your desktop, with the less-than-useful name, New Folder. You will want to give it a useful name to help you identify the kind of pictures you'll be storing in it.
3. Right-click on the new folder, and select Rename from the menu. Type in a new name, then click outside the folder to indicate you're done creating the name. You can always change the name later.
4. Now, simply drag folders and files — from either the Windows desktop or from Windows Explorer — into your new folder. From Explorer, find any pictures to be copied. Select them, right-click, and click Copy. Find your new folder (on the Desktop), select it, and click Paste.

To create a folder on your C drive, or other drive, follow these steps:

1. To use Windows Explorer, right-click on the Start button in the lower-left corner of your Windows desktop and select Explorer from the menu. Alternatively, from the Start Menu, choose Run, type **Explorer,** and press Enter. Windows Explorer opens.
2. Select the drive where you want the new folder. Choose File⇨New⇨Folder.

   A fast way of creating a folder is to select the drive, then hold down the Alt key and press F, N, and F.
3. Give the new folder a name and then drag those other picture-laden files and folders into it.

If necessary, you can add subfolders within the new folders by using the same procedure:

1. Open up the new folder, whether it's on the desktop or on a specific drive in Windows Explorer.
2. Choose File⇨New⇨Folder. (Or, hold down Alt and press F, N, and F.)
3. Continue creating all the subfolders and sub-subfolders you need. Figure 8-7 shows you an example.

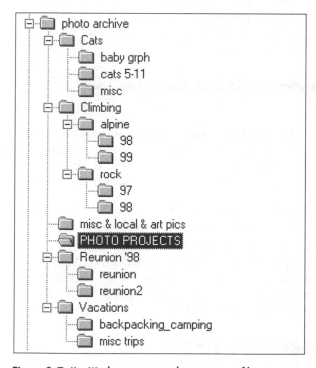

Figure 8-7. Use Windows to create whatever image-file organizational system works for you. This sample organization has six categories and several layers. Any system is better than none.

If you prefer a descriptive, subject-based organization, create folders like Family, Vacation, Pets, Beach, and so on. Or combine topical categories *and* years, using 2- or 4-digit numbers (for years) to define the subfolders (for example, C:/digital pictures/beach/2000).

Clarity and consistency in labeling *folders* are probably even more important than they are for individual digital picture files. Although browsing images in any one folder is relatively easy with AOL Picture Gallery (it shows all the pictures in a folder), it's much harder when you don't know which folder to start in. Creating descriptive names for folders (such as **Vacation 1998 New York** in a folder with pictures from New York vacations, **12th Birthday** in a folder devoted to pictures of a birthday, and so on) can make finding those folders a lot easier.

If you are using disks or other removable media to store pictures, make sure that you label them. (Label the plastic cases if you are using writable CDs.) You won't regret being consistent and even neat, especially if others will need to use your collection. Also, you may want to mimic your hierarchical file organization in the filing of the physical media as closely as possible. Using special labeling paper available from Avery, HP, and other vendors, you can print labels to make sure that they're legible and look good.

If you are a hobby photographer, you may want to create folders devoted to themes — landscapes, portraits, wildlife, or whatever topics make sense; such folders are matters of personal preference. You can always add folders for categories and move digital pictures later. The goal is not only to store images, but also to make finding them later as easy as possible.

Naming Consistently

Your system for naming files and folders should correspond to how you think of your pictures' *content.* For example, you might name your files like this: Claire_ hat for a picture of Claire wearing a silly hat.

Using Windows Find to Uncover Lost Pictures

Windows 95/98 comes with a handy way of finding any file on your hard drive, as well as any Zip, floppy, and CD drives. The value of a naming system becomes evident when you search for a specific picture using Find (or similar software).

1. From the Start Menu, choose Find⇨Files or Folders. The Find: All Files dialog box comes up; see Figure 8-8.

2. Click the Name & Location tab shown in Figure 8-8. Type all or part of a filename in the Named text entry box. You can use an asterisk (*) if you're not sure of the exact spelling of a file. For example, ***.jpg** retrieves all the JPGs on one or more drives.

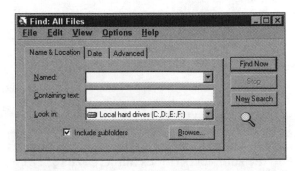

Figure 8-8. The Windows Find: All Files dialog box, available from the Start Menu at Find⇨Files or Folders.

3. Use the Containing Text box to search for word-processing documents that contain certain words.

Simply put, the Named box helps when you're searching for a file and know part of its filename. The Containing Text box helps when you know what's *inside* the document. In searching for a picture file, the Containing Text box won't do you a lot of good. If you want to create descriptions for your pictures, you'll want to use one of the specialized software packages described in "Managing Pictures with Specialized Software," a little later in this chapter.

The Look In box consists of a drop-down list of drives and disks that you can search: the C drive alone, the C through F drives together, the CD drive, the A and Zip drives, and the like. Searches can take a long time if you don't specify a drive to search. The choices available to you will vary with your system configuration.

Backing Up Digital Pictures

Many photographers keep their photographs in a different place from the negatives to decrease the chances of losing an image forever. Of course, digital pictures don't *have* negatives, at least if they were taken with a digital camera. In any case, you should retain backup copies of your important digital-picture files, and at the highest resolution, especially if you have no negatives for them. Though hard drives are much more reliable than they were a few years ago, they do sometimes fail. After all, if your hard drive crashes, retrieving data (including digital pictures) might be a hassle — if it's possible. Chapter 7 reviews the different kinds of storage media (such as Zip disks and CD-R/CD-RW disks), which you can use to archive your pictures. After your pictures are archived, you can remove them from your hard drive. For extra safety, make two backup copies, should anything happen to a backup disk.

Using Software to Manage Digital Pictures

For that growing collection of images, you may want to use software tools for organizing them. If you need to do any of the following activities, you will *have* to use such software.

▶ Store and associate descriptive text *(annotations)* with your images. Why would you want to do that? Partly to record exactly what is in the picture and the settings used to take it. Partly to do searches for digital pictures. The concept is simple. You assign keywords or descriptions to certain images, and then you can search for all images with which you have used the keywords or descriptive words.

▶ Convert files one at a time, or several at a time, from one format to another.

▶ Print out digital pictures as collections of small pictures, sometimes called *thumbnails,* to get a quick overview so you can begin associating filenames and picture content quickly.

▶ Catalog and sort image files and create albums of pictures dispersed across folders.

▶ Publish collections of images as Web pages.

All of these tasks can be carried out using a home graphics program such as MGI PhotoSuite III Family Edition or one of the leading products discussed in Chapter 9. Also useful are the more specialized products discussed later in this chapter.

Using Albums to Manage Pictures

An *album* is simply a collection of photos. The photos may be special simply because you like them, or they may have been brought together because they document some important event or place.

▶ *Online,* at "You've Got Pictures," albums make it easy to group related photos and share them with others. Chapter 5 goes into the details of creating and sharing albums, and of managing Buddy Albums (albums shared with you).

▶ *On your computer's hard drive,* an album is a very useful tool for keeping track of digital pictures that may be scattered across many folders. Albums on your computer can also be incorporated into projects such as family trees and wedding albums, which can be printed out or uploaded to the Web (see Figure 8-9). Popular programs like Print Shop and MGI PhotoSuite include templates for quickly creating such albums.

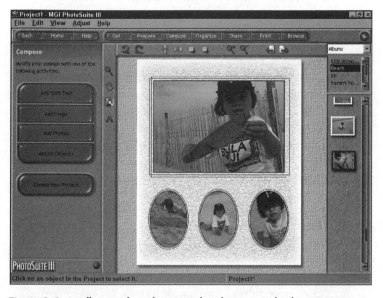

Figure 8-9. An album made to share your digital pictures with others (MGI PhotoSuite III).

In PhotoSuite (covered more fully in Chapter 10), it's easy to create an album. Click the Organize button on the toolbar (at the top of the main window). On the left side of the new window, click Albums. In the Master Albums box, click New, give your album a new name, and click OK. Now just click Add to add pictures — from any source — to your new album. Once you've created an album and filled it with photos, you can assign "properties" (keywords and annotations) to individual pictures to make it much easier to find them in the future. With an album displayed (Organize view), right click a picture, select Properties, and assign properties such as Title, Subject, Event, and so on.

Tip

The descriptive labels you can add to an individual picture in "You've Got Pictures" won't be retained when you download that picture to your PC. However, if you download all the individual pictures in an online album to your PC, you can then re-create the album on your computer. Use a program like PhotoSuite to give these downloaded pictures a home in a new album, along with complete descriptions.

Managing Pictures with Specialized Software

Some programs are made specifically for managing files. Such utilities are routinely integrated into scanner and digital-camera software. A few good standalone organizing products are described in this section.

▶ Xerox's Pagis Pro is designed to organize scanned images as well as text files. Why text? Pagis Pro includes *optical character recognition* (OCR) software. You use this kind of software to turn a scanned image of a word-processed document (such as a fax) into *editable* text (as opposed to a single image merely showing text). For your digital pictures needs, Pagis Pro provides thumbnail viewing and content searching.

▶ PhotoRecall Deluxe organizes digital pictures in a database. It enables you to store text and keywords describing each image. PhotoRecall lets you create albums, which can be printed out in various formats and published as Web pages. PhotoRecall enables you to store text and data along with your images. The software also enables you to search your own albums, drives, and the Internet. Finally, it provides a "darkroom" for editing digital pictures.

▶ ThumbsPlus, from Cerious Software, Inc. (www.cerious.com), offers outstanding tools for organizing, viewing, editing, and otherwise managing digital pictures. Unlike many of the products from bigger companies, ThumbsPlus lets you open dozens of file types and convert individual files or batches of files from one format to another. Along the left side of the ThumbsPlus window, ThumbsPlus displays folders and files — just as Windows Explorer does. On the right, ThumbsPlus displays thumbnails of individual digital pictures in a selected folder. A full suite of editing capabilities is included, so you can tweak colors, apply filters, and resize, crop, and rotate individual pictures. As with PhotoSuite III, you can add short descriptions to your digital pictures, so you can later search for digital pictures.

With Windows 98, you can now view *thumbnails* (small versions) of digital pictures. In the Windows Explorer window, open the folder that contains the pictures you want to view. Click the Explorer toolbar's View button and select As Web Page from the drop-down list that appears. Click a digital picture file to view a picture within the right-hand Explorer pane. Double-click the picture to view the picture within imaging software.

General-purpose database software can be used to store digital images as well as text. If you are comfortable using a program such as Access (Microsoft) or FileMaker (Filemaker, Inc.), you can quickly create a data table consisting of structured records for each picture. Each record would include the picture itself, a title, a file location, a subject, and so on. With such a database, you can more easily search for digital pictures, make them available to others, and update them systematically.

Summary

This chapter covered a lot of ground, but everything discussed took place on the familiar territory of your home PC. The basic chores described here — downloading files from digital cameras and scanners, then consistently naming and storing those pictures — can help you view and retrieve them later. Unless you have some sort of system, actually using your digital pictures can become an unnecessary hassle.

From here, the road is downhill, as in downhill skiing. With editing digital pictures (Chapters 9 through 10) and creating Web pages (Chapter 13), you can start getting creative with your growing and beautifully organized collection of digital pictures.

UNDERSTANDING RESOLUTION AND GRAPHICS FILES

A QUICK LOOK

Chapter 9

Understanding Resolution and Graphics Files

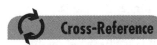

Cross-Reference

Chapter 10 takes the next step, applying the lessons of this chapter to the specific problems you can remedy with image-editing software.

Digital pictures offer a great deal more control of your pictures than you have ever experienced with photographic prints. Only in the most expensive digital cameras, however, does the camera itself provide this control. Usually, it takes image-editing software to bring out the best in your pictures. This software is easy to use, and software makers are learning how to simplify the process so that it serves as a true creative tool.

Understanding Images

Software for enhancing your digital pictures brings the control and creativity of the darkroom to the living room, and you won't have to breathe the fumes. With inexpensive graphics software, you can now remove red eye from your digital photos, turn up the contrast on washed-out scenes, and reduce the shadows in those unevenly exposed beach scenes. To use the software effectively, it helps to understand the basic relations between resolution, picture size, and file size.

Resolution and Picture Size

Resolution and picture size are closely linked. With digital pictures, *resolution* usually refers to how sharp an image looks as measured by pixels (picture elements) per image. *In general, the more pixels per image, the finer the detail collected (and the better the image appears when printed on paper or shown on-screen).*

There are exceptions to the general rule. For example, you can change the size of the picture without changing the number of pixels. Just like spreading butter, the thinner you spread the same number of pixels, the fewer pixels for each part of the picture. To the eye, the spread-out image is going to appear more "pixelated" — show more jagged lines, less continuous colors and tones.

A picture's size in pixels also makes a difference when you're using the picture on a Web page or for any on-screen use:

▶ For on-screen use, big files (in kilobytes) take long to download for people viewing the picture. That's why you'll want to use far fewer dots per inch for the Web — 72 or 96 dpi (dots/pixels per inch) — as compared to 300 dpi for prints.

▶ With a computer monitor's resolution unchanged, if you have two pictures to display, the picture with more pixels is simply going to need more space to display than one with fewer pixels. For example, a digital camera might enable you to take pictures at two resolution settings, such as 320 x 240 pixels or 640 x 480 pixels. The images appear as different sizes on a monitor. The 640-by-480-pixel image appears larger than the 320-x-240-pixel image. If you have a megapixel version of the same image, it will be larger than your screen and you'll have to scroll to the left and right to see the whole thing. The bottom line: A digital picture will rarely appear as sharp on-screen as on paper.

Note

It's possible to change the size of a picture without changing the number of pixels in the image, which is why it's not always true that the more pixels per image, the better the image's quality.

Note

When software can't display a complete image, it automatically adds scrollbars along the right and bottom of the window, so that you can move the picture right or left and up or down in order to see all parts of the image.

Tip

AOL 5.0 displays best at a screen resolution of 800 x 600 pixels or above. You adjust your screen resolution in Windows 95/98 by right-clicking the desktop, selecting Properties, opening the Settings tab, and moving the Desktop area lever to the right or left. When you have finished making adjustments, click Apply and then OK. Your screen may flicker momentarily, but don't worry.

Pixels and Resolution

A digital picture's *quality* — its sharpness and its richness of color and tone — depends on the number of pixels in an image and the number of colors that can be displayed by a single pixel.

What's a pixel? It's the small colored box that makes up the basic unit of every digital picture. The first of the following digital pictures shows pixels close up; the second gives you the whole picture.

A bit-mapped program is one that creates images made of pixels. A vector-based program (such as Adobe Illustrator or Macromedia Flash) creates pictures out of formulas that describe shapes; such programs are often used for creating art. This art can be rendered very large without reducing resolution, hence the principles of resolutions discussed here have to do with bitmapped images. The software products discussed in this book and commonly used online are bit-mapped.

Click to zoom in or out

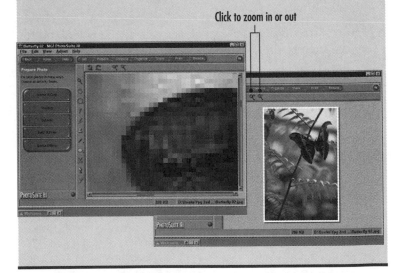

Resolution and File Size

The resolution of an image file (in pixels) affects its file size (in kilobytes). A higher-resolution image (640 x 480 pixels, as in the AOL PhotoCam) must obviously be bigger than a 340 x 260 image — just to store all those extra pixels.

Think of what happens when you jump to the megapixel cameras and three-megapixel cameras! Although good for prints, they're not much use for many on-screen uses. Three or four 1152 x 872 digital photos can weigh in at a megabyte or so. When you remember that the average floppy disk can only hold 1.4MB, even a handy camera like the Sony Mavica, which stores pictures right on a floppy disk, can max out on a megapixel picture.

Computers and Colors

In the world of magazines and four-color printing, colors are described as a mix of cyan (an intense light blue), magenta (a deep purplish red), yellow, and black ink. Each color can be defined as four numbers — one value each for C, M, Y, and K. The shorthand for this system of describing colors is CMYK — K is black.

Computers, however, describe every color in terms of a different model: as combinations of red, green, and blue (RGB) light. For any combination of red, green, and blue, software lets you set values such as *saturation* (density of color, from washed out and gray to fully and intensively colored) and *luminosity* (brightness of the color).

Definition

Computers describe every color as a combination of red, green, and blue (RGB) light. Each main color can assume any of 256 values (for example, from no red to solid red), and you can use software to adjust the density and brightness of the color.

Pixels and Colors: Who Needs 16 Million Colors, Anyway?

A pixel takes on color depending on how many bits it has to play with. A single bit can be black or white; eight bits can display up to 256 colors (2 to the 8th power). These days, pixels can have more than 24 bits. Because each bit can take up to two values, that makes more than 16.7 million colors (2 to the 24th power), which is more than the poor human eye can detect.

The two main Web browsers (Netscape Navigator and Microsoft Internet Explorer) share a *palette* of only 216 colors that can be reliably displayed in both browsers. Reducing a picture's *bit depth* (number of colors a pixel can display) is a good way to bring down its file size without reducing the number of pixels (resolution). A program like Macromedia Fireworks can help you adapt your picture's colors to the limited colors available on the Web.

Excellent information about file types is available on AOL. At AOL Keyword: **Help**, click the A-Z index. Under F, read the article called About File Types and Extensions.

Files saved in very common formats, such as JPG and HTML, can be opened by many different programs. AOL itself can open and play most common graphics formats, TXT (text) documents, MIDI and WAV sound files, JPG and GIF images, and HTML pages.

AOL has always offered members a way of viewing common graphics files, online and offline. With the AOL software open (but you don't have to sign on), choose File⇨Open. Browse to a specific JPG, GIF, or BMP file and double-click to view it. AOL's Picture Gallery lets you view all GIFs, JPGs, and BMPs in a specific folder.

What You Need to Know About Graphics Files

If you are planning to use your digital photographs in creative projects or on Web pages, it helps to get comfortable with file formats. This stuff reads like alphabet soup at first, but it becomes second nature quickly enough.

Digital pictures, like most kinds of computer files, can be saved in various file formats, which have been standardized to simplify their use by different programs as well as by different types of computers (Windows and Mac). A file *format* is indicated by the part of the *filename* that appears after the period (for example, beach.jpg and beach.gif). JPG and GIF are the two major graphics formats used on the Web, and they are the most important types of grapics files with which you should be familiar.

Based on the extension, your computer can usually figure out what program to use to open (or launch) a file.

In a filename like chapter6.doc, doc is the file type created by the Microsoft Word program. Open this file from Windows Explorer, and Word opens, too, with the document displayed. Likewise, if you have a Web page on your hard drive, its file extension is HTM or HTML. If you're connected to the Internet and open such a file, your default Web browser opens, displaying the file.

JPG

Usually pronounced "jay-peg," this format has a fairly compact file size but a high image quality, making it a good format for photographs. JPGs are particularly good for the Web because they can be compressed (decreased in size), can be downloaded quickly, and can be viewed with any Web browser, including Netscape Navigator and the version of Internet Explorer included with AOL. (JPGs get their name from the Joint Photographic Experts Group, the organization that developed the format.)

GIF

Usually pronounced "giff" with a hard *G* (and less commonly as "jiff," like the peanut butter), this format provides a reasonably small file size compared to JPGs, partly because a GIF pixel can't represent as many colors as a JPG pixel. GIFs work better for solid colors and simple black, white, and gray images — more than continuous-tone images, such as photographs, for which JPGs are better suited. GIFs are widely used on the Web for banners, line art, logos, and simple graphics. They are also used to create basic animations called *animated GIFs* (see the Glossary). GIF stands for Graphic Interchange Format. Figure 9-1 shows a JPG (the photo) and two GIFs (the logo and the button), side by side.

Note

GIFs can easily be saved with a transparent background (so that the background shows through, and so that the image doesn't clash with its surroundings). This format was used to exchange files on the Internet before the Web became popular.

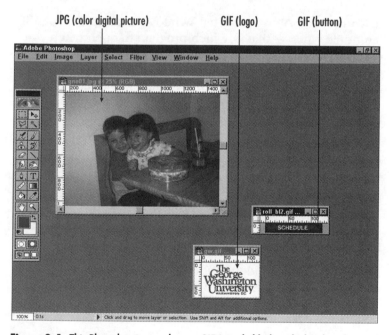

Figure 9-1. This Photoshop image shows a GIF (simple black-and-white line drawing) and a JPG (color digital picture).

ART

ART is AOL's own file format. To download certain Web graphics more quickly, AOL's Web browser converts them into this format. The AOL Picture Gallery can display ART files and convert them into JPGs and GIFs for use in other programs. ART works by compressing certain Web graphics, sometimes at the loss of quality. To turn off the automatic conversion to ART: choose My AOL⇨Preferences from the AOL toolbar; click the WWW button; click the Web Graphics tab; and make sure there's no check in the Use Compressed Graphics check box.

Telling Windows How to Handle File Formats

In Windows 95/98, you can tell Windows what to do with different file types — that is, which program to open when you open a specific document. If you like CorelDRAW, for example, you can double-click beach9901.jpg and have the picture come up in CorelDRAW. Or have the picture come up in AOL or Paint Shop Pro. In other words, you can edit your digital pictures with the software product of your choice — not the one chosen for you.

This useful procedure seems difficult because of the cluttered Windows 95/98 dialog boxes and the unhelpfully terse Microsoft language. These few steps can, however, go a long way to customizing Windows to suit your style. *Associating* a file with a program is the first step to making the file (and the program) useful.

1. While using Windows 98, choose Start⇨Settings⇨ Folder Options. Click the File Types tab. You'll see a window like the one shown in Figure 9-2.

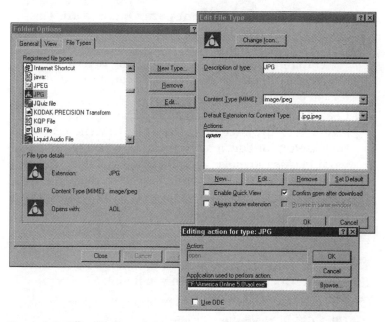

Figure 9-2. Telling Windows what program to open when you try to use a specific file. Here, I am "associating" files with the JPG extension with the ThumbsPlus program, discussed in Chapter 8.

2. In the list of Registered File Types in the Folder Options window, select a file type. In this case, JPG is selected. (The "registered" bit is a Windows thing, referring to the Windows 95/98 Registry, which keeps track of programs and their components.) Browse the whole list if you don't find what you're seeking. In the File Type Details box at the bottom of the Folder Options window, you'll see the following information for any selected file type:

   • **File extension(s).** The part of the filename after the period. In other words, you're telling Windows what to do when you try to open a file ending in .JPG, .GIF, or some other format. Chances are, most of the file extensions you'll use when working with digital pictures will end with .JPG, .GIF, .BMP, and perhaps a few others.

   • **Content type.** This is also known as MIME type (for example, text/plain).

- **Now, for the important part: Opens with.** This indicates which program launches when you try to open Beach.jpg. In this case, JPG files are currently set to open in AOL. Here, we're going to have them open in ThumbsPlus, where they can be annotated and edited.

3. Click Edit to open the Edit File Type box. (Refer to Figure 9-2.) If you see other words in the Actions box, such as Print or Edit, remove them by selecting each word, clicking Remove, and repeating until done. In the Actions box in the lower part of this box, click Edit to bring up the Editing Actions box. Use the dialog box shown in the lower right of Figure 9-2.

4. In the Editing Action for Type box, tell Windows to open a different program. To do so, click Browse and find the program with which you want to associate the file type. Double-click it when you find it.

5. Click OK to close the Editing Action box.

6. Click OK to close the Edit File Type box.

7. Test the new association by looking for an appropriate file (by choosing Start⇨Find⇨Files or Folders, searching for ***.JPG** in your system, and double-clicking a JPG file. The program specified in Step 4 should open automatically.

Software for Editing Digital Pictures

Cross-Reference

Chapter 10 shows how to use a single image-editing package to address a series of photographic problems.

Once performed only by trained graphic artists and other alchemists, editing photographs has gotten affordable, untechnical, and downright fun. Software for editing digital pictures is available in almost every price category. These programs can do just about everything from improving your digital pictures to creating bizarre effects that kids will love. Most of this software will let you create albums and create all sorts of projects.

Understanding Your Needs

With so much all-purpose software out there, understanding your primary needs is a good idea. Some programs — even if they purport to do everything — excel at specific functions, such as image-editing, creating special effects, or managing pictures. In evaluating software, make sure to assess:

> ▶ Whether you are creating for the Web or print; for your boss or your kids.
>
> ▶ The range of tools in the software.
>
> ▶ Platform support (Mac or Windows).
>
> ▶ Files supported and created by the software.
>
> ▶ Extent of Web integration. (Can images be optimized for the Web? Can Web pages be generated automatically from a digital picture, a collection of pictures, or a home project?)

Choosing the Right Package

Here are several leading digital-editing programs worth checking out if you want to set up your own digital darkroom. The list is not complete, nor will you find recommendations. Most of these programs are so complete that any one of them will suffice for most day-to-day needs.

Adobe PhotoDeluxe

Adobe PhotoDeluxe is a very popular program, and it is often included ("bundled") with both digital cameras and scanners. PhotoDeluxe is smaller and easier to use than Adobe Photoshop, the favorite of graphic artists, yet it still offers many of the Photoshop program's advanced features, such as layers. Basic editing tasks are made intuitive in PhotoDeluxe, unlike in Photoshop. PhotoDeluxe is oriented to rapid editing and easy incorporation of digital pictures into all sorts of photo projects. The PhotoDeluxe program includes templates to let you easily make calendars, cards, albums, and much more. PhotoDeluxe features step-by-step wizards that walk you through every task. As you'll increasingly find with other products, with PhotoDeluxe you can connect with several Web sites that give PhotoDeluxe users access to seasonal art and additional downloadable project templates.

Adobe Photoshop

Adobe Photoshop is a powerful, high-end photo manipulation and design program. There's not much you *can't* do with

Tip

AOL Keyword: **CNET** has the latest reviews of the latest versions of these programs. On AOL, you can purchase all the programs listed in this chapter at AOL Keyword: **Shop@AOL**, a virtual mall that includes big software vendors such as Egghead, Outpost, and Beyond.com. You can browse Shop@AOL for your hardware purchases as well.

Tip

One software feature to look for, no matter what your goals, is something called *TWAIN compliance.* TWAIN compliance means that the software in question is able to acquire (retrieve) files directly from a hardware device such as a scanner or digital camera. Load up the software; then initiate a scan or a digital-camera download from within the software!

Tip

For an outstanding introduction to PhotoDeluxe, see Julie Adair King's *Adobe PhotoDeluxe 4 For Dummies* (IDG Books Worldwide, 2000). Ms. King also wrote the highly informative *Digital Photography For Dummies,* 3rd Edition (IDG Books Worldwide, 2000).

Photoshop, from creating your own font to retouching your digital pictures a pixel at a time. As a commercial product (and as a fairly expensive one), Adobe Photoshop is extremely well supported with abundant information at the Adobe Web site (see the Adobe Photoshop Tutorial cited in Appendix A), plus a library of books in every price range, including *Adobe Photoshop 5 For Windows For Dummies* and *Adobe Photoshop 5 For Macs For Dummies,* both by Deke McClelland and both published by IDG Books Worldwide, Inc. While preferred by professional graphic artists for its range and depth of features and large third-party market of add-ons, Photoshop can be daunting for newcomers to digital pictures.

AOL GraphicSuite

Find It Online

Visit AOL Keyword: **GraphicSuite** for the latest details on the GraphicSuite CD.

AOL published GraphicSuite to put a variety of useful graphics programs and utilities from leading companies into an affordable package designed especially for AOL members who are fairly new to computer graphics. The suite includes versions of the following software:

- ▶ **@loha:** For adding animation and sound to e-mail
- ▶ **LivePix:** For retouching photos
- ▶ **MasterClips/Master Photos:** A collection of 6,000 clip-art images and 4,000 photos
- ▶ **PhotoVista:** For creating Web-ready panoramas from digital pictures
- ▶ **Print Shop:** A version of Broderbund Print Shop that can be put to work creating cards, posters, banners, and simple signs

Broderbund's The Print Shop

Cross-Reference

Wally Wang and Richard Hing unlock the possibilities of Print Shop in *The Print Shop Deluxe For Dummies* (IDG Books Worldwide, Inc.).

The names of many graphics-editing programs may seem to blur together in your mind (PhotoDeluxe . . . PhotoSuite . . . Photoshop . . . PhotoSoap), but The Print Shop has an especially precise name. The Print Shop is your private print shop. Choose any of the buttons in Figure 9-3, and you'll be able to select from a very wide range of *projects to make,* using any of the hundreds of built-in templates. Or start from scratch if you have a good idea of what you want to do. For every type of project and template, you will be walked through by a "wizard," which asks you to make a series of choices regarding everything from the way you want the paper folded (in a card, for example) to the backgrounds and digital frames. After you have specified the elements, the wizard creates the project for you. Presto. You can add text and digital pictures wherever you want, add digital "watermarks," and much more. Broderbund also makes a staggeringly big collection of Clickart (non-photographic clip art).

Figure 9-3. The Print Shop lets you put those digital pictures to all sorts of good uses.

Macromedia Fireworks

This product forms part of a set of Web-building products from Macromedia, a leading creator of tools for Web professionals: Dreamweaver 3.0 is an HTML editor, and Flash is currently the preferred means to produce animated, interactive graphics for the Web. Fireworks has much of the power of Adobe Photoshop but was developed with a focus on the needs of Web developers. It lets you optimize JPGs and GIFs, create animated and transparent GIFs, and (like Photoshop) build up complex graphics from layers, which can be individually edited.

MGI PhotoSuite

This versatile software comes in several versions and can be found packaged with some digital cameras and scanners; it is also available as a module within other software packages. In Chapter 8, Figure 8-9 shows the MGI PhotoSuite interface, as

Note

The AOL PhotoCam digital camera currently comes with an earlier version of PhotoSuite called *SE*. Because the newer version of the software adds so many features to SE and wraps them up in an easy-to-use interface, this book looks at PhotoSuite III Family Edition. The Platinum edition includes a CD with more than 30,000 digital photographs for you to use! MGI also makes VideoWave software for editing digital video.

do several figures in Chapter 10. *Versatility* is the operative word here. With PhotoSuite III Family Edition, you can do the basic work of editing digital pictures to sharpen contrast, enhance colors, remove scratches, and so on. For every tool, PhotoSuite provides a *wizard* (simple, numbered, on-screen instructions for using the tool effectively). In addition, as I mentioned in Chapter 8, you can use PhotoSuite to create albums on your hard drive — both albums for organizing your pictures (for yourself) and albums for displaying in an attractive layout (for others).

The MGI CD includes several hundred megabytes of templates and clipart for creating invitations, bookmarks, gift tags, announcements, collages, albums, magazine covers, and much more. The PhotoSuite Web site (part of www.mgisoft.com) has free downloads of seasonal and situational bookmarks, cards, posters, and more. On PhotoSuite III, you'll even find a handy (but somewhat poky) Web browser that takes you directly to the MGI PhotoSuite Web site for online help; from there you can browse anywhere you want.

Microsoft Picture It!

This popular product offers easy image editing plus more than 500 design templates and backgrounds ready to turn your photos into finished collages, cards, calendars, and more. In addition to basic image-editing tools, Picture It! can help you remove dust, scratches, and other blemishes from photos. It's a particularly useful product for organizing your digital pictures and making a set of images readily available for specific projects. Because it's Microsoft, Picture It! works smoothly with other Microsoft applications.

Paint Shop Pro (Jasc Software, Inc.)

Paint Shop Pro from Jasc Software, gives you a broad range of functions: viewing, converting, painting, photo-retouching, scanning, and screen-capturing. See Figure 9-4 for the main Paint Shop window. Among graphics enthusiasts, Paint Shop Pro has the reputation of packing much of the power of Adobe Photoshop without the daunting learning curve and abundance of complex features. For one thing, Paint Shop Pro supports a huge variety of file formats. It also includes an Animation Shop program and supports Adobe-compatible filters (also known as *plug-ins*), which let you apply photo-manipulation effects to any image. On AOL, you can download a shareware version; but to enjoy the full set of features and product support, you need to buy the program (currently under $100).

Figure 9-4. Paint Shop Pro (from Jasc Software, Inc.) comes loaded with powerful features. This figure shows an earlier version of this powerful, continually upgraded favorite.

Editing Software: Common Features

In the highly competitive market for image-editing software, software companies are piling more and more features onto products' editing capabilities, and they're adding functions that allow you to create projects and organize large collections of digital pictures. In tending to your collection of digital pictures, the key function is *editing* — the ability to make large-scale and pixel-level changes to digital pictures.

You'll find similar features in many products because the basic editing tasks are fairly standard, although the "depth" of any feature (for example, how many filters a program has) and its ease-of-use vary enormously. The current standard for feature depth is Adobe Photoshop; but for ease of use, you may want to use a consumer product like Adobe PhotoDeluxe or MGI

Tip

When shopping for image-editing software, look for the ability to create cool effects using built-in filters. With these tools, you can add character as well as cute effects to some of your images.

PhotoSuite, among the other products listed earlier in this chapter. Here are some common features:

▶ **Airbrush.** Mimics a real-life airbrush, which blows color on an image, creating a soft, indistinct edge.

▶ **Color Palette.** A map or chart you can click on to select a color to apply to a selected object.

▶ **Cropping.** Lets you cut out part of an image to focus on pertinent details or remove unneeded details.

▶ **Dodge and Burn (or Lighten/Darken) Tools.** Mimic the darkroom practice of *burning* (adding light) to darken a portion of a print or *dodging* (selectively withholding light) to lighten it. Compensates for underexposure and overexposure.

▶ **Eraser.** Erases an area of the image; sometimes various sizes and shapes are available.

▶ **Eyedropper.** Use to select a color already used in an image in order to apply that color to *other* objects by using paint and similar fill tools.

▶ **Fill tool.** Often depicted as a tipping can of paint, this tool fills in a selected mask or object with a color or pattern you specify (from a menu, palette, or eyedropper). A fill tool applies a color or pattern to an enclosed space in a digital picture or other graphics file.

▶ **Filters.** Use to sharpen and soften focus, distort, and apply other effects to digital pictures, mimicking traditional photographic filters. Filters are used in products like PhotoSuite, Paint Shop Pro, MGI PhotoSuite III, and Kai's PhotoSoap to create a very wide series of effects, such as embossing.

▶ **Layers.** Imaginary transparencies that enable you to place various elements in front or behind other items for aesthetic reasons or to directly edit a portion of the image without affecting other elements. Layers make a program like Photoshop difficult to learn but extremely powerful. PhotoDeluxe includes layers.

▶ **Hand.** Use to move images around (sometimes called *panning*) without editing them; for example, to position a large digital picture within a smaller frame.

▶ **Masking Tools.** Use to select objects of certain shapes (or freeform) or colors (or range of colors). With these tools, you can select a group of pixels to copy, cut, or edit in all sorts of ways, such as selectively applying a filter. A mask constrains edits. Without a mask, changes would affect the entire picture.

▶ **Paintbrushes.** Use to apply a color or pattern to an image or to touch up colors pixel by pixel. Sometimes also used to create "paintbrush" textures or other effects. You can often adjust the size, tip shape, and texture of the paintbrush.

▶ **Pen or Pencil.** Drawing tools; often, you can select the weight, pattern, texture, color, and other properties of the line.

▶ **Rotate.** Enables you to turn a selected object or area at either certain increments (typically of 90 degrees) or at any angle you select by rotating the image with handles provided or typing an angle measurement into a box.

▶ **Rubber Stamp or Clone Tool.** Use to copy the color or pattern of one area in an image to another area (for example, to remedy damaged portions or areas lacking in detail or color). Often, you can control the opacity, enabling you to blend the touch-ups into the background.

▶ **Selection Arrow.** To select an individual object, so that it can be moved or resized or otherwise edited. To start editing, you first select the item you want to edit! Chapter 10 goes into selecting in more depth.

▶ **Text Tool.** Use to enter and edit text. Usually, you can choose fonts, styles, colors, sizes, and other text attributes. After text has been applied, it often becomes an object that can be manipulated as a whole (repositioned, for example) or letter by letter.

▶ **Zoom Tool.** Usually, a magnifying glass for zooming in and out, to focus your editing efforts on a small part of an image.

Summary

The power of digital pictures lies in the control you have over the way they look and the ways they're used. To make the most of the software, it's helpful to know a little about pixels, colors, resolution, and graphics files; that's the stuff of image editing, just like words are what you play with when you use a word processor. In the next chapter, you get to start playing with this wonderful new software.

C H A P T E R

10

MAKING THE MOST
OF IMAGE-EDITING
SOFTWARE

A QUICK LOOK

Chapter 10

Making the Most of Image-Editing Software

The best equipment in the world can't arrange the clouds for you or remove the foot just within the frame of that otherwise perfect shot in the local playground. Sometimes, equipment flakes out. The flash misfires, or low batteries prevent an instantaneous shutter release when you click the button. And there are times when, in the excitement of the moment, the picture isn't composed quite right, and you've captured more in the picture than you may have wanted. These and many other common situations call for some repair work.

With image-editing software, you can remedy these and other problems. These days, software makers are going out of their way to make these tools fun as well as easy to use. The experience of using such software can be compared to budding photographers' excitement watching their first images come up in the developing tray in the darkroom.

Before Setting Out . . .

Image-editing software, with its big buttons and inviting interface, has the effect of a swimming pool on a sweltering day. It can be hard to stay out. Just as you'd probably want to change into a bathing suit before jumping into that pool, with any graphics software, you need to prepare a little first — you'll get better results in less time.

▶ **Save As. . . .** Save any digital picture you plan to edit with a different name before doing anything. (In most programs, you open the picture and choose File⇨ Save As.)

▶ **Free up hard drive space.** Make sure that you have a good chunk of unused hard drive space. Why? With software that manipulates big files, the software sometimes makes use of a chunk of hard drive space, sometimes called virtual memory or a scratch disk, to temporarily store the image being edited.

▶ **Learn to use the *selection tools*.** These tools let you specify exactly which parts of a picture you will be changing when you use the paint, cloning, and other tools. Precise editing and desired effects can be difficult without accurate selection.

▶ **Zoom in to see what you're doing.** With a selection made, use your zoom tools to see exactly what you're doing, close up. For removing dust, scratches, and red eye, and doing any pixel-level editing, the Zoom tool is a must.

Definition

A *scratch disk* retains previous versions of a file being edited so that any unwanted changes can be undone and prior versions restored. The only time you become aware of the scratch disk is when you lack space on your hard drive for routine editing, at which point you may be prompted to delete files and programs.

Editing Images with the AOL Picture Gallery

AOL's Picture Gallery is built right into AOL 4.0 and higher. It lets you view your digital pictures and make some overall edits. Online or offline, the Picture Gallery is available by choosing File⇨Open Picture Gallery. In the Open Picture Gallery window, browse to the folder that contains the images you

Definition

Think of a *gallery* as all the image files in a single folder on your hard drive.

Tip

The Revert button at the bottom of the Picture Gallery enables you to go back to the last saved version of an image, removing all changes made since then — not just the last change. In the Picture Gallery (or any other program), click Save after making any change you want to keep. Realize that no software lets you undo changes you've saved. That's why it's a good idea to save the edited images under a different name than the original images.

Tip

The Picture Gallery also lets you convert among common file formats (BMP, GIF, and JPG); but for additional conversion capabilities, you need a program like Paint Shop Pro or ThumbsPlus. JPGs tend to lose pixels and quality through repeated saves. They can be converted to TIFs before editing to preserve resolution, and only converted back to JPGs when you're done editing.

Tip

Play around with the Picture Gallery as with any image-editing software, but don't forget to first save your file with a different filename!

want to edit and click the Open Gallery button. You'll see a window with all the digital images in the folder, thumbnail-sized (small), six at a time. To see an individual image, just click it, and the image comes up in a new window (see Figure 10-1).

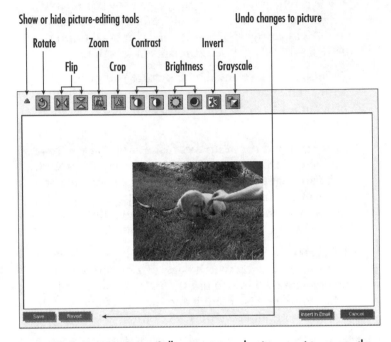

Figure 10-1. Use AOL's Picture Gallery to rotate and resize your pictures, crop them, mirror them, make them black and white, and adjust their brightness and contrast.

The Picture Gallery tools apply changes to the entire photograph, except for cropping, which (by definition) lets you remove those parts of a picture that don't add anything to your subject, creating, in effect, a new rectangular shape to hold your picture. These quick changes can improve photographs that weren't exposed or developed perfectly, and such changes can save you the effort of using more powerful but more cumbersome image-editing software.

▶ If you placed the picture the wrong way on the scanner (which is easy to do), use the horizontal or vertical flip buttons (refer to Figure 10-1).

▶ Use the cropping tool to remove anything in the picture that distracts from or competes with your subject (see Chapter 3).

▶ For those blurry shots, increase the contrast. For overly bright beach sun, decrease the brightness.

Solving Common Photography Problems Using MGI PhotoSuite III Family Edition

The following answers are based on MGI PhotoSuite III. You can apply, with minor modification, the following information to other image-editing programs, such as those listed in Chapter 9.

PhotoSuite III lets you perform a very broad range of functions:

▶ Organizing images (creating albums)

▶ Assigning keywords to digital pictures, making them easy to find

▶ Sharing images on Web pages

▶ Editing images (as you'll see in the next few pages)

▶ Creating a broad range of products (business cards, certificates, labels, and so on)

The navigation bar is at the top of every PhotoSuite screen. Its buttons give you access to PhotoSuite's main activities. For each activity (I call them *modes*), a different set of buttons appears on the Activity Panel, which is a group of buttons and boxes arranged alongside the left side of the screen.

For the Get and Prepare modes, you see a long, vertical strip of tools (the toolbar). Figure 10-2 shows the Activity Panel and toolbar for the Prepare mode. Play around, and you'll see how easy PhotoSuite is to use and how intuitive *most* of the naming is. To orient yourself to PhotoSuite, start with Figure 10-2.

Julie Adair King has written two books that include excellent discussions of editing: *Digital Photography For Dummies*, 2nd Edition, and *Adobe PhotoDeluxe 4 For Dummies*. Both books are published by IDG Books Worldwide, Inc. PhotoDeluxe and PhotoSuite share many features, though of course the step-by-step procedures differ.

A version of PhotoSuite is included with the AOL PhotoCam digital camera.

Note

If you'll be using PhotoSuite III, the following pages assume that you have installed the program. PhotoSuite III includes an excellent printed booklet on installing the software and using the features, and the context-sensitive on-screen help is outstanding. If you *won't* be using PhotoSuite III, you'll be surprised by how many of its features apply to a product like Adobe PhotoDeluxe. The interface and arrangement of features will differ considerably, however.

Tip

Like most big graphics-editing packages, PhotoSuite has built-in *wizards*. Choose any editing task, and a series of numbered steps guides you through the process. See Figure 10-5 for an example of a wizard and its numbered steps. The F1 (Help) key gives you context-sensitive help, so if the wizard's choices aren't clear, you get a fuller explanation of what's going on. For additional information, choose Help⇔MGI PhotoSuite Help.

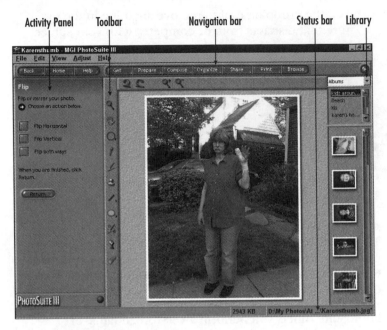

Figure 10-2. MGI PhotoSuite III.

The navigation bar gives you access to PhotoSuite's major functions:

▶ **Get:** Choose an individual digital picture to edit. (It's like the File⇔Open command, with more explicit instructions along the way.) You get a choice of places from which to retrieve your pictures, including your hard drive, your digital camera, and your scanner. When the picture opens, PhotoSuite switches to Prepare, where you can edit the just-opened picture.

▶ **Prepare:** Edit any digital picture. You needn't select an image first (by using Get). Instead, go to Prepare; then choose File⇔Open to select any digital image for editing. Prepare is the place to copy, resize, apply filters, and do pixel-level editing.

▶ **Compose:** Here's where you compose your digital *projects*, such as making stationery, albums, and calendars. First choose a project. (You'll need your PhotoSuite CD, with its many templates.) Then select the digital pictures to use for that project. Chapter 13 shows a few PhotoSuite projects.

▶ **Organize:** The place to create albums (PhotoSuite albums are discussed in Chapter 8), which you can use to either organize your pictures or share them with others.

▶ **Share:** From here, you can share your images via e-mail, on the Web, and in other places. Note that many of these places won't be available to AOL members. Kodak's PhotoNet, for example, is a sort of "You've Got Pictures" for non-AOL members, and PhotoSuite e-mail sharing does not work with AOL's e-mail.

▶ **Print:** Use Print Multiple to print out entire albums in well-formatted sheets, several pictures per page, or to create a page full of the same picture, so that (for example) kids can trade pictures.

▶ **Browse.** Use MGI PhotoSuite's built-in Web browser, which can be useful to view the simple Web pages you can create from individual pictures or albums by choosing File⇨Create a Web Page.

Common Photo Problems and Solutions

Here are just a few of the photo problems you can remedy with PhotoSuite III. You'll also find a smattering of useless things that are fun to do with PhotoSuite. Use the online help (or press the F1 key) to learn more about any feature.

How Do I Edit Just Part of a Picture? (Selection Tools)

Editing a digital picture often requires that you first select the exact part of the image to which you want to apply a certain effect, such as a color or filter. It's just like painting a window frame; you use masking tape to avoid getting paint on the window. In life and digital pictures, you don't want the colors to slop onto the wrong place. Often, the required digital effects apply to a small part of the image, sometimes just a few pixels or all the parts of the picture of the same color.

When you click the Print button, you're given the option to print one or more images at a time.

Use the Browse mode to explore the PhotoSuite Web site, where you can download card, poster, and other templates and get technical support.

Before doing any editing, choose File⇨Save As to save your digital picture with a different filename. For example, save `mountains2000.jpg` as `mountains2000a.jpg`. Saving JPG images as TIF images helps you preserve resolution during editing.

PhotoSuite gives you five selection tools to choose from. You'll find a similar set of tools in other graphics programs.

- ▶ Rectangle
- ▶ Ellipse
- ▶ Freehand
- ▶ Magic Wand
- ▶ Edge Finder

You open a digital picture by clicking Get on the navigation bar, selecting a source (usually, Computing), and then finding and double-clicking the file.

With the file open, you're automatically in Prepare (editing) mode. Click the Cutout button in the Activity Bar (on the left), to bring up the five selection tools shown in Figure 10-3. Alternatively, click the circular icon on the toolbar, shown in the same figure. The Activity Bar and toolbar work identically. Select a specific selection tool from either source, and a wizard appears in the Activity Bar to step you through the steps to use that particular tool.

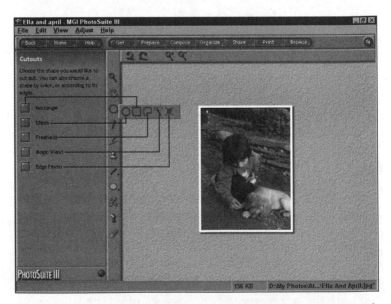

Figure 10-3. The same selection (cutout) tools are available in the Activity Bar and toolbar.

The process is similar from selection tool to selection tool, though the clicking-and-dragging techniques for each tool differ.

1. Start by choosing the tool that best suits the part of your picture to which you want to apply an effect. Each tool is described in the next few pages. See the sidebar "Deciding Which Selection Tool to Use," later in this section.

2. Create the part of the image that you wish to change.

3. Double-click when you're done making the selection.

Now, with the selection defined, you can:

▶ Leave the selection in place, and apply some effect to it: a special effect, a filter, or any editing adjustment available from PhotoSuite's Prepare mode.

▶ Move the selection to another part of the same picture, or to a different picture. There, you can apply some effect to the cutout selection. In PhotoSuite, a *cutout* refers to the technique of copying a selection from one place to another.

▶ Invert the selection and apply effects to the *rest* of the image. Inversion lets you select an area with a great deal of color and tone variety: select something simple and then invert it to apply some effect to the complex area.

Here's an overview of PhotoSuite's five selection tools:

Rectangle and Ellipse Selection Tools

The **Rectangle** and **Ellipse** tools let you click and drag across a rectangular or elliptical area of your choice. You see a *marquee* (dotted line) around the selected area. Such selections serve to isolate a geometrically simple area that you want to lighten, darken, blur, or otherwise enhance.

The Ellipse tool is underrated. Let's say you want to create a selection of a baby in the tub. Start by creating an elliptical selection on the arms. Holding down the Shift key, make successive, overlapping selections, working toward the edge of the body, using the rounded shape of the ellipse to match the baby's form. There really isn't a straight line on the human form, so you can keep creating ellipses from different directions to closely match the child's form.

Note

With a selection, you are not making any changes to the underlying image — until you actually (1) apply an effect to the selection and (2) save the image with the effect.

Tip

Use geometric selections to copy a portion of one image to another image without physically cropping the original and pasting it somewhere. Or, select a rectangular area to lighten up as the *background for text* that you want to include on top of your image.

The Freehand tool can be used to silhouette a product for which you are creating a promotional image. It can also be used for a collage you are creating, combining different photo elements into one image.

The Magic Wand works best for selecting an area with common tone or color. Hold down the Shift key while making multiple Magic Wand selections to select a really complex subject.

Freehand Selection Tool

The **Freehand** tool allows you to make precise selections around an area not otherwise defined by color. First, choose View⇨Zoom In to magnify the part of the picture around which you want to trace. By clicking and dragging along the edge of this area, you can achieve a very tight *mask* (the part of the image to which an effect is applied). The object of this method is to work your way around your subject until you get back to the starting point. When you're done, double-click to select the entire region you've just defined. Now you can apply any effect available in the Prepare mode to your selection.

Magic Wand Selection Tool

Use the very practical **Magic Wand** to select irregularly shaped and even dispersed parts of an image, as long as these parts have a similar color. Click on the part of the image with the desired color, or drag between adjacent parts of the image containing colors or tones similar to parts of the image you want to select throughout the picture. If you have a complex image with tones similar to the one you wish to select, it may take a while to get a *clean selection* (to indicate exactly what you want to select throughout the image).

Edge Finder

The fifth and final PhotoSuite selection tool is the **Edge Finder**, which works by looking for the border between areas of contrasting tones. Using the tool, you create a thin rectangle surrounding a border — for example, a border between the beach and the sea, or between a wall and the sky, or between a shadow and the sand. Keep the border *within* the Edge Finder's rectangular marquee as you go. The process is tricky, and not clearly superior to the Freehand tool, which is less awkward to use. Press Esc to start over. Double-click anywhere when you're done. The Edge Finder works fine when it has well-defined borders.

Deciding Which Selection Tool to Use

It's easy to describe the selection tools, but much harder to say which to use in a specific situation. Often, more than one tool will work.

> ► For a red-brick wall or other blockish shape, use the Rectangle or Freehand (outlining) tool.
>
> ► For any irregularly shaped but uniformly colored object (like the poppies in the meadow leading to Oz), drag the Magic Wand through several parts of the area to be selected. Double-click your heels when you're done.
>
> ► For human form or another non-geometrical shape, use the Magic Wand or successively applied ellipses (Ellipse tool). Hold down the Shift key to make multiple selections. Or select something simple with the Magic Wand or geometrical tools, and invert the selection.

How Do I Keep the Subject Focused and Keep Everything Else a Little Blurry?

You're talking about something called *depth of field*. It refers to how much of a scene is in focus. A narrow depth of field can be a very good way to call attention to the central subject of your picture — as long as the subject is in focus.

Many film cameras offer control of the aperture, which affects how much light is let in when you click the shutter button. The amount is measured by *f-stop*. A low f-stop lets in a lot of light and results in a narrow depth of field (with less in focus); a high f-stop lets in less light but creates a wider depth of field (with more in focus). With many point-and-shoot cameras, you may not have an *aperture* to use in defining depth of field.

But hey, all is not lost. The PhotoSuite selection tools let you select specific areas of your photos so that you can change the way they look. In this case, you can use the Magic Wand to select your subject (a portrait or a dog, for example). After you have selected the subject, you invert it (a simple click on the wizard, on the left part of the screen). Then you apply blur to everything except the selected subject. To apply blur, choose Prepare⇨Touchup⇨Touchup Filters. You'll want to apply the Soften filter to the inverted selection. The Intensity slider in PhotoSuite's Step 2 merely controls the amount of blur (try it and see!). See Figure 10-4 for the results.

Note

More-accurate tools, such as the Freehand selection tool, take a bit more work but provide the accuracy you might need. Zoom in to make a precise Cutout.

Tip

To *zoom in* (magnify part of the image for more precise editing) on any picture you're editing, simultaneously press the Ctrl key and the big plus (+) key on the numeric keypad. To zoom out, use Ctrl plus the big minus (-) key on the numeric keypad. Or just click the magnifying glass icons with the plus sign (to zoom in) or minus sign (to zoom out).

10

**Making the Most of
Image-Editing Software**

Tip

Until you click Apply, none of the effects are applied to your picture. Until you click Save, none of the applied effects are saved in your file.

Note

To use a slider, simply drag it back and forth, or click its endpoints.

Figure 10-4. Blur is applied to the background to emphasize the subject. These images are displayed in Jasc's Paint Shop Pro in order to show the before-and-after effect.

How Do I Fix Red Eye?

Beware the dreaded *red eye,* the red circles at the center of the eye in color pictures. Red eye occurs because most cameras today have a built-in flash that is very close to the lens. So close, in fact, that the light from the flash travels through the iris of your subject's eye and lights the blood vessels in the back of the retina. This shows up as a red spot on the eye where you would normally want a white highlight. Dogs and cats can be afflicted with red eye as well.

When this occurs on color prints, you can buy a red-eye reduction pen from your camera store and carefully dab its cyan dye onto the red spots until the effect is diminished. With a digital photo, you need to use software. Most editing programs offer a tool for removing red eye with the click of the mouse. These tools work by *desaturating* the red in the eyes (making the red in the eyes less intensely colored).

In PhotoSuite III, open your photo and click Touchup in the list of choices in the Activity Panel on the left, and then click Remove Red Eye. Zoom in on the photo and adjust the brush size, moving the slider in Step 2 back and forth. You want to make the red-eye tool about as big as the red color in the subject's eyes. Now, simply click the red portion of the eye until the red is gone. See Figure 10-5.

Red eye

Tool to remove red eye

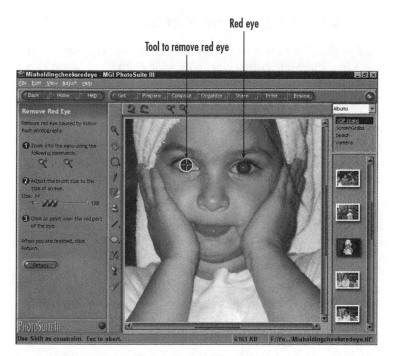

Figure 10-5. Removing annoying red eye requires you to size the brush so that it matches the diameter of the red circle in the subject's eye.

How Can I Make the Colors in My Picture Look More Natural?

The red-eye problem is related to larger problems with unwanted color casts, such as those that result from shooting under fluorescent lighting and getting an unpleasant green cast across the whole photo. Using the Get button, open your picture in PhotoSuite. Prepare mode's editing buttons come up. Choose Touchup⇨Touchup Filters⇨Color Adjustment. Now, clicking and dragging the sliders right and left, you can adjust the amounts and combinations of the three basic colors that make up every on-screen image (cyan-red, magenta-green, and yellow-blue). See Chapter 9 for more about colors.

This powerful control can make an unsightly picture look much closer to the one you intended. You can achieve remarkable results with a little patience and time. In the case of the photo with the green cast, you might start by sliding the Magenta-Green control toward the magenta end and the Cyan-Red control toward the red direction. Take your time and give your eye time to adjust to the changes. For some effects, you'll want to adjust two colors.

Tip

Software like Macromedia Firewords and Adobe Photoshop give you much greater control over text, but these programs are more expensive and more demanding to use.

Note

As soon as you click the Compose button on the PhotoSuite navigation bar, you're in Compose mode. See Figure 10-6.

How Do I Add Text on Top of the Picture?

Adding text is a snap with most image editors. Text on an image adds information to a photo as well as an interesting compositional touch. You would want to add text if you are making an ad for your business, for example, or creating a silly birthday-party invitation or a caption for a digital picture so that everyone will know what they're looking at. Or give the kids a chance to create their own cartoons. Words alone add information. Unusual fonts, colored letters, and shadow effects add pizzazz to your words.

To make such a picture in PhotoSuite, you start in a way that may seem backward. You first click Compose on the navigation bar and then choose a project to create, such as Photo Collage. After you have started a project — which will almost always require the PhotoSuite III CD and its templates — and have added a photo, you see the Add/Edit Text button in the Activity Panel. Click the photo, and a marquee box appears. A *marquee* is a box, outlined in dots, that indicates where any object will appear. The actual text is entered on the left of the screen (in the box provided), not in the marquee itself (see Figure 10-6). Type your text into the box on the left, and it appears in the marquee.

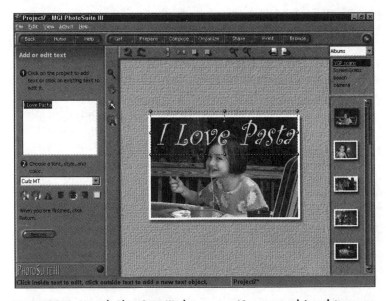

Figure 10-6. A simple PhotoSuite III photo project (Compose mode) applying text to a digital picture.

Now you can choose the font, style, and color by using the controls on the left. Using the marquee box on the picture itself, you can drag the box around, rotate it (for vertical text, for example), and resize it. Resize the text box by clicking and dragging one of the marquee's corners or any of the sides. Don't forget to use the Save As command when you're done.

How Can I Switch Parts of Two Digital Pictures?

In the graphics world, mixing and matching parts of different images to create a single, new image is called *compositing*. Kids use the effect to switch heads (of a dog and a little brother, for example). Graphic artists create attention-getting ads this way.

In PhotoSuite, the first thing to keep in mind is that you can show only one digital picture at a time in the program's on-screen workspace. So, in PhotoSuite, you need to copy a selected part of one picture, open the next picture, and paste in the part copied from the first picture.

Here's how to use the selection tools to edit a photo or photos for a special effect: Open your digital picture and click the Cutout button; you get a choice of five PhotoSuite selection tools. See "How Do I Edit Just Part of a Picture? (Selection Tools)," earlier in this chapter.

1. Select the Magic Wand from the Selection Tools on the toolbar (just to the left of the picture).

2. Select the Pointer tool, and adjust the Tolerance. (Hint: Try 100.)

3. Now, click and drag the wand tool across the face or other element to be selected. If any areas in the selection remain unselected, hold down the Shift key and click (to reactivate the tool), and click or drag across image parts until everything you want to select is selected.

Now, to move the selection to another digital picture, follow these steps:

1. Choose Make Cutout, the last step of the wizard procedure, on the left.

2. Select Copy to Clipboard.

Note

PhotoSuite saves your photo *projects* in its own Projects format (PZP), which means that you'll only be able to do further editing in PhotoSuite III. Other PhotoSuite changes (such as when you *get* an individual image and edit it) retain the JPG format.

10

Making the Most of
Image-Editing Software

3. Now, open the other picture and paste the cutout (choose Edit⇨Paste). You'll see the cutout in a marquee, with dotted lines, boxes for resizing, and a rotation handle.

By making a selection and copying it to another picture, you have just included a part of one picture in another! You can now proceed to edit the new picture in any way you want.

How Do I Add Special Effects Like Twisted Noses?

Open your digital picture and click the Special Effects button so that you can let your pictures twist and shout.

> Open the picture you want to muck around with (click Get). You'll automatically be taken to Prepare mode, for editing. Click Special Effects and then Effects to bring up a good-sized set of filters. Each category available in the Effects drop-down list has a different set of filters. In the Natural category, for example, you can choose from special effects such as fog, glass, and wind. For each filter, you can tweak the settings to determine the effect's intensity.

> Click **Preset Warp** to apply a much weirder effect — a horizontal or vertical wave, or a bulge, or a funhouse mirror — to the entire image. Again, the intensity of the effect can be controlled by using your handy wizard in Step 2 of the wizard on the Activity Panel (on the left side of window).

> Click **Interactive Warp** for a finer degree of control over the kind of Preset Warp's bizarre effects. Kids can use the tool to cause parts of a digital picture to shrink, grow, or melt. They will know just what to do with it.

The top photo in Figure 10-7 shows the fortress the way it was shot; the bottom photo shows it with dramatic clouds pasted in from another image. The effects were created with Adobe Photoshop to enhance the shadows on the castle.

Using selection tools, you can apply a filter to a small part of your picture. If you don't use selection tools, your effect is applied to the entire image.

To create the effect of a swollen head (or deflated ego for that matter), try the Interactive Warp tool. Adjust the size of the brush using the sliding tool in the wizard's Step 2. Click and drag in controlled subtle motions until you have the hang of it. The sensation is like dragging your finger through gelatin that hasn't quite set. You will notice that lower-resolution images quickly begin to *degrade,* a nice way of saying *look crummy.*

Figure 10-7. Photographer Len Rizzi modified a photo of an Italian fortress with a washed-out sky (top) using Adobe Photoshop to take a cloud layer from another picture.

How Do I Turn a Color Digital Picture into a Black-and-White One?

Much of the appeal of black-and-white photography is its ability to capture pattern and form and enhance shadows, which are good ways to emphasize the essential aspects of any subject. Color photography enables a higher degree of fidelity,

The black-and-white process is a snap on AOL. With the AOL Picture Gallery (refer to Figure 10-1), open a picture and click the Remove Colors button near the top of the screen. Because you're throwing away information in the process, make sure to save a copy of the image with another name before making the transformation.

You can selectively enhance color information, as well as remove it. One magical tool in PhotoSuite III is the Antique Effects Brush. To use it, display an image, click the Paint & Draw button, and click Effect Brush. Antique is in the list of Paint styles. Adjust the brush size and then carefully adjust the brush's tolerance. Brush over your photo to see the effect. Still using the Effects Brush, you can achieve lovely monotone effects by using the other paint styles, such as Moonlight, Sepia, and Warm. Sepia and Antique give your digital pictures an old-time look. *Remember to save each of your files with a different name before applying effects that you may not want to keep.*

Photo-editing programs make short work of removing dust and scratches. The Cloning tool makes cleaning up dusty scans easy, but it does require painstaking work. The same techniques can be applied whether the problem is with the picture or the scanner.

perhaps — in the sense of more information about the subject. Sometimes, however, color reveals the surfaces of objects while neglecting their significance. Most digital cameras render everything in color.

Here's a way of bringing the magic of black and white to the world of color (with apologies to Ted Turner):

1. Open your digital picture in PhotoSuite. You'll be in edit (Prepare) mode. Choose Touchup⇨ Touchup Filters⇨Fix Colors.

2. Use the Saturation slider to reduce the saturation to the desired effect. The red-eye tool (discussed earlier) does the same thing — reduces color in a part of the picture.

3. Return to the main Prepare menu by clicking Prepare. Choose Touchup⇨Touchup Brushes, and use the Colorize brush to adjust the saturation further, applying colors to the areas you choose (such as the backgrounds) to any degree you like. This tool allows you to apply creative effects to greatly enhance specific aspects of your photos, but you'll have to zoom in pretty close to get the exact effects you want.

How Can I Get Rid of the White Dust Marks on My Old Photos?

Dust is supposed to be everywhere, but all the dust with which I'm personally familiar tends to be on scanned images and old negatives. When scanning prints or film, take time to clean the scanner glass and remove all smudges and dust. Use glass cleaner and dust-free paper cloths. Look obliquely at the glass with the scanner light on so you can see all the dust particles. Then use either an antistatic cloth or an antistatic brush (or both) to carefully clean the original and neutralize any static charge it may have. Now you're ready to perform your scan.

To rid dust that's already in an old photo, follow these steps:

1. Open your digital picture in PhotoSuite III. You'll be in Prepare mode, where you edit pictures.

2. Choose Touchup⇨Clone.

3. Zoom in for good detail of those tiny (pixel-sized) white dots.

The Clone tool works by applying the color of one pixel to another pixel. The tool is the perfect way to turn a white pixel (or dust particle) into the color of a neighboring pixel. To use the tool, first click Reset Origin (the wizard's Step 1) and then click the part of your picture from which you want to take the color you will apply to the dust-pixel.

As with other tools, with the Cloning tool you can adjust the size of the brush you use to apply the source color (size 1 for pixel-level editing is great for eliminating dust); you can also alter opacity — how heavily you lay one color onto the other. Just move the sliders right and left with your mouse in Steps 2 and 3 of the Clone's wizard. See Figure 10-8.

Note

The concept here is not that you're choosing a specific color in order to re-color all your white pixels. Rather, you're choosing a distance and angle from the source color to the dust-pixel. With the Cloning tool, you can keep the source and dust pixels a couple of pixels apart so that the white pixel takes on the color of its neighbor.

10
Making the Most of Image-Editing Software

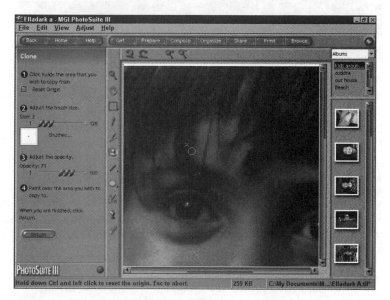

Figure 10-8. Use the Clone tool to remove those specks of dust from your digital pictures.

How Can I Get Rid of All the Extra Stuff I Don't Want in My Picture?

This issue has to do with the original composition of your picture. One of the first things to consider is *cropping* — removing part of the image to bring out the subject. Figure 10-9 shows a cropped version of the photo modified in Figure 10-7.

Note

It has become second nature to expect the computer to do things faster. When you're editing digital pictures, you're the one who needs to slow down, especially when it comes to correctly selecting the part of your image to edit and applying effects at as low a level as possible, pixel by pixel if necessary.

Tip

Adjusting brightness and contrast works especially well if you first select the area you are adjusting, using the tips provided earlier in this chapter in "How Do I Edit Just Part of a Picture?"

Tip

You can also adjust brightness and contrast in the AOL Picture Gallery, but only for the entire image. To selectively change either value separately, you need to use a program like PhotoSuite III, then make the appropriate selection, and then adjust either the contrast or the brightness (or both). In Prepare Mode⇨Touchup, select Touchup Brushes for another way to lighten or darken *parts* of your image. Simply select the size and opacity option and click and drag the brush over the area you are editing.

Note

Digital photos that are *overexposed* (too light) can be tougher to correct than ones that are *underexposed* (too dark).

Figure 10-9. This new version of Figure 10-7 shows the effects of both cropping and image enhancement.

How Do I Bring Out the Shadows and Details in My Pictures?

This is yet another annoying problem — but one that can be solved by following these steps:

1. First, open the image by clicking Get and identifying the picture's source (which will usually be Computer).

2. Then choose Prepare⇨Touchup⇨Enhance. This easy-to-use tool extracts all the value that can be extracted from a photo. If this doesn't work to your satisfaction, choose Prepare⇨Touchup⇨Touchup Filters⇨ Brightness/Contrast.

Is There Anything I Can Do to Fix a Washed-Out Picture?

When a photo is underexposed, you can lighten it to a degree because at least there is information within the photo (unless, of course, there is nothing but black, in which case you can't do much). When photos are overexposed, at best you might be able to use the Darken brush (one of the Touchup Brushes, when you're in Prepare⇨Touchup mode) to selectively darken the minimal information that is available. Use the Darken brush to gently darken specific details of your photo. If you expect to create a photo that looks normally exposed, you may as well spend your time looking for the Holy Grail.

How Do I Create a Blurry, Foggy, or Romantic Effect?

If you already have a photo to which you want to apply a similar effect, open it. Choose Prepare⇨Select Effects⇨Effects, and choose a category and effect (such as Lens and Moonlight). Try applying the effect to the background first (first selecting the background with the Magic Wand or other tool), and work your way toward the subject, gradually overlapping the subject's edge. A combination of effects allows you to build up the overall effect.

How Do I Make My Own Panoramas?

You can take a series of shots of some dramatic and predominantly horizontal scene like the mountains or a cityscape. Pivot smoothly, taking several digital pictures as you turn. Make sure that the images overlap by about 30 percent. Using a tripod helps enormously; most digital cameras, like the AOL PhotoCam, have a socket into which you can screw a tripod.

How Do I Sharpen a Blurry Picture?

Start by opening the picture in question in PhotoSuite, clicking Touchup and Touchup Filters, and selecting the Sharpen filter, to automatically preview the intended effect. You can sharpen the image further by clicking the Sharpen More radio button in the wizard. The changes won't be retained until you click Apply and then choose File⇨Save.

The Sharpening brush (choose Prepare⇨Touchup⇨ Paint & Draw⇨Effects Brush) works well, too, but use it gently as you *build up* (sharpen further) because your edits can become distractingly distinct. Just below the Brush Size adjustment slider in the wizard (which you drag back and forth to vary the effect), you see a box with a brush in it. If you double-click that box, the program shows you the available brush shapes. Start with a small brush size and a low

Tip

Combinations of softening and fog filters can yield a similar effect to the nylon-stocking trick. Don't be afraid to experiment and have fun.

Find It Online

For a useful Web resource on making panoramas, with examples and information on free software, check out PanoGuide (www. panoguide.com).

Tip

After you have all the images you need to work with, you can open the images in PhotoSuite or another editing program, crop them so that they fit together, and copy and paste them to make a long image.

10

Making the Most of Image-Editing Software

intensity, working on edges. Use the Darkening brush on dark adjacent areas to increase contrast and also increase the apparent sharpness, thus keeping the original integrity of the photo.

Preparing Pictures for the Web

"You've Got Pictures" solves the problem of getting, organizing, and sharing digital pictures on the Web. To use digital pictures on the Web, you must:

- ▶ **Download the digital pictures to your computer.** See Chapter 4 for details. Of course, if you've been stashing your pictures on your own PC, they will already be available to use on the Web.
- ▶ **Optimize them, if necessary, for Web viewing.** That's the subject of the next few pages.
- ▶ **Upload them to AOL Hometown as part of the Web-publishing process.** For uploading specifics, see Chapter 13.

Optimizing Web Graphics: File Format

Graphics on the Web need to be in GIF or JPG format. Chapter 9 goes over these and other graphics file types.

Preparing JPGs for the Web

Tip

Some folks edit with a format such as TIF that retains its pixels during editing. They compress the file as a JPG only after they've finished the basic work of resizing, cropping, and enhancing images.

Complex and colorful photos are best saved as JPGs. A JPG supports something called 24-bit color, meaning that each pixel can represent more than 16 million colors — overkill on Web browsers, which can display only about 216 colors. (Overkill for humans, too, who can't even *see* all those millions of colors.) JPGs thus tend to look better because the images' pixels carry more information. JPGs have another advantage: They can be *compressed* — reduced in file size for quick downloading. Compressing a JPG too much, however, causes its quality to deteriorate.

Editing software such as Adobe Photoshop and Macromedia Fireworks lets you determine the level of compression when you save a file as a JPG. In Figure 10-10, you can see two magnified versions of the same digital picture, shown in Fireworks. The image on the left is a TIF image with the following characteristics:

- ▶ **Resolution:** 1650 x 1759 pixels
- ▶ **Color depth:** 256 colors (grayscale) (8 bit)
- ▶ **File Format:** TIF

At 2.9MB, this file is completely inappropriate for the Web, and it cannot be displayed in a graphics program without your having to zoom out a couple of times. As a TIF, it can't even be used on the Web. So, we've got to make some compromises in choice of format and resolution.

The picture on the right, converted to JPG and greatly compressed, checks in at only 13K — a great improvement for Web use. Zooming in shows the image on the left to have smaller pixels with far greater continuity between pixels; the image on the right has bigger, less continuous, and more "jagged" pixels. On the Web, the image on the right will, as a result, display better at smaller sizes than larger ones.

Tip

When selecting a JPG compression level (the process varies with software), start with a middle setting in a program; then zoom in to check the results. If the image deterioration is minimal, increase the compression and check again.

10

Making the Most of
Image-Editing Software

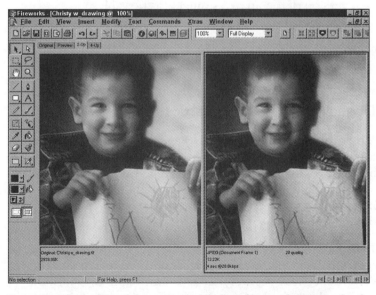

Figure 10-10. The original version (on the left) has a file size of 2.9MB (useless for the Web), while the one on the right is only 13K (Web-ready).

At AOL Keyword: **Animated GIF** (or AOL Keyword: **AGIF**), you can download animated GIFs plus software to create such images. Many Web sites offer free animated GIFs that you can download. One such site is MediaBuilder's Animation Factory (www.animfactory.com), with more than 10,000 animated GIFs to download. You can also create your own animated GIFs by using a special-purpose graphics program, such as Fireworks or Paint Shop Pro.

AOL's Web-creation tool, Easy Designer, gives you the ability to resize a graphic by simply clicking and dragging a corner. See Chapter 13 for more about Easy Designer. If you know HTML, you can use the IMG tag's HEIGHT and WIDTH attributes to specify exactly how big (in pixels) you want an image to be on a Web page. For more on HTML, see Ed Tittle and Natanya Pitts's *HTML 4 For Dummies* (IDG Books Worldwide, Inc.).

Preparing GIFs for the Web

Line art, clip art, button graphics, line drawings, and all simpler, nonphotographic images work better as GIFs, a file format that has two advantages over JPGs. Unlike JPGs, GIFs can be compressed without losing quality. Furthermore, they can display only 256 colors per pixel, making them much more suitable for the Web.

GIFs can be animated, interlaced, and made transparent. All of these effects can be created with more-advanced software such as Photoshop, Paint Shop Pro, and Fireworks.

▶ **Transparent GIFs.** Transparent GIFs don't have a colored rectangular background. Instead of an ugly rectangle on a Web page, the page's background appears to shine through an image, causing the graphic to blend with it.

▶ **Interlaced GIFs.** Have you noticed that as graphics on some Web sites load, they start as blurry images and get sharper as they build on your screen? This effect is called *interlacing*. The benefit of using interlaced GIFs is that you can provide viewers with a low-resolution version of the image as quickly as possible.

▶ **Animated GIFs.** Animated GIFs enable you to add movement to a Web page. These files consist of several slightly different images within a single file, shown in succession to create the effect of a simple cartoon.

Optimizing Web Graphics: File Size

A picture's *size* on a Web page refers to the amount of space it takes up on the screen. Even a picture with low resolution can be made to fill a page. *Size* also refers to the number of pixels used to create the image and the resulting file size in kilobytes. The two are related; the more pixels in a file, the bigger the picture.

To reduce an image's size (in both senses), crop it to display only the essentials. After you've cropped an image, you can then reduce less-important color information. On the Web, you can display only 216 colors. Using a product like Adobe Photoshop, Macromedia Fireworks, or JASC Paint Shop Pro, you can apply this minimalist "Web safe" color palette to reduce file size.

Another way to reduce the size of a Web graphic is to reduce the amount of its *color depth,* which refers to the number of colors that can be displayed by any pixel. 24-bit color lets you display far more colors than the eye can see or the Web can display. In PhotoSuite III, you reduce color depth as follows:

1. Choose File⇨Save As.
2. In the Save Photo box, select the Prompt for Options check box and click Save.
3. In the JPG Advanced Settings box, choose a lower Color Reduction Method (if the choice is available) and Picture Quality. Both have drop-down boxes. Reduce Picture Quality one step at a time (for example, from 7 to 6) before accepting the choice. It's easy to render JPG images indistinct by stripping them of too many pixels.

To see how the changed image looks on a Web page, use PhotoSuite. Just choose File⇨Create Web Page. You'll create a Web page showing just the image. The HTML page will automatically be created and its location will be indicated in a small dialog box. Then open the page within AOL, as follows: Choose File⇨Open, find the picture, and double-click the picture to view it in the AOL Web browser.

Summary

Chapters 9 and 10 introduced the world of images. The journey went from pixels (a picture's building blocks) to the software used to edit pixels. Beyond the basic work of removing dust, removing red eye, and improving brightness and contrast, you can have loads of fun with special effects and filters.

The next chapter proceeds from input to output — from getting digital pictures to printing them out on today's amazing and affordable printers, which you can use to make cards, T-shirts, gorgeous photographic prints, and much more.

Note

Digital pictures with a high resolution take up a lot of room on a Web page. Why? The computer devotes one of *its* pixels to each of the picture's pixels. Suppose that one of your viewers' monitors is set to a low resolution (the older, traditional 640 x 480 pixels, for example). Digital pictures with a resolution greater than 640 x 480 on a Web page exceed the size of the available screen area, and require the viewer to scroll the image to see the whole thing.

Tip

You can determine the size of a picture you want to use on the Web by using Windows Explorer. Right-click on the file and choose Properties. In the Properties dialog box's General type, you can see the digital picture's Type (TIF, for example) and Size (in kilobytes). In the Images box, you can see the picture's Color Depth.

A QUICK LOOK

Chapter 11

Printing Your Digital Pictures

IN THIS CHAPTER

What kind of printer do you need?

Understanding the types of printers

Figuring out your color options

Do you need a special printer just for photos?

What kinds of paper are available for your printer?

For convenience and portability, it's still tough to beat plain old prints — the kind you can stuff in your wallet or tape to the refrigerator door. Adding a color printer to your computer setup is like having your own darkroom, except there are no smelly chemicals, no plumbing or construction costs, and the printer and supplies cost far less than old-fashioned darkroom equipment. Just open up the desired image in your graphics software, load the printer with photo-quality paper, and click Print.

Understanding Your Printing Needs

Inexpensive color printers have been available for some years now, but for the most part, they haven't been photo-quality;

affordably reproducing the rich color and detail of a photo-graph is difficult. Fortunately, today you can buy a photo-quality printer for your PC or Mac that can turn out prints nearly indistinguishable from drugstore prints, for a few hundred dollars. If you buy an inkjet printer (more on inkjets later), you can use it for many purposes other than for printing photos; inkjets are good investments for home, for schoolwork, and for your small business — all at the same time.

Here are some questions that the DecisionMaker at AOL's Computing Channel (AOL Keyword: **Computer**), shown in Figure 11-1, can help you answer when you're selecting a printer:

▶ How much do you want to spend?

▶ Will the printer work with the kind of connections available on your computer? That is, is the printer designed for Windows or the Mac?

Find It Online

In AOL's Computing Channel, you can find a simple DecisionMaker that helps you choose a printer (see Figure 11-1). You answer a series of questions, and the guide searches its large product database looking for printers that match your needs. The guide also provides detailed specs for each printer to help you comparison shop.

Figure 11-1. AOL's Printer DecisionMaker helps you choose the right printer for your budget and needs. (Go to AOL Keyword: **Personalogic** and click the Printers link.)

11

Printing Your Digital Pictures

Note

As a rule, printing graphics on a printer that handles both text and graphics takes longer than printing text (the difference will vary with printers, of course). For greater speed and quality (in dpi), be prepared to pay extra.

Find It Online

AOL Keyword: **CNET** has loads of reviews of new products and tends to keep its older reviews available, too. Search for more information about specific models at AOL Search. To use AOL Search, type in your search term (such as **HP color**) in the text box on the navigation bar and then click the Search button.

▶ Is speed a concern? Printers are rated in ppm (pages per minute). Look for ppm for printing text versus printing graphics, and for printing at high quality versus "draft" quality (with quality measured in dots per inch — a measure discussed at the beginning of Chapter 9). Figure 11-3, later in this chapter, shows Hewlett-Packard's ratings for one of its own printers.

▶ How easy is the printer to use? Will kids be using it?

▶ Do you need a printer that handles text *and* graphics? If you want a printer primarily for text, consider a laser jet; for primarily graphics, consider an inkjet or dye-sublimation printer.

▶ Would you prefer to supplement your current printer with one that is optimized for photos? Consider a Photo Printer, while keeping your laser or inkjet for its current uses.

▶ How many pages do you want to print at a time? This answer determines what paper-holding capacity you want. Do you want double-sided printing?

▶ What kind of paper do you want to print on — heavy paper, transparencies, envelopes, glossy paper, regular paper.

It's a good idea to prepare a checklist of all the features that are important to you and then start to shop around. As you shop, you'll undoubtedly find a few more handy features that you must have. Take your time and keep your eyes open. Although a printer won't be your most expensive computer purchase, you don't want to be disappointed after you start using it.

Printer manufacturers seem to introduce new models every few weeks, sporting more features, higher-quality output, and a lower price than last month's hot printer. I can't possibly keep up with all the changing model numbers, but I should be able to point you in the right direction. Popular computing magazines and online resources such as AOL Keyword: **CNET**, shown in Figure 11-2, offer tests, reviews, and comparisons of current models, and generally provide cost comparisons for printing supplies as well as evaluations of quality and ease of use. I list some useful Web-based resources later in this chapter.

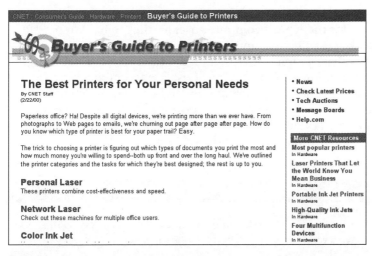

CNET Consumer's Guide Hardware Printers **Buyer's Guide to Printers**

Buyer's Guide to Printers

The Best Printers for Your Personal Needs
By CNET Staff
(2/22/00)

Paperless office? Ha! Despite all digital devices, we're printing more than we ever have. From photographs to Web pages to emails, we're churning out page after page after page. How do you know which type of printer is best for your paper trail? Easy.

The trick to choosing a printer is figuring out which types of documents you print the most and how much money you're willing to spend--both up front and over the long haul. We've outlined the printer categories and the tasks for which they're best designed; the rest is up to you.

Personal Laser
These printers combine cost-effectiveness and speed.

Network Laser
Check out these machines for multiple office users.

Color Ink Jet

• News
• Check Latest Prices
• Tech Auctions
• Message Boards
• Help.com

More CNET Resources
Most popular printers
In Hardware
Laser Printers That Let the World Know You Mean Business
In Hardware
Portable Ink Jet Printers
In Hardware
High-Quality Ink Jets
In Hardware
Four Multifunction Devices
In Hardware

Figure 11-2. CNET is one of the best places to stay up-to-date on new printers and new features. Start here, too, for comparison shopping.

Printers have improved rapidly in recent years, and prices have dropped, putting good-quality output within the range of home computer users. Factors that often determine cost are speed, resolution, image quality, and the number of colors offered. Fast, high-resolution color laser printers set you back the most money.

The Limits on Quality

When you start shopping for printers, you'll find resolutions of 600 dpi, 1200 dpi, and even more. These resolutions may be significantly better than what you need for the images you're planning to print. In general, if an image file has a resolution of 640 x 480, it won't look very good blown up to an 8-x-10-inch color glossy, but you can get a quality photo by printing it at a smaller size. You'll need a megapixel-quality image to print files at large sizes. For more about resolution, see Chapter 7.

Inkjet printers now produce remarkable graphics and good text at resolutions of at least 600 dpi (dots per inch) and in three, four, or sometimes six colors of ink. Prices are lower than for most laser printers — currently around $300 for excellent inkjets, and considerably less for very good models.

Tip

In some situations, image resolution, as measured in dots per inch (dpi), means less to print quality than it used to. That's because some printers can alter the size and shape of dots and perform other magic to improve quality. As a result, many of today's inkjets can produce graphics that look significantly better than the dpi number by itself suggests.

11

Printing Your Digital Pictures

For many years, laser printers have been considered the ultimate for the typical computer user — they're hard to beat for black-and-white text and graphics. They don't offer the same advantages to folks interested in color images, though. A high quality color laser printer may cost five to ten times the price of a good color inkjet printer, and at best may match the image quality of an inexpensive photo printer (basically, either an inkjet optimized for printing digital pictures or a special dye-sublimation printer; both are discussed later).

Tip

Check the Web site for your printer's manufacturer to download the latest driver software. For example (you may have to dig a bit to find drivers): www.pandi.hp.com, www.epson.com/printer, www.ccsi.canon.com, among many others. AOL Keyword: **CNET** also makes drives available.

Software You Need for Your Printer

One more thing that you'll need for your printer is software, two kinds of software to be precise:

▶ **Printer driver software:** You must have printer driver software to use a printer. Printer driver software is required to adapt the graphics that you see on-screen to the specifics of your printer, and many printers come with additional graphics software covering everything from image editing to fun arts and crafts projects. Drivers are included with your printer, as a rule.

▶ **Image-editing software:** The other kind of software is, well, nice to have, but luckily usually comes bundled with new printers. A friend's new laptop, for example, came with a free Canon bubble jet, which in turn came with a version of PrintMaster, software for editing digital pictures and creating projects.

Choosing the Right Type of Printer

All different types of printers are available, and they vary in the ways you'd expect — in price, technology, and quality. The basic choice boils down to laser versus inkjet. Laser printers cost much more but do a better (faster and sharper) job. As you'll see, the two differ in underlying technology. Beyond this basic choice, a number of speciality printers, such as photo-quality printers and dye sublimation printers, serve the needs of photo enthusiasts and pros.

What Color Is Your Printer?

Nearly all color printers depend on a color system known as CMYK, or the *four-color process,* as it's known in printing businesses. Cyan (a kind of blue), magenta (a reddish violet), and yellow are combined to form all the colors of the rainbow, and black (the *K*) is used to vary color intensity and provide pure black when needed. Some of the less expensive inkjet printers use only the three colored inks, which are combined in equal amounts to create a brownish black. This can waste a lot of colored ink, because most people print a lot of plain-black text. Four-color printers add a separate black ink cartridge. This gives you the best of both worlds, and if you print a lot of black text, your ink cartridge costs will be lower because you can use black instead of a combination of other colors. Some of the newest photo printers claim to use six colors, but actually, they have two cyan inks, two magentas, one yellow, and one black. The extra cyan and magenta inks are used to produce richer colors.

Inkjet and Bubble Jet Printers

Inkjet printers are by far the most popular type of printer for the home market. (*Bubble jet* is the name of the inkjet printers manufactured by Canon.) You'll find general-purpose color inkjets that produce excellent photos, as well as special inkjet photo printers (discussed in "Considering Photo Printers").

As the name implies, ink is sprayed onto the page from one or more easy-to-replace cartridges that move back and forth across the page. Unlike a laser printer, with its dry toner, inkjets use liquid ink, an important factor to remember when caring for fresh, wet prints. While inkjets may seem to sport the same features, it's important to look at the specifics before buying one; they can differ in details such as the size and types of paper they support, the number of sheets they hold, and their color and black-and-white print rates. Manufacturers typically provided such detail, as HP does at its Web site, shown in Figure 11-3.

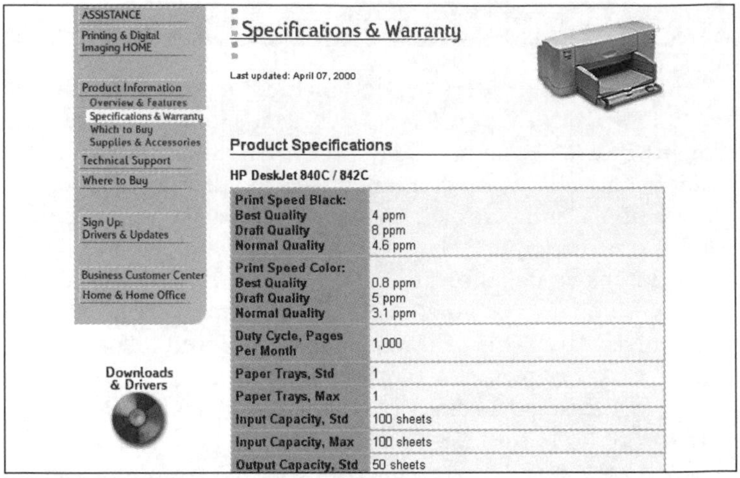

Figure 11-3. At vendors' Web sites, you can count on finding detailed specifications and illustrations. Here is information on an HP DeskJet color inkjet printer.

The most common setup is a two-cartridge printer, with a black ink cartridge and a second color cartridge equipped with three sets of nozzles, one set for each of the three CMYK colors (see the sidebar "What Color Is Your Printer?"). The marketplace is starting to see inkjets with four cartridges, which enables you to replace each color as it runs dry. These printers can be cheaper in the long run than two-cartridge models, because you don't have to toss-out a three-color cartridge that still has lots of ink left for the other two colors. Epson has a two-cartridge, six-color printer that produces superior results, but other printer companies have achieved similar results with conventional four-color systems.

Inks from different inkjet vendors differ in quality. Some manufacturers' cartridges can last twice as long as others', despite a similar price. Some inks are water-resistant, while others run and bleed if they get slightly damp. Some manufacturers offer higher-priced ink cartridges intended for photos, which you can use interchangably with cheaper cartridges intended for less-demanding uses. What's true in all cases is that photos require a great deal of ink, and that ink may take a while to dry after the print is finished. When you consider the costs of the paper and ink, one 8-x-10-inch photo print can cost over $1.

Considering Photo Printers

A new crop of inexpensive *photo printers* addresses the needs of digital photographers. Epson, HP, and Fuji make photo printers based on inkjet technology (described earlier in this chapter in "Inkjet and Bubble Jet Printers"). Other printers are based on dye-sublimation technology, described in the next section.

Many models include extra connections so you can connect your digital camera or camcorder directly to the printer. You'll still want to be connected to a computer, where most of your files are probably located, but if you just want to spit out a few snapshots, it may just be a matter of plugging in your camera and printing directly!

Photo printers often accept a wide range of printing media, too, including many kinds of special paper, transparency materials, iron-on transfers, cloth, and sometimes rolls of paper so that you can print banners or odd-sized prints with a minimum of trimming.

One disadvantage to photo printers is that they're sometimes equipped to print *only* photos — and in at least one line of printers, photos of a certain size (4-x-6-inch). That's not so wonderful if you have your heart set on an 8-x-10-inch color glossy. In addition, the special paper often required by these printers can be more expensive than the normal paper you use on an inkjet or laser printer.

Dye Sublimation Printers

This category of photo printers is based on one of a few thermal dye (sometimes called *dye sublimation*) processes, which typically provide excellent printed images. These machines create continuous tone images by applying color from ribbons, rather than approximating an image (as a digital camera does) using tiny dots of color. Dye-sublimation printers are expensive to run, with estimates of up to about $1 per print, but deliver near photo-quality output. Prices seem to be coming down. Figure 11-4 shows a photo printer from Olympus, which (according to CNET's comparison-pricing guide) can currently be purchased for less than $400. Like Olympus digital cameras, this printer works with the SmartMedia memory

Because of the use of ink, fresh prints can be runny. Don't pull them as they're being printed out (as you can with a laser). Avoid smudging them. Use good printer paper.

A small amount of lubricant is included in ink to prevent jets from clogging or spraying too much ink. You may want to be wary of remanufactured or incompatible ink cartridges, using only the new ink cartridges recommended by the manufacturer.

Some manufacturers, including Epson, Vivitar, and Hewlett-Packard, offer photo printers as part of a complete digital camera outfit that may include software and other coordinated components. PC manufacturers, too, often offer free or heavily rebated printers with new PCs.

11

Printing Your Digital Pictures

card (see Chapter 7), from which it can print directly. You'll get outstanding images from such printers, but be prepared for printing rates of fewer than 1 to 2 pages a minute or slower.

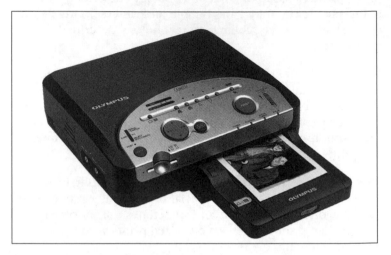

Figure 11-4. The Olympus P-330 photo printer.

Laser Printers

The important thing to know about laser printers is that they produce excellent results, but at a cost, especially for color lasers and hence digital pictures. These printers shine laser beams of colored light on a drum, which picks up an electrical charge in the process. The drum then rolls through the powdery toner in your cartridge, picking up toner corresponding to the pattern of charges produced by the laser. The toner is directly applied to a piece of paper, and a fuser melts the toner onto the page. Laser printers are faster than inkjets, they can print just about any font, and they typically print at a higher resolution. They also have internal memory, unlike inkjets. Color laser toner (ink) is often supplied in four bottles, one for each part of the 4-color process. You can buy a new inkjet printer for the price of one new laser printer drum, so be careful not to scratch it!

Color laser printers can deliver fine graphics at resolutions of 1200 dpi x 1200 dpi and higher. They enjoy many of the traditional laser printer advantages — greater print permanence, higher speed (prints per minute), lower cost *per page,* and razor-sharp text output. For the most part, color laser printers are too expensive for home use, but can be a very good choice for an office network. Expect to pay at least $1,500 or even more. If it's just photos you want to print, however, and you don't make your living from photography, you may want to compare an expensive color laser with a top-of-the-line inkjet. You might be surprised at the comparable results. Especially if value is a consideration, inkjets make a lot of sense.

Printers That Also Copy, Scan, and Fax

Small-business owners and even home users may appreciate combo printers, which can include a plain paper fax, a rudimentary scanner, and a color inkjet printer, all in one package. Thanks to the built-in scanner, you can use these machines as copiers, too. Check the specifications for these machines carefully. Some won't measure up to the demands of digital photography, but others may be quite adequate. AOL Keyword: **AOL Store** often features a reasonably priced all-in-one unit. The best thing about these machines is that they do so much in so little space; see Chapter 5 to get an idea of what they look like.

Ink, Toner, and Other Consumables

When you shop for a printer, it pays to consider the prices of all supplies and the estimated lifespan of those supplies. They can be a big "gotcha" when you get your printer home.

Most inkjet printers require two ink cartridges, each of which typically costs $25–$35. A big part of the price is the precision-made ink nozzles and electrical contacts needed to connect the cartridge to the rest of the printer. These nozzles can be damaged if mishandled and can clog if your printer is used heavily or is hardly used at all. Be sure to follow all the manufacturer's instructions for handling, installing, aligning, and cleaning your printer in order to get the longest life and best performance.

Depending on the printer's manufacturer and the kind of items you print (for example, photos need far more ink than plain text), you may get 1,000 to 2,000 pages from a single set of cartridges. Ink cartridges are not standardized, so be sure to buy the correct replacement for your make and model of printer.

Dye sublimation printers typically use ribbon-like sheets covered with colored dyes. You have to change these sheets frequently, but the process requires no sloppy liquids or other mess.

Color laser printers have a variety of maintenance supplies, including toner (four different colors, usually supplied in bottles) and print drums. These printers are not nearly as simple to maintain as the typical black-and-white laser printer, which usually has a single cartridge that contains toner and a drum. Cleanliness is very important with color laser printers. You don't want to spill toner, and you have to be careful when replacing the waste toner container.

Printer-Buying Tips

Here are a few tips for choosing a printer:

▶ Look closely and trust your senses. Consider bringing your own picture files to print when you go to the computer store.

▶ Take printer speed specs with a grain of salt; they refer to the print engine's rated (maximum) speed and don't take into consideration things like the speed of data transfer and processing. Photos take far longer to print than "spot" color, too. Look for special technologies that support photography such as super-small ink-drop size (something measured in picoliters — a trillionth of a liter).

▶ Ask for data on printer resolution and test printer resolution *on plain paper,* as opposed to glossy paper, stock, or specialty paper. See "Printing on Different Kinds of Paper."

▶ Consider the cost of consumables in your printer price. Some printers print best on special (costly) coated paper, and some have expensive print cartridges or cartridges with short life spans. Technical reviews in magazines and online often provide such cost estimates. How much do cartridges cost for the printers you are reviewing? CNET's reviews are a good place to start.

▶ Color printers run most economically if you can independently change the toner or ink cartridge for each color instead of changing the entire cartridge.

▶ If your needs are mostly for printing text and occasionally in color, consider buying a laser printer rather than an inkjet, for better speed and quality. For the occasional color job, use an inexpensive inkjet or service bureau (see "Making the Most of Service Bureaus," later in this chapter).

▶ Compare the software that comes with different printers, especially those programs aimed at photo printing. What image-editing software, if any, does the printer include?

▶ Consider carefully whether saving a small amount up front is worth the hassle of having to frequently change cartridges on an inkjet in order to print (black) text.

Printing on Different Kinds of Paper

The difference between a drab, low-quality photo print and a snappy, impressive print can be as simple as using the right paper. Take a trip to your local office supply store, and you'll find a staggering variety of paper types. Which paper works best for your photos depends on your printer and your purpose.

Selecting a Paper Type

The first step in selecting the best paper is to check the manual that came with your printer. Quite often the printer's manufacturer recommends specific types of paper and may even point out those that you should avoid. Keep in mind, however, that it is generally acceptable to purchase brands other than those recommended, which may be unavailable or too costly.

Next, note your printer's capabilities. Is your printer limited to paper that measures the standard 8½ x 11 inches or can it accommodate larger sizes? Can it handle heavier paper for business cards and projects? What is your printer's maximum resolution in dpi (dots per inch)? Also note your printer's make and model.

After you've tracked down all these details about your printer, take a trip to your local office-supply store. Or look online for a multivendor outlet such as AOL's ShopDirect (AOL Keyword: **AOL Store** or **Shop@AOL**), shown in Figure 11-5. Look for paper types that claim to be good for photo printing; such paper usually comes in small quantities (20 sheets or so per package). Now match up your printer's specifications to the available paper types. With a little luck, this exercise can help you narrow down your paper selection to two general types of paper: glossy photo paper and greeting-card paper.

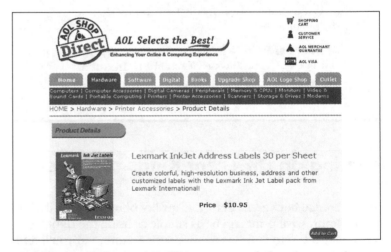

Figure 11-5. At AOL Keyword: **AOL Store**, you can find a wide variety of printer accessories (glossy paper, special paper, cables, and so on).

Why Use Special Paper?

What's wrong with using copier-quality paper for digital photos? Conventional paper (even the conventional paper designed for inkjet printing) can be too absorbent for high-quality photos, or it may have an irregular surface.

Even though it's hard to see without a microscope, ink may be soaked up by the paper's fibers, leading to a blurred image or washed-out appearance, or the laser toner may not be deposited smoothly. Photo paper has special coatings or smoothed surfaces to ensure that the images are sharp and bright.

Glossy Photo Paper

By far the most popular paper for printing photos is glossy photo paper. This type of paper offers the traditional look and feel of a photo (you can even get genuine Kodak photo paper with that ubiquitous Kodak logo on the back). Generally, glossy photo paper produces the best photo images, because it's formulated specifically for photos. Look for paper that is

▶ Fast drying to help prevent smearing

▶ Bright white (90+) for sharper image contrast

▶ Extra heavy weight to stand up to full color ink coverage

You can purchase glossy photo paper in a variety of sizes, from as small as 4 x 6 inches to as large as 11 x 17 inches. Photo paper is also available in super-gloss finishes and in matte (non-glossy) finishes.

Greeting Card Paper

If you want to create greeting cards, postcards, or trading cards (for kids), you'll find a wide variety of heavy paper intended for color photos. Most greeting card paper comes pre-perforated or pre-scored, or both, making your job that much easier.

If you intend to print a large, full-color image on your cards, it is best to avoid cards that require printing on both sides (two-up cards). Most greeting card paper isn't heavy enough to withstand ink coverage on both sides. Instead, look for greeting cards that fold twice (one-up) and require printing on just one side of the paper. These cards feel more like traditional greeting cards.

Photo paper is expensive. If you feel the need to run a test print, use a cheaper color printing paper and use the good stuff only when you're satisfied with your print.

When printing on glossy paper, be sure to select glossy paper in your Print dialog box. Also be sure to let freshly printed paper dry for a few minutes before touching it, because the ink may smear. Using the wrong paper or wrong ink can result in the image not drying at all.

11

Printing Your Digital Pictures

Other Paper Types and Formats

With the recent surge in photo printing, many different types of photo paper have come onto the market:

- ▶ Regular weight (24 lb.) paper specially coated for color printing
- ▶ Presentation-quality paper (40 lb.) with or without a glossy finish
- ▶ Glossy photo-quality labels in sizes ranging from return address size to full-size 8½-x-11-inch sheets
- ▶ Postcards and business cards, available in glossy and matte
- ▶ Glossy folders that can be printed and constructed

If all this variety seems overwhelming, look for a paper sample pack, which may offer many of the paper types and formats mentioned in this section. These sample packs are a good way to try out various types of paper and choose the one that works best for your purposes. You can find samplers at a local office-supply store, on the manufacturer's Web site, at AOL Keyword: **ShopDirect**, or in the box of labels you just bought.

Tip

Check the back of a paper's packaging for printer compatibility information before you buy it.

Printing on Transparencies, Fabric, and Other Strange Materials

Why limit yourself to printing on paper when you can show off your special photos in more creative ways? From see-through transparencies to iron-on shirt transfers, your printer can probably do the job.

Transparencies

In general, transparency film isn't ideal for photo printing. Even on high-quality transparency film formulated for color printers, photos may seem washed out and grainy. Transparencies still have their uses, of course, such as during presentations or for craft purposes. If you need to use transparency film, it is essential that you select one that indicates it will work with your printer. Also keep in mind that transparency film is quite expensive (currently about $1 per sheet).

An alternative to transparency film is special photo-quality glossy film, as it's called, formulated specifically for photos. As you can imagine, this film is even more expensive and harder to find.

Iron-on Transfers

Yearning to put your sweetheart on a shirt? Or your aunt on an apron? You may be able to with the help of printable iron-on transfers. The transfer material isn't cheap (about $1.50/sheet), but it is a creative way to make photo gifts at home.

If you're unsure how to format images for iron-on transfers, look for a starter kit, which usually comes with detailed directions, software, iron-on transfers, and a T-shirt to try.

Fabric

Yes, you may even be able to print directly onto fabric, but only special types of fabric designed specifically for inkjet printers. The fabric material, which is usually called *canvas,* is ideal for craft projects. How about a photo pillow, or a custom fabric bag, or a digital quilt?

Other Materials

As more consumers purchase color printers for home use, more creative and innovative printing materials are introduced. You can find many of them at your local office-supply store, but you should also check craft stores as well. Here are a few of the more unique materials onto which you may be able to print photos:

▶ **Magnets:** You can get magnetized, coated paper in sheets, which you can cut to whatever size you like.

▶ **Window clings:** Want to see sunlight shining through your children's eyes? Print a photo of them on special window cling material, cut it to size, stick it on a window, and watch their eyes light up!

Tip

Before you print your iron-on transfer, select Mirror Image or Flip in your Print dialog box (if such an option exists). If you print a mirror image of your photo on the iron-on transfer material, the image will transfer to your shirt in the correct orientation.

11

Printing Your Digital Pictures

▶ **Clear decals:** Show off your grandkids or your latest product by printing it onto a clear decal and placing it in your vehicle's window.

▶ **Laminated ID cards:** Print out your employee or club members' photos onto special cards, fold back the special lamination, press it into place, and voilà!

Ordering Prints from "You've Got Pictures"

AOL's "You've Got Pictures" offers photo-quality prints up to 8 x 10 inches and a variety of other photo-customized merchandise, including T-shirts and coffee mugs. If you order "You've Got Pictures" service when you develop your conventional film, all you have to do is go online, identify the pictures you want printed, and place your order. Family and friends with whom you've shared pictures using "You've Got Pictures" can do the same thing. If you have your own digital camera or scanner, you can upload your photo file to "You've Got Pictures" and then place your order. (Images may need to be of a certain resolution for use in prints.) See Chapter 4 to learn the basics of "You've Got Pictures" and Chapter 6 to learn about the printing services offered at the "You've Got Pictures" store.

Making the Most of Service Bureaus

Tip

Kinko's and AOL are teaming up to offer AOL members a variety of printing services. These new services may be available by the time you read this. Check out Kinko's on the Web at AOL Keyword: **Kinkos** or go to www.liveprint.com

A *service bureau* is a professional copy shop that can handle a variety of printing needs. You may want to go to a service bureau when you need something printed in a large quantity, or at the highest quality; or you may have a project you simply can't do effectively on a home printer (glossy posters, for example, or attractively bound booklets). Service bureaus are cropping up on the Web. Figure 11-6 announces Kinko's teaming with liveprint.com to offer custom printing services for business and home.

Figure 11-6. Online printing services are becoming conveniently available from any place and at any time.

With just a little shopping around, you can probably find a service bureau in your area that can turn your graphics files into top-quality prints. Kinko's is probably the best-known company in this business, offering 24-hour, 7-day a week service. Because graphics files can be very large, you'll need a Zip drive, a recordable CD (CD-R), or other high-capacity removable storage medium on your computer. Make sure that the service bureau can handle that kind of disk. Most service bureaus are also equipped for Internet or modem access, if you prefer to send the files electronically. It's a growing market, so keep an eye out for small vendors in your area, or on the Web, that might provide just the services you need.

More Information

AOL offers a wide lineup of resources that can help you turn your digital pictures into prints. AOL's Computing Channel (AOL Keyword: **Computing**) is the best place to start. You can find printer reviews, pricing, and background information from CNET and HP's Print Central.

Many service bureaus have large-format color printers that can print posters and banners with ease, and high-speed printers for the kind of job that would keep your printer churning for many hours.

11

Printing Your Digital Pictures

AOL Keyword: **Digital Photo** takes you to AOL's Digital Photography Community, where you can find live chats, classes, message boards, and links to many digital photo resources, including AOL's Graphic Arts Community (AOL Keyword: **Graphics**), which addresses a broad range of topics aimed at the beginner and professional alike.

Summary

Using a printer to make your own photographic prints gives you more control than having the drugstore make your prints. This chapter presented the basic printer choices available to you, with enough information to help you choose a printer and figure out your paper choices. The final part of this book looks at *what* you print — all the amazing photo projects possible with digital pictures.

12

PROJECTS FOR HOME AND SCHOOL

A QUICK LOOK

▶ **Using Digital Pictures to Celebrate Important Events**　　**page 236**

Popular image-editing software, such as MGI PhotoSuite, Adobe PhotoDeluxe, and Broderbund Print Shop, can jump-start your creative activities as you create cards, certificates, and other projects celebrating the big events in life, including birth, graduation, and marriage.

▶ **Following Your Roots as Far Back as They'll Go**　　**page 243**

The Internet has attracted family researchers for a long time. First, you find tools for creating and making your family tree available on the Web, complete with pictures of all sorts. Second, you find searchable church, death, and governmental records. Finally, you can link up with other researchers, learn the arts of research, and perhaps meet a long-lost family member in the process.

▶ **Tapping Kids' Potential with Digital Pictures**　　**page 248**

Kids can do all sorts of things with digital images. They can use paint and draw programs and upload their creations to AOL Keyword: **Blackberry Creek**. They can take existing digital pictures and add goofy features, for no particular purpose. They can use images in their homework and create things for their lives — ID cards for clubs, birthday invitations, and T-shirts, to name a few.

▶ **Parental Controls**　　**page 256**

AOL provides the controls many parents want to make sure that kids with their own screen names stay safe on the Internet.

Chapter 12

Projects for Home and School

IN THIS CHAPTER

Celebrating events with announcements, invitations, cards, and calendars

Putting digital pictures to work in day-to-day uses like creating an inventory for insurance purposes or adding pictures to your AOL Address Book

Doing genealogy and related projects with digital pictures

For students: polishing homework, hanging out, and staying out of trouble

Old-fashioned photographic prints can be *seen* just about everywhere, but digital pictures can *do* just about anything, which makes them, for many people, more fun. You can use digital pictures in greeting cards, company newsletters, announcements, calendars, fun ID cards, and every sort of refrigerator art. Using one of the many excellent graphics software packages listed in Chapter 9, you put your pictures to good use, delighting your kids, friends, and significant others in the process.

Celebrating Major Events

Suppose your daughter just got engaged, *you* just got engaged, you just shot your first hole in one, you grew a prize pumpkin, you got a new job, the lab just had pups, or you have some other good excuse to celebrate. With your collection of digital pictures, you can share these events with anyone online. With a printer, you can reach everyone who's not online by using cards and announcements bedecked with digital pictures.

Weddings

Take plenty of pictures at the next wedding you attend. Using "You've Got Pictures," send individual pictures, with messages, to the couple and any of the guests who happen to be online. Or create albums and share them. These shots can be more personal and more effective than all those expensive, posed photographs, so share them! If the wedding was yours or a loved one's, why not use "You've Got Pictures" to order prints to send to those who couldn't attend the big event? Don't forget to edit your pictures to highlight the people and events you most want to remember — cropping or blurring the background, or both, as explained in Chapter 10.

Births

If the little guy or gal isn't yours, consider offering to distribute digital pictures along with the good news as a helpful favor to the harried new parents. If you have a creative impulse, send a customized announcement along with cute baby pictures. Other milestones worth photographing and sharing include baby's first tooth, first step, first haircut, first birthday, first day of school, first lost tooth, and so on.

Birthdays and Holidays

Surprise your friends, relatives, and peers by marking birthdays with a digital greeting and copies of the latest digital pictures. Pictures of your place decked out for the party or the holidays are also worth sharing online. Many software packages allow you to create your own birthday, holiday, and greeting cards easily. Figure 12-1 shows a card that took about a minute to make in PhotoSuite III. (The digital picture was ready to go, of course.) Or just remember the event by using "You've Got Pictures" to send digital pictures to grandma or others.

Tip

Programs like Broderbund Print Shop and MGI PhotoSuite III come with ready-made designs for wedding albums, to which you can add pictures and share the results on the Web. PhotoSuite III also comes with templates for making wedding cards, albums, VHS videotape covers (for those videos), and Web pages. AOL's Web tools, 1-2-3 Publish and Easy Designer, have useful wedding-related templates as well.

Tip

Desperate to celebrate but lacking a good excuse? Try AOL Keyword: **Fact a Day**; then click the Today in History link. Why not celebrate Shakespeare's birth, Stalin's death, Elvis's reappearance, or your child's first tooth? Another such page comes to you daily from the Library of Congress at memory.loc. gov/ammem/today/ today.html.

12

Projects for Home and School

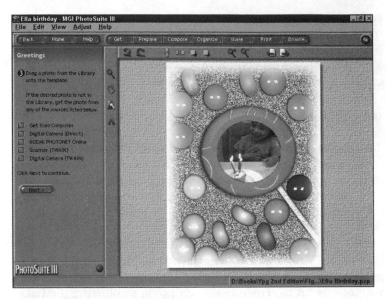

Figure 12-1. Happy birthday!

Feeling Blue?

Have you ever contemplated having a theme party for no reason other than perhaps the next holiday or vacation is just way too far away (the "tax season blahs" — that long stretch between holidays in the early spring when most of us are broke and grumpy)? Or is morale down around the office? How about setting up and promoting an event with an online invitation? Add some old and silly pictures of your friends or workmates. (Silly cards and bad humor work well in such occasions.) Use the special effects filters in Kai's PhotoSoap or MGI PhotoSuite III to create your weird pictures.

Day-to-Day Uses for Your Digital Pictures

Special events demand special cards, invitations, certificates, and the like. Daily uses of digital pictures help you tap the real usefulness of digital pictures.

Personalizing Your Calendar

Talk about day-to-day! Software and your digital pictures give you the tools to personalize calendars by using digital pictures and custom text. Many programs let you create calendars. The calendar shown in Figure 12-2 was made with PhotoSuite. Adobe PhotoDeluxe and Broderbund Print Shop offer a wealth of calendar-making templates, too.

Figure 12-2. A face a month — what better way to remember anniversaries, birthdays, holidays, and other events.

From the main PhotoSuite window, I clicked Compose (new project). With the CD in the drive, I clicked Calendar from the list in the Activity Bar on the left. With the Calendar template displayed, I simply clicked Add Photo and retrieved the digital picture from my hard drive. This particular digital picture began life in a 20-year-old Nikon single-lens-reflex (SLR) camera. I had the picture developed at my local photo processor and delivered online through "You've Got Pictures," so I could download it and edit it slightly.

Romancing the Web

If you're feeling oppressed by all these baby pictures, or are suddenly single, or are still searching — and not the kind of searching you do with a search engine — try posting your digital picture on Love@AOL. On AOL, this personals area can be found at AOL Keyword: **Love@AOL**. On the Web, you can visit the area at `love.aol.com/LoveMain`. In either case, you can post pictures, submit a personal profile, hope for a match, and (in the meantime) search for your alter ego.

Creating a Home Inventory

Consider keeping a collection of digital pictures in case you ever need to report a burglary or file an insurance claim. You can use digital pictures to keep a record of all the valuable and important objects around the house or office. To do so, you must first get digital pictures of the items in question (see Chapter 2 if you're still unsure how to do that). Beyond that, you probably already have the software you need.

▶ In Microsoft Word, create a table by choosing Table⇨Insert Table. Select enough columns to include all relevant information for your inventory, such as Name, Picture, Location, and Description. For the Picture column, you can drop in digital pictures by choosing Insert⇨Picture⇨From File, and then finding and double-clicking the picture. After the picture has been inserted, you can drag it around and resize it. You will probably need to switch to View⇨Page Layout to see the pictures on the page. Now, write a paragraph or two describing the item, with details about its size, value, condition, and so on.

▶ If you are comfortable with Microsoft Excel or another spreadsheet program, you can use the spreadsheet grid to create a larger and, if you want, more complex inventory. For each item, supply information (in separate columns) about its size, value, condition, and so on.

To protect your inventory, consider giving a copy to a friend, or putting it in a bank safe, or uploading it to AOL Keyword: **My FTP Space**, explained in Chapter 13. That way, if you lose everything, you'll still have your inventory!

Pictures for Your Address Book

If you send and receive e-mail, sooner or later you will want to take advantage of AOL's built-in Address Book. With a message open and nothing selected on the message, just click Add Address to include the sender's address in the Address Book. At any time, you can add an address to the Address Book by choosing Mail Center⇨Address Book from the AOL toolbar. One of the Address Book's little-used features is the capability to add the picture of someone with their e-mail address. Here's how:

1. Open the Address Book (choose Mail Center⇨Address Book from the AOL toolbar).

2. Select the name of someone whose e-mail address has already been included in the Address Book, and click Edit.

3. Click the Picture tab. (See Figure 12-3.) Click the Select Picture button and navigate to the picture you want to include. Then double-click the picture.

4. If the digital picture is large, you'll see a message asking whether you want to resize the image before inserting it into the Address Book. Click Yes or No, and you're done!

Note

To include someone's picture in your Address Book, you must, of course, have already acquired the digital picture, and you need to know where it's located on your hard drive.

Figure 12-3. Paste that digital picture right into your Address Book.

Making Digital Mischief

Do you have any pictures that cry out for graffiti, a dunce hat, Groucho's glasses, or Spock's ears? To get these effects, you can write text or apply digital "paint" directly on the image itself; then you can attach it to your e-mail message, or you can place it right into an e-mail message if your recipient is on AOL. If your digital picture is a JPG, GIF, or BMP file, you can open it in the Windows Paint program and add text and other effects, such as spray paint, directly to the picture (though programs like PhotoDeluxe and PhotoSuite give you a lot more control).

For more fun, buy yourself (or your kids) one of the many programs for children that allow for the creation of warped, stretched, and otherwise distorted faces. PhotoSuite's Family Edition includes many such special effects. Kai's SuperGoo is tremendously popular among kids. Figure 12-4 shows a couple of kids hamming it up while taking a popcorn shower at the breakfast table. It was made with Crayola Make a Masterpiece software.

Figure 12-4. Crayola Make a Masterpiece (from IBM) is for special effects that kids can make by themselves.

Planting a Family Tree

Curious about your family's history? You can find information about your kin online, create digital family trees, and publish the results on the Web — perhaps learning about and meeting distant relatives in the process.

You begin by gathering photos and information about your grandparents, parents, siblings, nieces, and nephews, or maybe just your own immediate family. Then, ask others to sift through their personal archives. Make sure to use a variety of media while doing your research, including digital pictures, old pictures (which you'll need to scan), and videotaped interviews, which you can mine for stills using video-editing software such as MGI Video Wave.

In addition to the basics — dates and places for key life events for each family member — don't forget to collect information about occupations, education, military service, hobbies, community service and awards, pets, favorite jokes, and the like. Don't worry about getting exactly the same sort of details on each person; everyone's story requires different details after all.

After you've gathered and organized your photos and text information, you can always dip into your archive to use this information for other purposes, like making homemade personalized birthday cards or creating a family newsletter.

Your family photos will probably need to be scanned. With today's technology, that's the easy part. You can now get a color scanner for less than $100. Of course, if you're using "You've Got Pictures," you have an easy way of getting digital pictures of living family members: Photograph them, have the prints posted to "You've Got Pictures," create an online album as explained in Chapter 5, and send it (or the individual pictures) to family members who are online.

Then, assemble a family tree with the help of your computer and AOL. The easiest way to do so is with special-purpose software. See "Choosing Genealogy Software," later in this chapter.

Even if your own interest in family history is limited, a family tree, either printed and framed or shared online, can make a special gift for parents or others. Creating a family tree with

Find It Online

Philip Greenspun's Photo.net, one of the best general photography sites on the Web, includes a detailed guide called "Storing Slides, Negatives, and Photos" (www.photo.net/photo/storage.html).

Tip

For a complete introduction to online genealogical research, pick up any of the following books published by IDG Books Worldwide, Inc.: *Genealogy Online For Dummies,* 2nd Edition; *Your Official America Online Guide to Genealogy Online,* 2nd Edition; and *Family Tree Maker For Dummies.* The first two books are available at AOL Keyword: **AOL Store.** The Family Tree Maker book can be purchased, along with the software, at AOL Keyword: **Shop@AOL.** (Search for **Family Tree Maker.**)

Tip

Scanning old or damaged photos by using a flatbed scanner is likely to expose them to less wear and risk than other methods of scanning them. After such photos are scanned, photo manipulation software can help fix and conceal damage to these old pictures.

digital pictures can bring it to life, especially if you can un-earth stern-faced portraits of your great-grandparents. The family tree can help your kids learn who's who and how people wound up in so many different places. If published on the Web, a family tree can help everyone stay in touch cross-country, and can help you discover new leaves for your tree.

Doing Family Research: AOL's Genealogy Forum

If you have a passion for genealogy, you'll find true community at AOL Keyword: **Roots**, which has been one of the most popular forums on AOL for years, staffed by more than 140 volunteers.

A click away from AOL Keyword: **Roots** is the forum's Web site, directly available at www.genealogyforum.com (see Figure 12-5). The forum and Web site provide access to all sorts of Internet resources and guidance in using them, including the following:

Tip

Mapping your genealogy requires much more than old pictures and a scanner. You can also search for and scan citizenship papers, letters, diaries, certain pages of old high school yearbooks, obituaries, birth certificates, and other documents you can uncover. With these pictures and documents you can begin to reconstruct their lives, inviting others to fill in missing details.

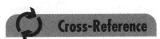

Cross-Reference

A *mailing list* consists of a group of people who can communicate with each other by e-mail about a specific topic. You can take part in Roots-L, to which more than 7,000 people belong, by sending an e-mail message to roots-l-request@ rootsweb.com; in the subject area, type **subscribe**; in the body, type **subscribe**. When you're done, send the message. For all you need to know about mailing lists, see Chapter 12 of the *America Online Official Internet Guide,* 3rd Edition, also published by IDG Books Worldwide, Inc.

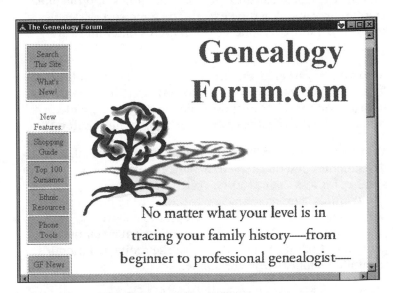

Figure 12-5. AOL's Genealogy Forum.com on the Web.

- ▶ Web sites organized by topic (for example, Mayflower, Maps, Religious Resources)

- ▶ Web sites organized by nationality and ethnic group (French, Jewish, and so on)

- ▶ Mailing lists by topic (for example, Indian-Roots-L)

- ▶ Tons of AOL message boards (online bulletin boards where you can read and post public messages about dozens of topics)

- ▶ Links to related Web sites, available throughout the forum and the Web site

That's not hardly all AOL offers. From the Families channel, check out the Genealogy Family History area (AOL Keyword: **Genealogy**). This area, sponsored by Ancestry.com, offers the opportunity to search several large genealogical databases for traces of your ancestors, some of which are fee-based.

Choosing Genealogy Software

A wide variety of software is available to help you with genealogy research and family trees. One of the best-known programs for genealogists is Genealogy.com's Family Tree Maker Deluxe Edition II, which currently comes packaged with, count 'em, 20 CDs. What do you find on those CDs? The FamilyFinder Index lists more than 220 million people who appear in several centuries of state and federal records. Four CDs include 60 million records from two popular genealogical research services. Five World Family Tree CDs include tens of thousands of family trees contributed by family history enthusiasts from around the world. Two Social Security Death Index CDs provide birth and death dates, Social Security numbers, and residential information for some 55 million people. And that's just for starters. Family Tree Maker's Web site itself (as shown in Figure 12-6) is a massive resource for genealogists, and for users of the software in particular.

Also highly rated is Generations Beginner's Edition 8.0 from SierraHome.com (www.sierrahome.com), which likewise provides tree-creating tools, Web space for your family tree, and voluminous research resources.

Cross-Reference

At AOL Keyword: **Roots**, click Resources. In the list box that appears, double-click Genealogy Forum File Libraries Center. Here, you find an entire file library devoted to genealogy shareware and utilities. Using the forum's message boards, you can get advice about the best software for your purposes.

12

Projects for Home and School

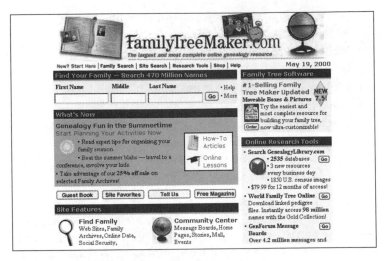

Figure 12-6. The Web site for Family Tree Maker software.

Plant Your Tree on the Web?

If you're inspired by your family picture project, how about taking it online? It's a great way to let your distant relatives check it out at almost no cost, bring your family closer together, and let your kin share those rare, valuable photos. It may also persuade them to dig into their own archives and contribute to the project. A really public family tree can serve as a kind of magnet for old documents boxed up in other people's attics. It can also help identify errors and gaps in a family tree.

To create your genealogy pages, you may want to start with the easy-to-use and attractive templates available through 1-2-3 Publish and Easy Designer (see Chapter 13 for the details on using these page-building tools). For information about genealogy and research techniques, type AOL Keyword: **Web Centers** and look for the Research Your Family Tree link (as shown in Figure 12-7). Visit that area for tips and lessons, as well as for the opportunity to search state records, church records, and other resources. All the details are available online.

Find It Online

Elsewhere on the Web, two large sites provide inspiration, advice, software, perhaps a few insights into your own family, and a very large number of links. The first site is RootsWeb at www. rootsweb.com. The second site is Cyndi's List of Genealogy Sites on the Internet at www. cyndislist.com. The latter site offers a comprehensive overview of Internet resources of interest to family researchers on the Net.

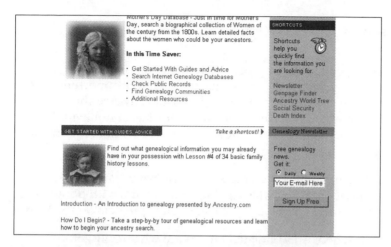

Figure 12-7. Part of the Research Your Family Tree area of AOL.com.

Making a Family Album

Image-editing and project software like MGI PhotoSuite III makes it easy to create a *printed* family tree, arranging pictures of family members in a nicely designed layout. Other project software, such as Printshop, offers very similar features. This example looks at PhotoSuite because the software is introduce elsewhere (Chapter 10).

1. Open PhotoSuite, and click the Compose button to create a new project.

2. From the list of buttons on the left, choose Photo Layouts⇨Family Trees.

3. With your PhotoSuite III CD in the drive, choose a template for displaying your family's digital pictures.

   You can edit the template's text depending on the number of people you wish to include on the page created from the template. Then, create additional pages for anyone you want to include.

Each page can then be saved as an HTML page by choosing File⇨Create Web Page. A dialog box will tell you where the HTML file (the Web page) can be found on your hard drive. Now, upload the Web pages and any associated digital pictures to AOL Hometown, as explained in Chapter 13.

12

Projects for Home and School

Note

For now, many of the online areas for kids' art provide opportunities to share digital drawings made with paint and draw tools. Many kids don't have cameras, or their parents don't let them use theirs. Digital drawing and painting is probably the best way for children to get comfortable working with digital images, an ideal way of getting ready for the excitement of digital photographs.

Tip

Microsoft Word has always made it simple to insert a graphic, then resize and edit it, by using the Insert⇨ Picture⇨From File command.

Tip

Parents and teachers may want to consider purchasing inexpensive drawing or painting programs, such as AppleWorks or Knowledge Adventures' Kid Works, both of which include word-processing *and* picture-making modules. With Kid Works, kids can create illustrated stories, using digital pictures to stimulate their narrative and writing skills.

Digital Pictures for Kids Only

Kids spend their early years coloring, sculpting, making collages, and painting. They seem to have fewer opportunities for creative expression as they grow up and advance through the school system. Perhaps that's why they feel at home in the world of multimedia — they're given free reign to follow their creative urges wherever they lead.

Kids can put digital pictures to use in many ways. School uses are pretty obvious. Kids can illustrate reports with photos and maps, create charts, and publish science projects on the Web.

After-school uses of digital images are what really get elementary-age kids excited. With programs designed for kids, such as Broderbund KidPix, Crayola Make a Masterpiece, and AppleWorks (formerly ClarisWorks), kids can create the following:

- ▶ Collages (using a combination of digital pictures, text, handmade and scanned pictures, and computer-generated art)
- ▶ Silly pictures
- ▶ Birthday invitations
- ▶ Valentine's Day cards
- ▶ Club ID cards and newsletters
- ▶ Mazes, crossword puzzles, and other games
- ▶ Stories illustrated with pictures, silly and otherwise

Broderbund's KidPix is the granddaddy of creative programs for children, and its wild design and creative features have kept it on the short list of the best children's software for years. On AOL, a special area is devoted to the software at AOL Keyword: **KidPix**, where you will find dozens of ideas for using the software, plus good deals if you don't already own it. Some kids use KidPix as the world's coolest doodling machine. Others actually put their doodles to good work, making comic books, thank-you cards, stamps, jigsaw puzzles, and abstract art suitable for display by impressed adults.

Many KidPix activities require kids to print out their work, then color it in, paste it together, and do other things. An inkjet color printer is indispensable for regular KidPix use.

KidPix files can be saved as BMP files (PICT on the Mac), and thus can be used in other programs. After the files are converted into JPGs and GIFs, these pictures can be used in kids' Web pages.

Kids Sharing Art at Blackberry Creek

Kids' art used to make it no further than the classroom bulletin board or refrigerator door. Now, kids can make their work available for just about anyone by using AOL's Blackberry Creek (AOL Keyword: **Bcreek**). Kids have fun looking at each other's work, and parents and teachers should see this as an opportunity for kids to learn skills from others. Blackberry Creek's Art Shop (AOL Keyword: **BcreekArt**) lets kids draw pictures of themselves, animals, and any of dozens of themes, and then upload their digital doodles for everyone to see.

At Blackberry Creek, children have the opportunity to download one of the cool templates available (for example, one such template has a beach and sky in the background but no people), which they can fill in using any graphics program, including any of the image-editing programs mentioned in Chapters 9 and 10.

Starting an Online Club

At a certain age (eightish and above), kids start to love clubs: creating them, surrounding them with elaborate rituals, keeping others out, and admitting only certain kids. AOL kids in particular create clubs of every kind: fan clubs, girls' clubs, boys' clubs, Pokémon clubs, video game clubs, and many more. A list of these clubs for the pre-teen and teen sets is available at AOL Keyword: **Youth Tech**; click Message Boards to visit and take part in the Web-based boards.

Making Things for Your Club

With digital pictures and your computer, kids can create all the paraphernalia required by any self-respecting, real-world club:

You can import digital pictures into KidPix by using the File⇨Import a Graphic menu; and you can use pictures in any KidPix activity, including the Stampinator, which lets kids do things like create flying bugs that flutter aimlessly around a digital picture.

For special effects and just mucking around, programs like KidPix, Kai's SuperGoo, and Crayola's Make a Masterpiece will keep kids busy making funny pictures. Without being aware of it, they'll also be organizing their ideas for presentation to others, working with a variety of computer equipment, and learning the basics of image editing. Just don't say it's good for them.

Parents, be sure to read Blackberry Creek's Privacy Notice — type AOL Keyword: **Bcreek** and then click the Privacy Notice link.

Tip

At Blackberry Creek, templates (picture-starters) are available for both PC users (the file format is `.bmp`) and Mac users (the file format is `.pict`). Graphics can be created with *any* software that allows a child to save their work as `.bmp` or `.pict`. Windows Paint, for example, or KidPix work fine. After the kids download and edit the templates, they can upload their contributions to Blackberry Creek to share with others.

Note

AOL's Web-publishing tools (1-2-3 Publish and Easy Designer) cannot be used by screen names assigned to the Kids Only or Young Teens categories (see the discussion of Parental Controls later in this chapter). Kids will need to work with an adult to create a page of their own.

▶ **ID cards.** Kids can use a word processor to create a simple table, and then use each cell for a single club member, pasting in a digital picture, name, and other information. The kids can print the finished document on cardstock; then use a paper cutter to separate the ID cards. Broderbund Print Shop and MGI PhotoSuite have templates for creating business cards that can be easily adapted for kids (as shown in Figure 12-8).

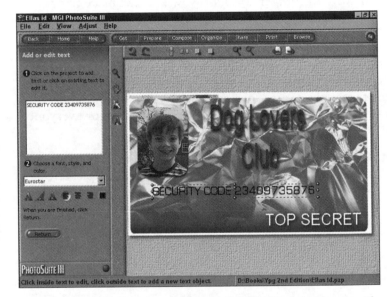

Figure 12-8. A fun ID project made by using an AOL PhotoCam digital picture with a PhotoSuite III template and then playing with the text and arrangement.

▶ **A club newsletter.** With nothing more than a word processor, your child can edit the club's newsletter, profiling a different club member each week or month and covering club events. Using a product like the Broderbund Print Shop PressWriter, sophisticated-looking newsletters (using digital pictures, clipart, and neighborhood journalistic talent) can be churned out in no time. Even Microsoft Word or Publish, with its support of digital pictures and multicolumn text, are perfectly fine for creating a club newsletter.

▶ **Web sites.** What would a club be without a Web site these days, created by using 1-2-3 Publish or Easy Designer and decked out with digital pictures, a counter, links to related sites, and stories and poems by club members? If the site is a celebrity club, it will have to have photos and links to similar sites, plus an e-mail link so that other fans can write back.

Homework with Horsepower

Every kid has homework. Few kids *like* doing homework. Parents, teachers, and anyone who works with them can help them use digital pictures to make their homework more motivating, more fun, and maybe more effective.

Most word-processing programs let you insert digital pictures in the text and create tables and charts. If your daughter has to write a report on South Dakota, she can find simple facts and pictures — such as the state flag and local scenes — to add to her report. Encourage her to use photographs and clipart to create informative diagrams and charts for science and math classes — the pictures may also help her understand the material better. Make sure you can put her findings in her own words and explain them to others.

Kids and Digital Cameras

Digital cameras are coming down in price, while a whole new category of kids' digital cameras has started to flourish (JamCam from KB Gear for Kids, Barbie and NickClick cameras from Mattel Media, and others). Even elementary-age kids can be encouraged to start documenting the world around them with such digital cameras, disposable cameras (using 35mm film), and inexpensive point-and-shoot film cameras.

More meaningful than a postcard from a field trip, for example, would be a series of digital pictures taken of, and shared with, the group. Taking more than one picture creates the framework of a story and opportunity to do some writing.

Tip

The Web has dozens of *homework helpers,* sites that link to the core subjects about which children must write reports and do homework. AOL has brought together a large and highly selective group of such sites at AOL Keyword: **AOL@School**. The sites are organized by subject (math, science, and the like) and by level (primary, elementary, middle school, and high school).

Tip

For a guide to the dozens of specialized collections of digital pictures on the Web, one of the most valuable starting places is the Digital Librarian at www.servtech.com/ ~mvail/images.html. Assume that any picture found on the Web is copyrighted: Ask for permission to use an image and explain the purpose; then cite the source accurately, as you (or your child) would with any resource used in a paper.

12

Projects for Home and School

Or, kids can capture the following:

▶ The week-by-week progress of a season

▶ The month-by-month maturation of a dog

▶ The day-by-day melting of a snowman

Taking pictures of local plants and animals, and making the results available on a Web page, can provide the starting point of long-distance friendships among students in the same grade but different schools. Some teachers of younger students like to take the kids on a walk around the school, photographing everything along the way, as a record and a point of departure for classroom discussion. Using digital cameras lets kids see the results on the spot and makes them more aware of exactly what they're seeing.

Projects, Projects Everywhere

Find It Online

Kodak's Digital Learning Center includes a large set of Digital Learning Projects. Finding it on the huge Kodak site is not easy, though. Start at the Kodak Learning Center (www.kodak.com/US/en/digital/dlc/plus). Click the DLC Plus link, and you're there.

Software can simplify routine homework assignments. It can also jump-start those creative projects, too, to the point where it now makes more sense to create printed and digital products yourself than to buy something less personal and more commercial. Kids can now crank out professional-looking calendars, cards, and the like in a few minutes.

Stickers, Yes

Kids love stickers — as rewards at the dentist's office, decorations for clothing, and markers for calendars. Now, kids don't have to wait till they visit the dentist to get stickers; they can create their own, using their own designs. Making stickers requires three things:

▶ Software to design the sticker images or import the digital pictures

▶ *Sticker paper* (precut removable stickers on heavy, adhesive stock)

▶ An inkjet color printer

A leading maker of sticker gear, Avery (Avery Dennison Corp.) is also a leader in the label business, and you can get a full overview of sticker-related products, including Disney's Stickers & Stuff Software, at `www.avery.com/kids`. Avery also sells the all-important paper for making stickers, labels, and name badges, in sheets suitable for home printers. If you can't find the paper at a local office-supply store, you can order it directly at the Web site.

T-Shirts for All Seasons

Here's a project that makes good use of *transfer paper*, a type of specialty printer paper from companies like Hewlett-Packard and Kodak. How do you go from a digital picture to a T-shirt or canvas bag? Simple. First, you'll need a special kind of paper — transfer paper — for your photo-quality inkjet printer. Then, set the printer's preferences to "reverse" and print your digital picture, or anything else for that matter, such as your company's logo and Web address. Now, print the image directly onto the transfer paper. Finally, iron the paper onto a white T-shirt to transfer the image. Many photofinishing businesses and service bureaus, such as Kinko's, can also produce T-shirts for you.

Greeting Cards

For every greeting card sold in the drugstore, there's a digital card that offers much more room for customization and personal expression, not to mention the fact that digital greeting cards are less expensive. Graphics programs, such as MGI PhotoSuite (see Figure 12-9) and Adobe PhotoDeluxe, make creating cards of every kind — invitations, holiday greeting cards (from Father's Day to Kwanza), thank-you notes, birthday cards, general-purpose cards, and blank cards — very simple.

Broderbund's Print Shop offers perhaps the largest assortment of cards and options for customizing them. Select Greeting Card, and you can then choose from dozens of types of greeting cards (birthday, romantic, sympathy, and on and on). Choose one of them (invitation, for example), and you get another two dozen choices of types of invitations. Figure 12-9 shows one that I recently used. Print Shop gives you control of the entire card, so you can add words (in any style),

Tip

Transfer paper can be used for all sorts of things, such as creating your own wrapping paper or tote bags. You can add text to a digital picture to make your designs more personal and direct.

12

Projects for Home and School

watermarks, frames, textures, digital pictures, and clipart. The trickiest part is getting the thing to print in such a way that it can be correctly folded, but Print Shop helps there, too, by printing your pictures and words in a variety of formats, allowing for folding in half (vertically or horizontally), or folding in quarters (all possible combinations).

Figure 12-9. Yes, we have birthday cards. These were quickly worked up with MGI PhotoSuite and Print Shop.

A Solution to the Pokémon Card Problem

Why should kids buy expensive cards when they can make their own sports cards, postcards, and other trading cards? Why should they settle for others' images when they can make their own? A program like Print Shop lets kids create custom cards with their own digital pictures — a great idea for clubs, hobbies, and sports teams. Images are, for that matter, the one really personal touch missing from most business cards, too.

For both trading and business cards, you will need to print your work on *card stock* (heavy paper for your printer) at the highest possible resolution.

Cartoons

Transforming pictures into cartoons, which can be printed out and colored in, is a neat little feature built into MGI PhotoSuite SE, the older software included with the AOL PhotoCam digital camera and also available on the Net as shareware. Open the software, and from the opening MGI Activity Guide, select Fun with Your Photos. Click Turn a Photo into a Coloring Book. Select a picture, and it comes up in outline form. Play with some of the controls to bring out as much of the outline as you want.

Slide Shows to Go

If you have Microsoft PowerPoint, consider creating a slide show to show off your digital pictures in presentations. See the info on presentations in Chapter 14. A *slide show* is a series of "slides" into which you can insert text, pictures, video, and audio files. PowerPoint lets you automate slide shows so the pictures flip by themselves. You can gather everyone around your computer, or share them in many ways:

▶ After the next family reunion or other event, collect your digital pictures in a PowerPoint slideshow and send the PPT file to others. Saving the slide show as a PPT file that can be read by earlier versions of PowerPoint deprives you of the fancy effects of PowerPoint 2000 but makes the file more widely usable.

▶ Viewers are available at the Microsoft Web site for people without the PowerPoint application. With a viewer, you then can use a PowerPoint slide show file without having the software. The address: www.microsoft.com/office/000/viewers.htm.

▶ Saving your presentation as a series of Web pages (choose File⇨Save As Web Page), and then uploading the pages to AOL Keyword: **My FTP Space**, gives anyone access to your slide show. Chapter 13 goes into the uploading process in more detail, and Chapter 14 discusses slide shows in more detail.

12

Projects for Home and School

Find It Online

Complete online safety guidelines are available at GetNetWise (www. getnetwise.org). Another valuable site with similar information is Safe Surfin' (www.safesurfin. com).

Child Safety Online

Much has been written about the perils of the Internet, but not much about the countless, valuable, fun, completely safe, and occasionally educational activities for kids on the Net. Yes, there are dangers, including predators and unseemly adult diversions. But AOL and the Internet industry offer many lines of defense against these real, but managable, risks:

▶ Monitor your kids' Internet use without completely getting in their way. Help them make good choices.

▶ Be a model. Gently suggest the kinds of sites where your kids might want to hang out: the Kids Only Channel (younger kids); YouthTech and the Teens Channel (older kids); Web sites like MaMaMedia, or any site available through AOL Search for Kids. Click the Search button on the toolbar. From the AOL Search page, click Kids Only.

▶ Nonetheless, lay down the law. As an adult, tell kids that they should

- Never give anyone their AOL password, ever

- Never give out contact information

- Never accept gifts (files, links in e-mail, and the like), solicited or unsolicited, from an adult

- Never agree to meet in the real world a stranger met online

- Always report objectionable language to an adult

▶ Use AOL's Parental Controls, a collection of content filters that you can apply to any screen name on your master account.

Parental Controls are available in many places on AOL (the main Parental Controls screen is shown in Figure 12-10):

▶ AOL Keyword: **Parental Controls**.

▶ A button on the Welcome screen.

▶ My AOL⇨Parental Controls.

▶ AOL Keyword: **Neighborhood Watch**. This area pulls together all of AOL's major safety areas, including Parental Controls. Here you can learn about computer viruses, too.

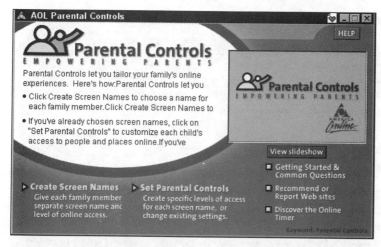

Figure 12-10. AOL Keyword: **Parental Controls** leads to many sources of information about child safety, and to AOL's tools for keeping your kids safe.

AOL Keyword: **Parental Controls** is a major line of defense in keeping kids safe online. To set up controls for a child, you must first create a screen name for him or her at AOL Keyword: **Screen name**, along with a password for the screen name. Every *master account* — an account set up by an adult — can have up to seven associated screen names (usually for different people and different purposes). Each screen name has its own password, its own Favorite Places, its own electronic mailbox, and so forth. Keep a record of your account's screen names and passwords in a safe place. They are easy to forget, and you shouldn't rely on someone else to remember them.

After you've created the screen name, click Set Parental Controls from the main Parental Controls window. A window similar to the one shown in Figure 12-11 appears. Your window will vary from the one shown here, because this one shows screen names (available from the drop-down menu) for a particular account, and yours will show screen names under your account.

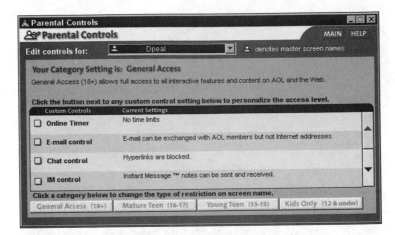

Figure 12-11. Set controls for specific features (like e-mail and Instant Messages) and specific screen names (available from the drop-down list).

Finding Your Child's Level

The first step in using Parental Controls is to assign a child to a category. You make this choice kid by kid based on a combination of age and developmental factors. Each category has an associated group of settings for major features on AOL:

▶ **Kids Only** access restricts young children to the Kids Only Channel (available from the Channels menu). A Kids Only account cannot send or receive Instant Messages (IMs), cannot enter member-created chat rooms, cannot use premium services (games paid for on an hourly basis), and can send and receive only text-only electronic mail. That is, kids cannot send or receive either file attachments or embedded pictures.

▶ Parents of teenagers may want to select **Young Teen** (aged 13–15) or **Mature Teen** (aged 16 and 17).

  • *Young Teens* may visit some chat rooms, but they may not visit member-created rooms or private rooms.

  • *Mature Teens* can download files and use IMs.

- Both teen categories are restricted to Web sites appropriate for their respective groups.

- Both teen groups are also blocked from downloading files from newsgroups and from reading certain newsgroups. Nor can they use AOL's premium gaming services. The choice between "young" and "mature" is a judgment call that depends more on a child's maturity than age; it also depends on your concerns and readiness to work with your child to use the Net.

▶ The **18+** category provides unrestricted access to all features on AOL and the Internet. All master accountholders are automatically included in this category.

With screen names established for each child and access levels assigned to each screen name, you're ready to start editing your Parental Controls. In the main Parental Control window (refer to Figure 12-11), you can do the following:

▶ Select the screen name for which you want to change the settings. (Use the drop-down list at the top of the window.)

▶ Change, if you want, the category to which the screen name belongs (for example, allowing a child to graduate from Kids Only to Young Teen).

▶ Change the settings for any of the individual controls. Currently, you can adjust the settings for e-mail, chat, instant messages, the Web, downloading, newsgroups, and premium services (games). Just click the little square to the left of the control's name; then, follow the on-screen instructions for setting the controls. If you make any changes to any of the controls for a particular screen name you must click Save on the window for that control, in order for your changes to take effect. Close the Parental Controls window(s) when you're done.

 Note

Parental Controls and the specific controls are discussed in more detail in Chapter 3 of the author's *Your Official America Online Internet Guide,* 3rd Edition (IDG Books Worldwide, Inc.).

12

Projects for Home and School

Summary

This chapter opens the door to possibilities awaiting you after you start exploring digital pictures. With a digital camera, a scanner, or a regular film camera (and "You've Got Pictures"), you can start using digital pictures throughout your life. Skim these pages for some specific ideas such as creating a home inventory, posting a picture to Love@AOL, making a family tree, and helping your child design school projects that go beyond both the assignment and the school's walls. The next chapter explores ways to include digital pictures in Web pages, which can be used for home and school, as well as office and business.

13

TAKING YOUR DIGITAL PICTURES TO THE WEB

A QUICK LOOK

Chapter 13

Taking Your Digital Pictures to the Web

Some people consider the World Wide Web the "visual" part of the Internet. On AOL, you have all the tools you need to create your own contribution to the world's largest mosaic. AOL Hometown (AOL Keyword: **Hometown**) is the home on the Web for AOL members and nonmembers alike. At AOL Hometown, you'll find two tools — 1-2-3 Publish and Easy Designer — for quickly creating a personal, family, or business Web page. Easy Designer in particular offers a great deal of flexibility if you want to share your digital pictures with a bridge club, a Brownie troop, an aerobics class, an extended family, a neighborhood, or a group of potential customers.

You and the Web

You're no doubt familiar with the World Wide Web. Web addresses — h-t-t-p this and h-t-t-p that — are as common as,
well, photographs. Perhaps you've considered the Web a fad.
Perhaps you can't imagine why you would ever need your
own Web page.

Think again.

> ▶ A digital version of your résumé, enhanced by your dig-
> ital picture, would be readily available to every poten-
> tial employer and would be easy to correct and to
> continually refine.

> ▶ A Web page can help promote a home business to your
> customers or potential customers. Think how much
> more exciting your message would be with pictures of
> your products and a few happy customers!

> ▶ A Web page with digital pictures can also be a great
> way for everyone in your extended family to see the lat-
> est pictures of the kids and to catch up on the family
> events. It's the easiest way to supply the entire family
> with the latest pictures of the kids.

> ▶ Your personal Web page (your *home page*) is a good
> way for you to connect with like-minded folks or that
> as-yet unmet special someone. AOL Hometown consists
> of dozens of small (and some large) communities of re-
> lated pages, making it easier for you to connect with
> like-minded people.

> ▶ Your Web page provides an easy way to voice an opin-
> ion or share research. For many people, the Net's real
> value comes from its many different voices. With AOL
> Instant Messenger Remote (discussed a little later in
> this chapter), you give people the chance to talk back.

You may think of creating a Web page as a way of joining a
conversation more than as a way of creating personal or professional billboards.

Before You Start . . .

AOL makes getting started on a Web page so easy that it's worth the effort to think through your purposes and otherwise get prepared for building a page. Why? As easy as it is to make changes to your page, you can save a lot of time and hassle by doing a bit of initial design work — planning.

What Are You Trying to Do on the Web?

Here are some questions to ask yourself before getting started with your Web page:

▶ **What is the purpose of your page?** The most important factor in any Web page or *Web site* (a collection of pages) is its purpose. Purposes don't have to be serious, just clear. Why? With so many millions of pages competing for everyone's attention, your readers may disappear as quickly as they arrived — if they don't know what you have to offer as soon as possible after arriving at your page. Giving your page a title that matches its purpose is a good place to start.

▶ **What sort of impression do you want to make?** Given your purpose, what personality do you want to project — professional, knowledgeable, welcoming, whimsical, or something else?

▶ **How important is visual interest? What kind of visual interest?** What needs to be illustrated? What colors support your intended purpose and impression? Do you want to include much text in your page, or mostly digital pictures?

▶ **Where will the content come from?** Do the pictures and words you need exist, or must you either create them or collect them elsewhere?

Don't sweat the details if you don't have specific design ideas at this point. You can always use one of AOL's thematic, fill-in-the-blank templates to get started and then alter things to your liking later. Editing is easy with AOL's Web-publishing tools.

Tip

Most people who create Web pages continuously learn from each other's work. On AOL, the place to start to see others' work is Hometown (AOL Keyword: **Hometown**), a small city, with many neighborhoods, for Web pages.

Groups@AOL: Sharing Photos in an Online Group

Groups@AOL (AOL Keyword: **Groups**) provides a wired home on the Web for the close-knit communities in your life, no matter how far apart everyone lives. Think of a *Group* as a meeting place where you can share ideas, information, and (you guessed it) digital pictures with a small group of people.

Groups@AOL is open to anyone, AOL member or not. Only AOL members can *start* a Group, but they can invite non-AOL members to join.

What do digital pictures have to do with Groups@AOL? Imagine a Group formed by an extended family, or a neighborhood organization, or a Cub Scout troop — under the guidance of a parent, of course. Any member of your Group can upload pictures to the Group's photo collections, where the pictures will be instantly available to the other Group members. Hometown pages can be included in a Group's list of Favorites. To view and post pictures in a Group, click See Photos from any Group's main page.

Instead of being called *albums* as in "You've Got Pictures," in Groups, related pictures are called *collections*.

To add photos to a Group, you first create at least one collection to hold them. Here's how:

1. In the Current Photos section, shown for a sample Group in the preceding figure, click Create New.

2. In the new page that comes up, enter a name for your collection and then click Add a Photo. This page appears:

Continued

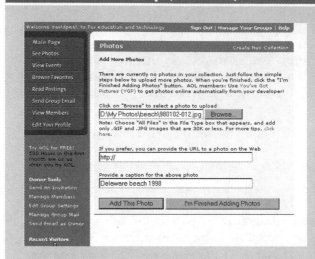

Groups@AOL: Sharing Photos in an Online Group *(continued)*

3. Add a photo by clicking the Browse button and then finding and double-clicking the picture file on your hard drive.

4. Add a caption, if you want, which will appear with your photo.

5. Repeat Steps 2 through 4 to add additional photos and click the I'm Finished Adding Photos button when you're done.

Cross-Reference

The first step in gathering your digital pictures is to create a new folder or folders. For each Web page, consider creating a special folder for all your text and pictures. You can download pictures from "You've Got Pictures" or from a digital camera or scanner into this folder. See Chapter 8 for downloading procedures, guidelines for keeping track of digital pictures, and instructions for creating folders on your hard drive and desktop.

What Pictures Will You Need?

Early in the Web-page-building process, you'll want to gather any digital pictures (along with any text) that you want to include in your page and keep all the files in one folder (or a manageable number of folders) on your hard drive. Make your Web-publishing tasks more efficient and rewarding by beginning with good organization.

If you have any pictures or artwork in unusual file formats, convert them right away to GIFs or JPGs. You may need to use graphics software, such as Paint Shop Pro or ThumbsPlus, both of which are mentioned toward the end of Chapter 9. Programs like these will open your images and let you save them as GIFs or JPGs.

Welcome to AOL Hometown

AOL Hometown provides a home on the World Wide Web for
AOL members and nonmembers alike. Here's what you can
find in this bustling virtual metropolis:

- ▶ **Web-publishing tools:** 1-2-3 Publish (super-easy) and
  Easy Designer (super-flexible), which simplify the creation of pages featuring your digital pictures.

- ▶ **A Web site:** Here, anyone can make any number of
  Web pages available. *To make pages available* simply
  means to copy your pages to Hometown, where they
  can be viewed and searched for by anyone with Web
  access. You find out about copying (uploading) later in
  this chapter.

- ▶ **Storage space:** AOL Hometown furnishes visitors with
  enough storage space to hold up to 12MB worth of digital pictures, Web pages, and anything else they want to
  make available to others. This storage space is actually
  very handy for sharing word-processing files, spread-
  sheets, and other documents for school and work. You
  get this space in addition to your space on "You've Got
  Pictures" and Groups@AOL; it is the storage space you'll
  use when uploading pictures to Groups@AOL.

- ▶ **Rich learning and reference resources:** AOL provides resources for learning the ropes of page-building,
  whether you're new to HTML (the language used to
  build Web pages) or want to acquire more advanced
  Web-building skills.

Choosing the Right Tool

Each of AOL's tools takes a different approach. Choosing a tool
does not necessarily prevent you from using a different tool. If
you start with 1-2-3 Publish, it is easy to continue editing the
same page with Easy Designer, which offers more flexibility. If
you start with Easy Designer, however, you can't edit pages in
1-2-3 Publish. (Though if you're comfortable with Easy
Designer, you probably wouldn't want to use 1-2-3!)

▶ 1-2-3 Publish is the fastest way to create a page and publish it quickly in AOL Hometown. Choose a template, add your digital pictures and other content, put in some links, and you're done.

▶ Easy Designer lets you go further than 1-2-3 Publish does. With Easy Designer, you can add pictures wherever you want on your page.

▶ You can use any Web page editor and upload the files to a special area (AOL Keyword: **My FTP Space**) from which they can be added to AOL Hometown.

1-2-3 Publish: Fastest Path to the Web

The fastest way to create a simple Web page on AOL is with 1-2-3 Publish. Just go to AOL Keyword: **123**, choose a fill-in-the-blanks template, and you're off!

1-2-3 makes it simple by starting you off with a template, which makes a few decisions regarding the ordering of elements such as digital pictures, lists, text, and headings. You just fill in the blanks with your own information, an approach you'll appreciate if you are in a hurry. Currently, 1-2-3 offers about five dozen different templates for you to use.

Tip

1-2-3 Publish has a variety of templates suited to a range of interests. Choose from templates about yourself, your family, your hobbies, your favorite sports teams, and so on. Yes, there's even a Photography template. You can find a list of templates on the first screen that appears when you use AOL Keyword: **123**.

If you are a photographer, you might want to show off a sample image by using the My Photography Page. Or create a page showing a specific use of digital pictures — such as an auction page (to show off those Roman coins) or a genealogy page (to post restored digital pictures of corseted or be-whiskered ancestors). When 1-2-3 Publish opens a template, it's a blank sheet, at first. Your job is to fill it in with your own information. Figure 13-1 shows the first step of a genealogy template.

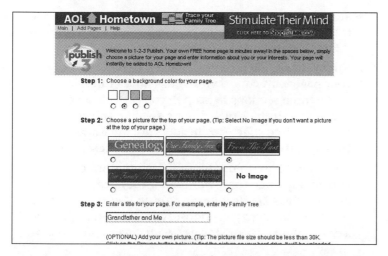

Figure 13-1. 1-2-3 Publish! The top part of the fill-in-the blank genealogy template.

Following is an example using the template called Our Genealogy Page. Exact steps vary by template, so this procedure is provided only as an example. None of your choices is permanent, by the way, so don't get hung up on the details. Later, I'll show you how to make changes to your page.

▶ In **Steps 1** and **2** for this template, shown in Figure 13-1, you are asked to choose a background color for your genealogy page and a *banner,* a graphical image that characterizes the purpose and content of your page.

▶ In **Step 3,** enter a title for your page. The words in your title (the official term for this Web element is *header,* actually) appear below the banner, in large bold type. Type your header into the blank provided. Keep your title short!

In this template, as the second (and optional) part of Step 3, you can add a digital picture. Here's your big chance to show off your imaging wizardry. With a digital picture on your hard drive (either downloaded from "You've Got Pictures" or acquired from a scanner or digital camera), you're ready to go. Any digital picture you select is uploaded only when you choose to preview your 1-2-3 page at the end of the process (click Preview at the bottom of the template). Your page plus any associated pictures are uploaded at the same time.

Note

Uploading to AOL Hometown involves a different process and different destination from uploading to "You've Got Pictures". If you'll be using a digital picture from "You've Got Pictures", you must first download the picture to your hard drive, following the steps in Chapter 4.

▶ **Step** 4 lets you choose a horizontal divider to separate the short sections of your page-to-be. In Web lingo, this thingy is called a *rule*.

▶ Now you get down to the business of personalizing your page with your own words and pictures. In each of the three sections in **Step 5**, you provide a header and a paragraph or two about a specific subject. In this case, the three *suggested* headers are My Family Heritage, My Ancestors, and My Current Research.

You do not have to use these three titles but can choose any three (or fewer than three) headers you want, such as *The Infamous Family Reunion of 1992*. Whatever headers you choose, you do need to provide a description of your stories or whatever else you have to say.

▶ *Links* are the bits of clickable text that allow your users to visit pertinent Web sites of your choosing. No Web page should be without links, according to most Web surfers. In **Step 6** of the Our Genealogy Page template, you can add up to three link names (the clickable text) and link addresses (the Web addresses), as well as a title for your collection of links.

▶ Finally, in **Step 7,** you can choose to include a special communications tool called AOL Instant Messenger-Remote at the bottom of your page. AIM-R consists of a series of buttons (as shown in Figure 13-2). These buttons allow visitors to your site to send you messages by AOL Instant Messenger or by e-mail, or to join (effectively, to create) an AIM chat room related to your page and its subject. Anyone viewing the page can also add you to their AIM Buddy List by clicking a button. What a great way to stay in touch with your extended family!

Tip

If you later import this page into Easy Designer, you can add many more links and many more pictures, and you can create clickable pictures as well.

Note

A Web address, or *URL* (short for Uniform Resource Locator), has several elements. In the example in the text: `http://` means that this is a Web page. `hometown.aol.com` tells the browser software *where* (on what Internet computer) the page can be found. The rest of the address says exactly where the page is on that computer (in what folder). (It's like a path on your own hard drive, such as `c:/americaonline5.0/download/photos.exe`).

Figure 13-2. With AOL Instant Messenger-Remote, people visiting your page can send you e-mail, or an instant message, or create a chat room.

After you've gone through each step, click the Preview button to see what your page looks like. If you want to make more changes to your page, click Modify at the top of the preview page. Make any changes, and click Preview again. When you're happy with your page, click the Save button instead of the Modify button.

Publishing Your 1-2-3 Page

Every page created and saved by using 1-2-3 Publish is automatically registered at AOL Hometown when you click Save. After clicking Save, you'll see a page notifying you of your new page's Web address:

```
http://hometown.aol.com/screenname/myhomepage/
heritage.html
```

Instead of `screenname`, the folder would actually have *your* screen name. Make a note of the address so you can share it with friends. Ask them by e-mail to visit your page, or use it on your business cards or in the annual family newsletter. That's it! Now, anyone can visit your home page.

When your page is published, you'll get official notification right away by e-mail. The useful e-mail message includes information about the Hometown message boards, instructions for updating your page, and more. Save this e-mail message!

Editing Your 1-2-3 Publish Pages

Before you publish your page, you have a chance to modify it, as outlined in Step 7 in the previous procedure.

After you publish a page, the process is similar, except that you must first, of course, retrieve your published page. To do that, simply type in the Web address of the page in the text box on the AOL navigation bar. Then click Go. When the page appears, scroll to the bottom and click Page Created with 1-2-3 Publish. The page appears, with the Modify and Save buttons at the top.

> ▶ Click Modify and then make any changes in your digital picture, links, or text.
> ▶ To make the revised version available, click Save.

To add information *about* your page so that others can more easily search for it, go to AOL Keyword: **123**. In the next window, click Add Pages and follow the on-screen steps. At the end of the process, you'll be notified that your page has been added to your community of choice.

Tip

Whenever you stumble across an AOL Hometown page that you especially like, you can tell a friend about it by clicking E-Mail This Page (at the top of your page), which summons up a fill-in-the-blank form. Enter one or more recipients' e-mail addresses, type your message, and click Send. The clickable link will be automatically included in the message. Take advantage of this easy way to notify your friends when you create a Web page.

Tip

What are others doing on Hometown? Check out each week's Top Picks, available from AOL Keyword: **Hometown**. From Hometown's opening page, click Member Hall of Fame for the best of the best.

At AOL Hometown's Web-based message boards, you can ask questions and read answers to others' questions. These boards, as well as links to Web chats, are available from the Talk About It link, available at AOL Keyword: **Hometown**. Or, you can always use the Easy Designer Help menu to get help on specific procedures.

Note

Perhaps you've heard of Java, the innovative computer language invented at Sun Microsystems, which is used for creating small programs that can be shared on the Internet. Easy Designer is a Java application. Because Internet Explorer's Security settings take a wary view of Java, you may see a message saying `Warning: Applet Window`, as shown at the bottom of Figure 13-3. You can safely disregard the warning message when using Easy Designer. Because Easy Designer is built with Java, Easy Designer won't be available instantaneously; it may take a minute or two to download first.

A Step Further with Easy Designer

AOL's new Web-publishing tool, Easy Designer (AOL Keyword: **Easy Designer**), offers more control of layout, page elements, and content than 1-2-3 Publish does. Easy Designer even opens up your 1-2-3 pages in Easy Designer so you can continue to edit them. Why would you want to do that? 1-2-3 Publish lets you quickly create something on the Web; Easy Designer lets you lavish more attention on your creation. Now's the chance to add all those great digital pictures you've been salting away on your hard drive. When you're all done, your Easy Designer pages, just like your 1-2-3 Publish pages, can be stored in AOL Hometown and viewed by anyone with access to the World Wide Web.

How is Easy Designer different from 1-2-3 Publish? Easy Designer lets you do the following:

▶ Add as many blocks of text and images, including digital pictures, as you want

▶ Move text and images anywhere you want

▶ Format and style your text and digital pictures, linking any element to your other pages or pictures in order to create a true Web site

▶ Add HTML script if you're comfortable with HTML

Using a Template to Create a New Page

When you use AOL Keyword: **Easy Designer**, you'll be asked whether you want to create a brand new page (click Create a New Page) or edit an existing page, such as a page started in 1-2-3 Publish (click Return Here).

▶ If you click the Create a New Page link, your first job, as with 1-2-3, is to choose the template that best meets your needs. See Figure 13-3 for the templates at your disposal.

▶ With Easy Designer open, choosing File⇨New likewise prompts you to select a template.

Instead of choosing a template, you can choose Blank Page, an option shown in Figure 13-3. You'll be taken to a window that

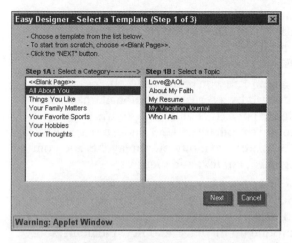

Figure 13-3. Select an Easy Designer category and topic, and you're ready to create your own page.

looks like Figure 13-4, where you'll be making a lot of use of the Add Text and Add Image buttons, described in the "Editing Text in Easy Designer" and "Editing Digital Pictures in Easy Designer" sections, later in this chapter.

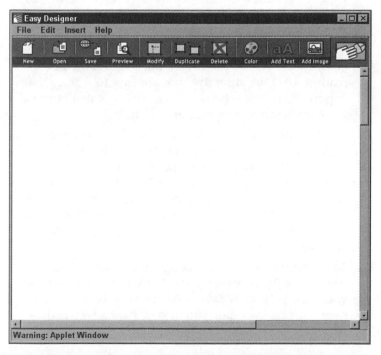

Figure 13-4. Easy Designer gives you great flexibility in filling in a blank page with your own words and images.

Note

Don't worry if you later change your mind. With your page displayed in Easy Designer, you can at any time click the Color button on the toolbar to change the color scheme or create a custom scheme.

Tip

A *visited link* is a link that someone viewing the page has clicked already; an *unvisited link* has yet to be visited. On the Web, unvisited and visited links are usually displayed in different colors to help your users realize where they've been and where they've not yet been.

1. When creating a new page, the first thing you see is a list of available templates, as shown in Figure 13-3. Select the topic and category that most closely match your needs. After selecting a template, click Next.

2. If you use a template, you're offered a choice of page layouts, indicated by a series of thumbnail images. You'll notice at once the complexity of the pages, as opposed to the simplicity of 1-2-3 Publish pages. Easy Designer templates use multicolumn layouts and complex arrangements of text and pictures.

   Choose the page layout that appeals to you. Don't worry about getting locked into a particular layout. With Easy Designer, you can later change layouts, move elements around on the page, add new elements, and so on. After selecting a page layout, click Next.

3. Next you're offered a set of color schemes for your template. A *color scheme* defines a combination of colors designed to work together: a background color, a text color, and a pair of colors for your visited links and unvisited links. Click a scheme's name in the left side of the Select a Color window to see how the scheme looks on the right side. Click OK after selecting a color scheme.

   Color schemes are a matter of looks, of course, but also have a strong impact on your page's usability. Certain color combinations can make your pages difficult to read; others look attractive *and* are easy to read. AOL's expertly matched schemes can greatly assist in improving your pages' appearance and usability.

   After selecting a layout and color scheme, your template appears (as shown in Figure 13-5), ready for you to start adding your own elements (digital pictures, links, and text). These procedures are described in "Editing Digital Pictures in Easy Designer" and "Editing Text in Easy Designer." The specific toolbar choices are described in "Editing a Published Easy Designer Page," also later in this chapter.

4. To see your page before making it available on Hometown, click Preview on the toolbar. When you're happy with your page, click Save. After the page is saved, a message pops up informing you of your page's Web address.

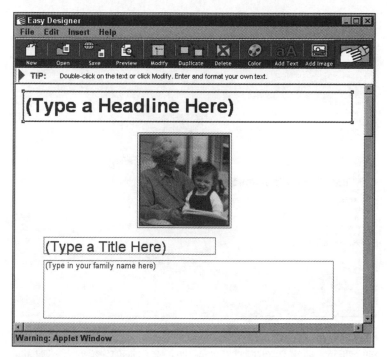

Figure 13-5. Your template, ready to go; just fill in the blanks, move things around, add your own elements, and you've got a page.

Editing Digital Pictures in Easy Designer

When using templates, you will want to replace the template's images with ones of your own, as follows. You'll thus be *editing* images that came with the template — swapping them out and using your own.

1. Select the digital picture you want to replace.

2. Click the Modify button on the Easy Designer toolbar.

3. In the Picture Gallery box (not to be confused with the AOL Picture Gallery, discussed in Chapters 8 and 10), click the Upload Picture button, as shown in Figure 13-6.

4. When the Upload Picture window, click Browse and find the desired digital picture on your hard drive. Click Upload Picture when you've selected the correct digital picture. In Step 3, you can also look through Easy Designer's collection of more than 5,000 images to find one that might suit your needs.

Click this button to see the Upload Picture window.

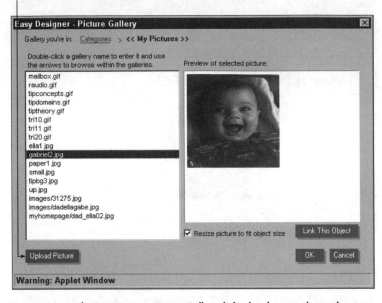

If you find that your pictures appear on top of your heading (or other objects are in the same place), Easy Designer warns you with an `Overlap` warning message inside objects. Just drag the intruding objects so they're no longer overlapping other objects. You won't be able to save a page with overlapping elements.

Figure 13-6. The Easy Designer Picture Gallery dialog box lets you choose the picture you want from either your hard drive or the clip art and photo collection provided with Easy Designer.

Both the Text Editor and Picture Gallery window give you the ability to link your words or pictures to another Web page. This means that someone viewing your pages can click some text or a picture to jump to a related page. You have three different ways to add a link. (1) You can type in the URL for any page to which you want to link. (2) You can link to a page on Hometown AOL (if you've published one or know the URL of someone else's). (3) You can create a link to an e-mail address — your own, for instance, if you want your visitors to be able to send you e-mail messages about your page.

You can resize a digital picture by simply selecting it and dragging one of its sides or a corner. Be careful not to distort it by changing its *aspect ratio* — the height and width relative to each other. Move one side of the picture frame, for instance, and the picture appears squashed; move the other side, and it pulls like taffy. To avoid such distortions, right-click on the picture after you've resized it and choose Maintain Aspect Ratio from the pop-up menu that appears. If you'd like to restore the picture to its original size, you can do so from this menu, too, by choosing Restore Original Size.

You can also add a picture, including a picture still on your hard drive, by clicking the Add Image button and following the simple on-screen instructions.

Editing Text in Easy Designer

The first thing you'll probably want on your Web page is a headline. Double-click in the box where you see `Type a Headline Here` (or something similar). The text box shown in Figure 13-7 appears and lets you enter some text. You use the same text box whether you're creating a headline or typing paragraphs of body text.

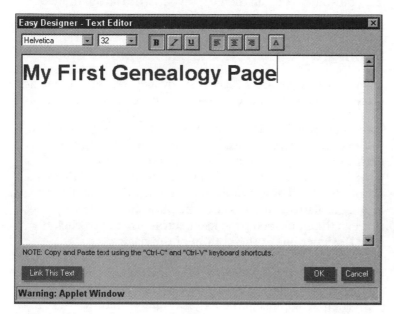

Easy Designer - Text Editor

Helvetica　　32　　**B** *I* <u>U</u>

My First Genealogy Page

NOTE: Copy and Paste text using the "Ctrl-C" and "Ctrl-V" keyboard shortcuts.

Link This Text　　　　　OK　Cancel

Warning: Applet Window

Figure 13-7. Easy Designer's Text Editor gives you control over the appearance and placement of text.

In the Easy Designer Text Editor, you can do the following;

- ▶ Add your own words and edit them until they're just right
- ▶ Style the text, making it **bold,** *italic,* or <u>underlined</u>
- ▶ Align the text along the right or left side of the box
- ▶ Change the font size and font type
- ▶ Adjust the size and shape of the text box

Just be sure to click OK when you're done!

You change the shape of a text box by simply clicking any side or corner and dragging in the direction you want. Notice also how your mouse arrow changes shape as you pass it across different parts of the box.

To edit the *contents* of any text box, double-click inside the box. You can delete the existing text: Highlight the text and press the backspace key. You can now add your own text, setting the font face, size, styling, and alignment as you wish. When you're done editing your text, click OK to close the Text

Tip

If you know HTML, you can add some custom scripting. From the Insert menu, select Advanced HTML. Any code you add will not appear until you preview your page.

Tip

By resizing the text box, you can create long, skinny columns of text and create other effects. Some templates offer columns; when editing a page built with such a template, you can adjust the column width and height.

Tip

If you want to center the title of your page, clicking the Center button in the Text Editor is not enough. That action merely centers text in the box. You'll want to visually center the box on the page by moving it right and left until it *looks* centered between the Easy Designer window's right and left sides.

Editor and return to Easy Designer. For longer text blocks, consider writing and editing your text in a word processor (saving it if you want); you can then copy your words from the word processor and paste them into the Text Editor.

Editing a Published Easy Designer Page

Editing an Easy Designer Page is exactly like creating it in the first place: You use the same tools to do the same kinds of things.

To edit an Easy Designer page, as with a 1-2-3 page, you first retrieve the page. Go to AOL Keyword: **Easy Designer**, and click the Open an Existing Page link to edit the published page. You need to know the page's filename in order to select it from the list that appears after you click Open an Existing Page. Alternatively, if you know the published page's address, retrieve the published page itself, scroll down, and click the Easy Designer link at the bottom of the page.

1. From the Open Existing Page box, select a page and click Open.
2. The page opens in the Easy Designer window (shown in Figure 13-4), which has the same buttons and works the same way whether you're creating a new page or opening an existing one.

   Note that when your 1-2-3 page opens within Easy Designer, it appears just as you left it last in 1-2-3. Click any element on the page (picture, text, horizontal bar, and the like), and you can then drag the element around the page, resize it, delete it, and so forth.
3. Right-click on any block of text, digital picture, or other element, and you can choose to modify, duplicate, or delete it.
4. Click Save when you're done.

Here are some other useful tasks available from the Easy Designer toolbar that you can use when you're editing your page:

▶ **Modify.** With an object selected, click this button to open the text or image editing window. Use the available tools to make any changes. Refer to Figures 13-6 and 13-7.
▶ **Duplicate.** This tool is handy if, for instance, you want to use the same graphical divider several times on the same page or repeat a tiny GIF bullet in a list. Instead of clicking Add Picture for each copied image, just highlight the

Note

When you use 1-2-3 Publish or Easy Designer, the HTML is automatically created for you, behind the scenes. The HTML is there, but you don't really need to know that it's there.

Tip

Every Easy Designer template-based page automatically includes AOL Instant Messenger-Remote (AIM-R) at the bottom of the page (refer to Figure 13-2). AIM-R gives visitors to your page the capability to send you e-mail, add you to their Buddy List, pop you an instant message, and take part in a chat discussion related to the topic of your site; the button bar is included at the bottom of your published page. If you're not using a template (that is, if you are starting with a blank page), use Easy Designer's Insert menu and select AIM-Remote. Your visitors must have AIM-R, a free program always available to AOL and non-AOL members at www.aol.com/aim.

box containing the picture or text that you want to copy
and click Duplicate. A copy of the object appears, and
you can drag that copy to the place where you want it.

▶ **Delete.** Use this option to get rid of an unwanted object,
for example a digital picture used in a template. Select
the picture or other element; then click this button.

▶ **Color.** If you decide that your template's color scheme
doesn't quite cut it, click this button to select another
scheme or to create your own custom scheme. You can
also add your own background image to your page.

▶ **Preview.** This button shows you the page as others
will see it.

▶ **Save.** When you're happy with your page, this button
lets you publish your page in AOL Hometown.

When you finally save your new Easy Designer page, you will
be notified of your page's address on the final Web page (after
clicking Save) and then by e-mail. Just as with 1-2-3 Publish,
your new Web address will be something like:

```
http://hometown.aol.com/YourScreenName/
index.html
```

Uploading Pages *Not* Created with 1-2-3 Publish or Easy Designer

To publish a page made with an HTML editor, you can make
use of the free space AOL makes available to every AOL member and to all nonmembers who publish pages at AOL
Hometown. This space is called My FTP Space. (*FTP* is short
for File Transfer Protocol, a pre-Web but still-popular standard
for exchanging files on the Internet.) When you use 1-2-3
Publish or Easy Designer, you're using the same space, but all
the uploading takes place automatically, so you don't have to
give the process a second thought. Uploading to My FTP
Space requires, well, a second thought. Here's how to upload a
page to your free Web space:

1. Create the page by using your HTML editor and save
the page on your hard drive. (HTML pages have a file
extension of .HTM or .HTML.)

Definition

HTML stands for the
HyperText Markup Language.
HTML files contain both content (words and pictures) and
tags — special instructions
for browsers, like Netscape
Navigator and the AOL
browser, on how to display
the content. When you
browse the Web, all you're
doing is downloading HTML
files from an Internet computer to your own computer.

Tip

When you use an *HTML editor* — such as Macromedia's
Dreamweaver — you create
Web pages (and the underlying HTML files) visually. Just
add the effects you want
without worrying about the
underlying HTML — just as in
Easy Designer. However,
HTML editors *also* give you
direct access to the HTML
code so that you can create
elaborate and sophisticated
effects if you know HTML and
other scripting languages,
such as JavaScript and (my
favorite) Cascading Style
Sheets.

Tip

You can upload any kind of file — not just HTML files and digital pictures — to My FTP Space. For example, I often make Word documents and *PDF* (Portable Document Format) files available for my work colleagues to read.

2. On AOL, go to AOL Keyword: **My FTP Space**. In the window that first comes up, click See My FTP Space (or another clearly marked button or link that leads you to your FTP space).

You'll see a window similar to the one shown in Figure 13-8. (Figure 13-8 shows my own uploaded files; yours will show your uploaded files, of course, or no files at all if you've never used AOL Hometown.)

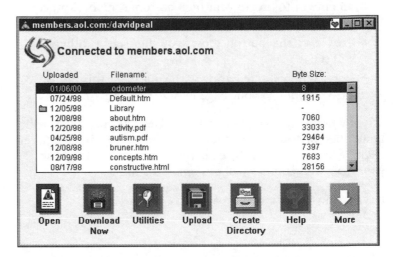

Figure 13-8. AOL Keyword: **My FTP Space**. On AOL, it's your free online storage space.

3. Click the Upload button. In the new window that appears (as shown in Figure 13-9), type in the Remote Filename. You can safely use the same filename (ending in .HTM or .HTML) you used for the Web page after you created it on your own computer. Click Continue.

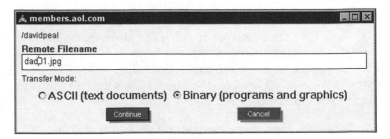

Figure 13-9. Specifying a file to upload to My FTP Space.

4. In the Upload File box, first click Select File; browse to
   the file on your hard drive and select it. Back in the
   Upload File box, click Send to copy your file to your
   online storage space. After the file has been uploaded,
   its Web address will be

```
http://hometown.aol.com/yourscreenname/
yourfile.html
```

A Web page uploaded to AOL Hometown in this way is not
yet registered with AOL Hometown, nor is it searchable or included in a Hometown community. For all that, you need to
add the page to AOL Hometown as described in the following
section, "Adding Pages to AOL Hometown."

Tip

You can register any pages
with AOL Hometown, no
matter how you created
them. Add *all* your pages to
AOL Hometown, and AOL
gives you 12MB of storage
space to use!

Adding Pages to AOL Hometown

When you create a page with either 1-2-3 Publish or Easy
Designer, the page is automatically registered with AOL
Hometown. The first thing to do with any *other* HTML page is
to register it with AOL Hometown. If you've registered your
page, people who either share your interests or know you personally stand a chance of finding it. Being found is, well, the
whole idea of creating a page.

To expand your personal Web page offerings on AOL, go to
the main AOL Hometown window (AOL Keyword:
Hometown) and click the Add Pages link at the top of the
page. From the Add & Manage Pages window, you can do the
following:

▶ Add other pages (or *all* your pages) to AOL Hometown

▶ Move your pages from one AOL Hometown community
  to a different one

▶ Add and edit descriptions of pages, to make them more
  easily searchable

From just about anywhere in AOL Hometown you can add
pages by clicking the Add Pages link. Adding your HTML pages
to AOL Hometown takes (currently) five simple steps, which
are well documented at every point on-screen. Remember that
these are the pages made with visual editors other than 1-2-3
Publish and Easy Designer and then uploaded to My FTP
Space.

Tip

Deleting either 1-2-3/Easy
Designer pages or pages
made with other editors is a
manual process. At AOL
Keyword: **My FTP Space** (refer to Figure 13-8), you select
the HTML file to delete. Click
Utilities and then click Delete.
Your file will be removed
(without the chance to confirm your desire to delete it).

Tip

Make sure that you register the index.htm page (the default name of a page made by 1-2-3 and Easy Designer, and the default page opened when someone types in a URL but leaves off the specific file name, as in www.aol.com). This page also has links to all your other pages. That way, people who find your page on AOL Hometown will view it the way you intended. If you want all of your published pages to be searchable in AOL Hometown, even though they're not all listed individually, return to the Add & Manage Pages screen and click Add All. You can increase visits to your Web site by making all the pages searchable, thus increasing the likelihood that people seeking your information can find it.

Note

Moving pages from one community to another involves an almost identical process. Select a page and choose a new category and subcategory.

1. AOL shows you all the pages you have uploaded to My FTP Space. Select the one you want to add. You can add several pages, but you must add them one at a time. Click Next to open a new window.

2. Write descriptive text about the page, if you want, and then click Next.

3. Select a category. AOL Hometown currently has such categories as Business, Careers, Culture, Education, Entertainment, Family, Food, and Hobbies. Click Next.

4. Select the subcategory where your page best fits. Click Next.

5. Select a community within that subcategory that would make the best home for your page. Click Next to plant your page in a suitable Hometown community.

Finding Other People's Pages in Hometown AOL

While you create your own pages, other AOL members are creating Web pages devoted to their sundry passions and possessions. AOL has already opened 1-2-3 Publish and Easy Designer to anyone on the Internet, giving members and non-members alike the opportunity to add pages to any of the AOL Hometown communities, where they are searchable.

You can search AOL Hometown pages for key words or phrases — words used in people's descriptions of their own pages. Or, you can search for pages created by a particular screen name.

The Hometown AOL home page (directly available at AOL Keyword: **Hometown** or at hometown.aol.com) puts these search techniques at your fingertips. To search pages by key word or screen name, type a screen name or key word into the Search Pages box at AOL Hometown's opening page, then click Search. Next, you'll probably see a list of pages (if you don't, try modifying your search words). Click any page to visit it directly. In addition to searching at AOL Keyword: **Hometown**, you can also browse AOL Hometown by burrowing through categories and subcategories and on to communities in quest of the pages that interest you.

Summary

You've seen here how many ways you can make your pictures available for everyone to see. On AOL, you've got Groups@AOL, 1-2-3 Publish (for instant pages), and Easy Designer (for flexible pages). Or you can build your page in any HTML editor you please. Hometown gives you a lot of space for your pages and pictures, and it also gives you the services that add value to your pages, such as the capability to add them to communities of similar pages and to make them searchable.

The final chapter explores ways of using Web pages to meet the needs of a growing business. You'll find out, among other things, how to integrate a Web site into a larger collection of business materials, all of which are created from digital pictures.

A QUICK LOOK

Chapter 14

Digital Pictures at Work

Many people are going it alone today, working at home instead of in cubicles or setting up home-based businesses. If you're one of a growing number of such people, you can use digital pictures to produce professional stationery, business cards, custom marketing materials, effective Web sites, and much more. These materials can help define your image, create your brand, and enhance your business, regardless of its size, sector, or location. Many of the ideas in this chapter can be used in different settings, whether you want to make a mark in your job, stretch your departmental budget, or make a contribution at a professional or trade association event.

Most of the software mentioned elsewhere in this book, such as MGI PhotoSuite, is primarily for home use, but some of these programs can also handle business projects with ease, and some even come in business versions. Broderbund Print Shop Professional, for example, includes business-specific templates to help you create attractive stationery, effective flyers, and other essential materials. This chapter focuses on a few of the applications included in Microsoft Office, including Word, PowerPoint, and Publisher; all these programs greatly simplify the creation of business materials, with some offering business-specific templates.

New products are introduced all the time. An excellent way to stay up-to-date is to go to AOL Keyword: **CNET**, where you can find reviews and price comparisons. For your shopping needs, start at AOL Keyword: **Shop@AOL** (AOL's online mall).

Creating Visual Business Materials

Did you ever consider creating your own stationery and business cards sporting your own logo, a picture of your product, or a memorable image to get the attention of prospective partners or customers? With the right equipment, you can be your own designer and production shop. An inexpensive inkjet color printer and a powerful word processor can help you design your own materials and print them out whenever you need them.

The examples in this chapter come from Microsoft Office applications. Not only is this software broadly available, but specific applications such as PowerPoint and Publisher come with templates that support business needs and enable you to create business materials.

Even if a graphic designer got you started, inexpensive software, plus an inkjet printer and the appropriate paper, can give you the flexibility to customize, update, and print your materials at a moment's notice. Suppose you want to adapt your stationery or flyer for a local street fair. Start with existing materials, add a digital picture showing last year's fair or an appropriate product, and you're ready to go.

Figure 14-1 shows the Microsoft Publisher interface and some of the business-related templates at your fingertips.

Your Own Letterhead

All of the major imaging programs have similar capabilities that help you create great letterhead from scratch or by using the programs' tools. You can get excellent results without having previously used the software, because all such programs

Tip

You can easily create letterhead by using a program like Broderbund Print Shop or Microsoft Publisher, both of which offer templates for creating customized business stationery. With these types of programs, you create a project into which you can import a digital picture, such as a graphic (to use as a logo), a photo (to use as background), or a decorative image (to use as a banner across the top of your stationery). Then you use the text and art tools to finish the job.

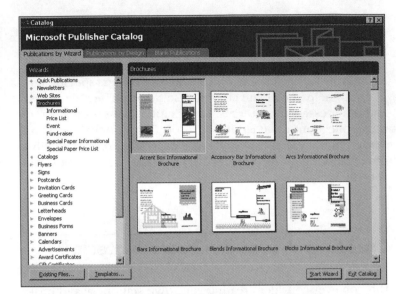

Figure 14-1. A sampling of Microsoft Publisher's business templates.

Small Business @ AOL

Here are a few general AOL and Web resources that offer guidance for managing a growing business:

▶ AOL's WorkPlace Channel (Type AOL Keyword: **Work** or click the WorkPlace link on the Welcome screen's Channel menu)

▶ Start-Up Businesses (AOL Keyword: **StartUp**)

▶ Doing Business Online (AOL Keyword: **Doing Business Online**)

▶ Business Research Tools (AOL Keyword: **Business Research**)

▶ Professions (AOL Keyword: **Professional Forums**)

▶ Monster.com (AOL Keyword: **Monster**)

▶ Business Know-How (AOL Keyword: **Business Know How**)

▶ U.S. Small Business Administration home page (AOL Keyword: **SBA**, or www.sbaonline.sba.gov)

offer fill-in-the-blank templates and ample on-screen instructions. Make sure that you print your letterhead and envelopes on quality stock and at the highest print resolution, or take your printouts to a service bureau such as Kinko's. Figure 14-2 shows custom stationery created by photographer Len Rizzi for his studio.

Figure 14-2. Make your own business stationery with Microsoft Publisher.

Your Own Business Cards

Business cards can quickly say a great deal about your company. In general, business cards provide essential contact information and come in a near-universal size and format (paper weight). Customers expect you to have a card and are likely to hold onto it for a long time.

Here are some general tips for making an effective business card:

▶ Get creative by using colors other than white and textures other than smooth, for example. Keep your company's image in mind when you do so, of course.

Printing on an inkjet printer is fine for small runs and quick address changes, but laser printers provide the sharpest results. At a certain point, depending on your audience and volume, professional reproduction may be cost-effective.

When image quality really counts, such as in a print ad, save the original graphic elements in a common file format such as TIF or JPG. If you save your creation in a nonstandard file format (such as an MGI PhotoSuite PZP project file), your service bureau may not be able to work with it. On the other hand, service bureaus are more likely to be able to use Adobe Photoshop's PSD/PDD format, because it is a standard among graphic-arts professionals.

Use AOL Keyword: **PaperWorks** to find paper products for all your business needs.

Make your life easier with Avery Wizard software, a free download from www.avery.com/ software. This Microsoft add-on, from the company that sets standards for labels and stickers, can be used to design, format, and print business cards and other types of identification pieces. Avery also makes stock paper that can be used with an inkjet printer to create business cards.

A consistent look in your printed materials helps you create a *brand,* what marketers call the unique blend of image, name, and reputation that people won't easily forget. Digital pictures or other graphical designs can go a long way in defining a brand.

▶ Use a digital picture of you, your product, your location, and so on. Such images aid recall.

▶ Make sure that key information is legible (especially if it's set in a smaller font than other text on the card): your company's logo and type, address, phone number, fax number, and e-mail address.

▶ Print on high-quality card stock or go to a service bureau (Kinko's, for example).

If you're laying out a Word document to produce business cards, here are some tips for setting up the document:

▶ To print many cards on a single sheet of stock paper, set the top, bottom, right, and left margins to 0.5 inches.

▶ Create two columns with a column width of 3.5 inches and a gutter of 0.5 inches. You should be able to get five 2-inch-wide cards per column. Expect to do some fiddling to get the results you want. In Word, you can easily insert, edit, resize, and rotate small digital pictures. (To add pictures, choose Insert⇨Picture⇨From File.)

You can buy sheets of perforated card blanks at office supply stores and then print out your text and graphics by using your desktop printer. This card stock typically comes in fancy, colorful, and plain versions. Fancy and colorful cards are handy if you have only a mono-color printer and need a splash of color; the plain cards help you project a serious image. Make sure that the blanks you buy fit your printer. Also, these cards often show a somewhat rough edge after they are separated at the perforation. The amount of roughness varies, so check out samples in advance.

Some printers, including most lasers, can handle card stock or even heavier paper, but some newer inkjets are every bit as capable, and are even designed to manage diverse paper types. With an inkjet printer, it's best to use a good-quality paper recommended by the manufacturer. Paper quality makes a difference in the impression you convey, so choose your paper just as carefully as you lay out your design.

Figure 14-8, later in this chapter, shows a simple business card made with Microsoft Publisher.

Using Digital Pictures in Business Materials

Consider using digital pictures in business documentation, presentations, proposals, and custom marketing materials.

Documentation

If you teach a course or produce a toy, for example, that requires any kind of step-by-step instructions, consider adding digital pictures to make your instructional materials that much easier to follow. Image-editing software lets you add text labels and arrows right on the pictures. Even if your document is only for internal distribution, adding a few pictures can make it more informative. Remember that every question the document answers is a question you don't have to spend time answering. Good documentation is a simple and neglected way of adding value.

Presentations

Many graphics programs let you create built-in slide shows. A computerized *slide show* is a way of automatically displaying a series of related digital pictures. A picture is displayed for a certain amount of time (which you can easily set to be longer or shorter), then another picture is displayed, and another, until the last picture is reached, at which point the slide show either stops or loops back to the beginning. You can also operate a slide show manually and advance the slides in sync with a presentation. Think of a slide show as an album (see Chapters 4 and 7) that displays images — manually or automatically — in a specific sequence.

When you attach your computer to an overhead projector, such as an InFocus device, a slide show enables you to show your pictures and other information to a group of potential customers, students, new employees, or conference-goers. Even non-presentation software such as Cerious' ThumbsPlus (described in Chapter 8) lets you adjust the background, the

Tip

Do you have a presentation to make? Don't forget the old-fashioned transparencies that you use with overhead projectors. You can purchase special transparency paper to use with your printer. You can print digital pictures as well as the standard lists of bulleted items. Transparencies are less useful for printing digital pictures, but can effectively convey schematic illustrations (line art), bulleted text, and simple images.

14

Digital Pictures at Work

amount of time between pictures, the picture size, and other factors. You can also create home- and small-business presentations with MGI PhotoSuite III's Family Edition, although your options are more limited.

For important presentations, a special-purpose program such as Microsoft PowerPoint, shown in Figure 14-3, is a big step up from general-purpose graphics software.

Note

When using text and pictures in a Microsoft PowerPoint presentation, it's best to keep the text simple (bullet points are often all you need for a strong presentation) and make the photos large enough for people to see from the back of the room. Instead of Microsoft's occasionally cliché (and frequently used) clip art, consider using creations you made with image-editing software (see Chapter 10).

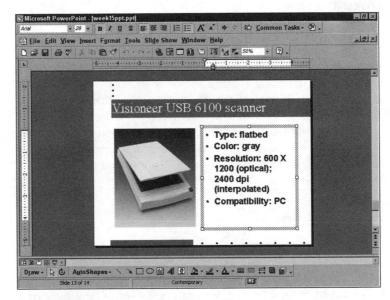

Figure 14-3. Creating a PowerPoint slide. To add a picture, choose Insert⇨ Picture⇨From File and then find and double-click one of your digital pictures to include it on the slide. You can also insert clip art, if you want, as well as add sound files and video clips to your presentation.

Note

PowerPoint 97 had the same feature (saving a presentation as a Web page), but the Web has evolved in many ways since then, and the Web files created in PowerPoint 2000 support a range of more sophisticated effects.

Proposals

If you're submitting a formal proposal for a job or even a casual letter of interest, consider whether you can improve it by adding digital images — product and site photographs, pictures of your production operation, maps, charts, team photos, workflow and timeline diagrams, and the like.

Presentations on the Web (Microsoft PowerPoint 2000)

Want to show your business presentation on the Web, for anyone to see at any time? PowerPoint 2000 greatly simplifies the job of making attractive Web (HTML) versions of your PowerPoint presentations, with links and attractive formatting. Follow these steps to show a PowerPoint presentation on the Web:

1. Create a PowerPoint presentation. The presentation file will have the .PPT file extension.

2. Save the PPT file as HTML (choose File⇨Save As Web Page). PowerPoint creates a new folder on your hard drive and converts the PPT file into a slew of HTML and related files.

3. In your online space (AOL Keyword: **My FTP Space**), create a folder to hold all these files. Then upload all the presentation files into this folder. (See Chapter 12 for details.) Unfortunately, you'll have to upload the many automatically generated files one at a time. Keep the filenames the same, because the Web files often link to each other in complex ways.

Tip

In Word or PowerPoint, you can do simple graphics editing such as resizing and repositioning the picture, adding text and a border, and so on. To do so in Word 97, right-click on the digital picture and choose Show Picture Toolbar; in Word 2000, the toolbar pops up automatically. To see what each button on this toolbar does, move the mouse arrow over the button until a short text description pops up (Image Control, More Brightness, Crop, and so on). Because Microsoft packs so many effects into its picture-editing features, one of the best ways to learn how to use them is to try them out.

14

Digital Pictures at Work

Marketing Materials

In the age of one-to-one marketing, you can create effective marketing materials for any occasion or client, and flyers tailored to a specific conference, season, or part of your market. Figure 14-4 shows a handout that could be mailed or posted on local bulletin boards — the real kind with thumbtacks, not online message boards. The handout was made by using the clip art included with Microsoft Office. You can even individualize your marketing materials for specific clients. Similarly, you can build goodwill with targeted materials for current customers.

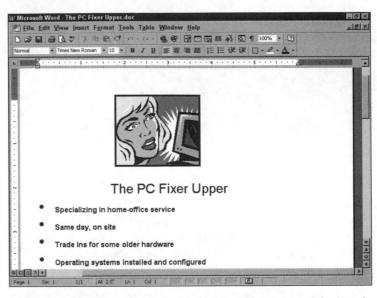

Figure 14-4. This flyer was created in Microsoft Word; the image came from Word's color clip art. Whenever using anyone's clip art, make sure to get explicit permission (see AOL Keyword: **Copyright**).

Using Digital Pictures in Web Promotions

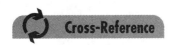

Cross-Reference

See Chapter 13 to find out how to create and publish a Web page on AOL.

To most people, online business means first advertising and then selling products and services on the Web. In today's glitzy world of e-commerce and multimedia, simple business considerations often get lost in the rush to create a fancy site. Here are some tips for using digital pictures to sell your products and services on the Web:

▶ **Be generous with product information.** Because people may not be familiar with your products, include digital pictures of them. You can save PowerPoint slides, like the one shown in Figure 14-3, as Web files and post them to AOL Hometown (see Chapter 13).

▶ **Provide questions and answers about your products or services (a *FAQ,* or Frequently Asked Questions document).** Consider using digital pictures that show different uses for your product or including a digital picture of your product that identifies its parts and how they work.

▶ **Use e-mail (mailto) links on your Web site to provide one-to-one customer service.** Online businesses often overlook customer service, so providing it is a good way to set your business apart.

You can add the following HTML to a Web page to enable customers to send you e-mail messages:

```
<a href="mailto:harrycrabgrass@pcfixerup-
per">Let us know what you think!</a>
```

Insert your own e-mail address in place of harrycrabgrass@pcfixerupper. And instead of Let us know what you think!, insert the text you want your customers to see on your page. The customers can then click this link to send you an e-mail message.

▶ **Reach your local market through mutual linking arrangements with neighborhood organizations, churches and synagogues, local companies, restaurants, key individuals, and so on.** The principle is simple: You link to their sites if they link to yours. You can trade links with these organizations or trade other services; you're neighbors, after all. To help your local marketing efforts, consider including a map to your location or digital pictures of customers and coworkers with big smiles.

Web sites offer several advantages over other forms of advertising:

▶ You have a better chance of reaching your specific target market, and potential clients can check the site at any time, from any place.

▶ You can provide more information on a Web site than with any ad, in a more engaging and interactive format, especially if you include digital pictures.

Note

Although a Web site can be inexpensive to create, it can be time-consuming to maintain. Customers expect up-to-date information and a regularly refreshed look.

Getting Your Web Site Noticed

It's no secret that there are now a gazillion Web sites (make that a cool billion or so) on just about every topic. So how do you get your business site noticed?

Advertise Your Web Address

Prominently include your Web site address (URL) on your business cards, letterhead, proposals, and other business materials. Because of the enormous number of Web sites, you need to get the word out that you have a site online, or your effort may be wasted. Consider paying for ads in the local paper or on a local cable TV station. Choose the papers and TV stations that best target your audience.

Include Your Web Address in E-Mail Signatures

Make sure that you include your Web address in your e-mail signature. AOL's e-mail program now offers a built-in feature for adding a *signature* at the end of each message, an automatically appended message with your name, phone number, URL, and business contact information. Follow these steps to add a signature:

1. Click the Write icon on the AOL toolbar to open the Write Mail window.

2. Click the right-most button in the Write Mail window, just above the big box where your message goes; the button shows a pencil point.

3. Choose Select Set Up Signatures to open the Set Up Signatures dialog box.

4. Click the Create button and then give the signature a name in the Signature Name box, so you can later identify it, use it, and edit it. You need to *identify* a specific signature because AOL lets you create several signatures, for different purposes. For each message, you can use one of several signatures.

5. In the Signature box, type in your signature and any other information you want to include. You may not want to add any styling (text type, size, color, and so on) because non-AOL members won't be able to view it.

Using Images in Business E-Mail

Thanks to its immediacy, low cost, flexibility, and speed, e-mail ranks right up there with the telephone as an important business tool. Consider using digital pictures to add some pizzazz to your business e-mail. Because many of your customers won't be AOL members, it's safest to attach pictures to your messages instead of inserting them into the text itself.

Consider including documentation, flyers, and other materials mentioned in "Using Digital Pictures in Business Materials," earlier in this chapter. Attractive item-incorporating digital pictures should include the address of your Web site. Use JPG images, as opposed to proprietary formats or standard but high-resolution TIF files, to keep the attachment size small.

Creating Integrated Business Materials: Katie's Candles

My neighbor Katie has always enjoyed making candles for holidays and other special occasions. Over the years, friends would comment that her candles were so good that she should sell them. Eventually she decided to give the candle business a try on a limited basis, selling her candles mainly in her local community.

Using Microsoft Publisher, she created a basic flyer that introduced her candles and provided a Web address for people to find out more about her candles and prices (Figure 14-5 shows the flyer, and Figure 14-6 shows the Web page). Katie used the same strong photographic image, created by a professional photographer, in all her materials. At the bottom of the flyer, she provided small tear-off strips that included her name, phone number, and Web address.

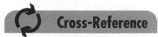

Cross-Reference

Chapter 5 goes into detail about inserting and attaching images.

Tip

Be responsive. If you have a Web site that lets prospective customers send you e-mail or if you typically contact customers by e-mail, check your mail often and respond promptly. Web surfers who are interested in the vacation cottage listed on your site will assume you check your e-mail, and they'll be frustrated if you don't get back to them quickly.

Tip

If someone inquires about a product or service and gives you an e-mail address to respond to, then by all means attach a picture illustrating your product or service. Make sure that you describe the attachment in your message.

14

Digital Pictures at Work

Figure 14-5. A flyer Katie created in Publisher to reach her core market quite literally where they live.

Because her business is predominantly local, Katie posted her flyers in local stores, the YMCA, and schools. Periodically, Katie visited the locations where she posted her flyers and replaced ones in which the tear-off strips were gone. Looking at the number of torn-off strips provided invaluable marketing information about where her potential customers were.

After putting up her flyers, Kate used Publisher to create a sophisticated-looking but easy-to-make Web page to provide photos of her candles, along with pricing and ordering instructions. The Web page was also a good venue to tell visitors about herself and why her candles are special.

Katie used a Microsoft Publishing Wizard to create the Web site. Figure 14-6 shows a draft of the page as it was shaping up. The wizards do all the fancy work behind the scenes, including the relatively advanced Web tasks of creating navigational elements, adding sound, and creating fill-in-the blank forms.

Tip

All the software applications in Microsoft Office 2000 — as well as many other programs — allow you to save any formatted, program-specific file (such as a PowerPoint PPT or Publisher PUB) as a generic HTML file — a Web page, in other words. The Web page, together with the files for any digital pictures used on the page, can then be uploaded to My FTP Space, as described in Chapter 13.

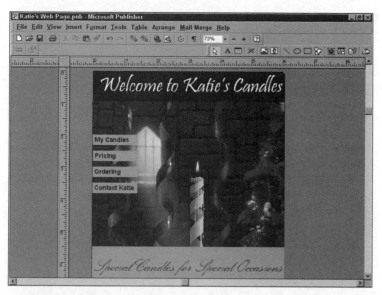

Figure 14-6. The home page of Katie's Web site, created in Microsoft Publisher and saved as an HTML file.

For the photographic image that dominates the home page, Katie enlisted the help of her photographer friend. By using an existing photo for her cover page, she was able to quickly put her site online and then add catalog photos as she produced them. (Adding a photo means changing the link on a page and uploading both the changed page and the new photo.) When potential customers requested photos of candles that she had not yet finished, Katie used her digital camera to photograph the candles when they were complete and then e-mailed the digital pictures to the customers. She then added those photos to her Web page.

Web sites require maintenance and updating. Katie chose to have a small site closely tied to an emerging business need (showing her work in progress) — *and* to promote her work beyond the local community.

Photographing Candle Light

As Katie photographed her new candles to create new photos for her page, she noticed that her flash created a somewhat harsh, flattened result. She also noticed that the flame did not show up in the photo.

In cases like this, you may get better results by using available light instead of flash. First, make sure that you have enough available light for a proper exposure. Katie started by setting her candle in a pleasant location with a festive feel that did not compete with her candle. The closer she got to the candle, the more likely the background went out of focus and thus did not compete with the subject. She placed the camera on a tripod and turned off the flash. She chose a viewpoint where light hit the candle in a pleasing manner and showed the detail and color well.

Katie eventually started taking two photos of each candle, one for the candle and one for the flame. She then copied the good flame to the good candle by using *compositing*, a technique simplified by many image-editing programs (see Chapter 10). She eventually realized that she could use the photo of the good flame and paste it onto many subsequent candle shots. This way, she focused on the candle and the surrounding scene instead of repeatedly struggling to get the right flame effect.

Next, Katie needed a large jar label (shown in Figure 14-7). The label's purpose was to provide company contact information and to list the candle's name and provide any anecdotes or stories about its origins (such as the little tags that come with collectible plush toys). By including this label on her product, Katie created an image for herself and her candles while providing company contact information for later orders. The label also served as a way for her business to grow by word of mouth because customers could pass this information on to friends who were also interested in the candles. For zealous collectors and traders, such tags and labels assume intrinsic worth. In this case, it's all that's left after the candle has been used!

Figure 14-7. A label for each of Katie's candles.

After designing her label, Katie was ready to print it out on her inkjet printer. Microsoft Publisher gave Katie the option of printing on standardized (Avery) labels, but in this case, she chose to use specialty paper to give her labels a personalized feel. Remember, she has to print only a few of these labels at a time. As she develops her style and look and grows her business beyond the local market, she can make changes as she goes.

Finally, when Katie created her business cards, she developed the theme used on her flyer. She chose sheets of pre-cut business card paper from a specialty paper company. She quickly designed her business card with Microsoft Publisher, as shown in Figure 14-8.

Cross-Reference

See Chapter 11 for more about different types of paper.

14

Digital Pictures at Work

Figure 14-8. It's official. With her own cards, Katie's in business.

Because Katie printed the cards herself, she took advantage of her company's evolving identity — and her growing collection of digital pictures. Each holiday season or special time of the year, she can create flyers and cards with the same theme, and she plans to make a complimentary calendar showing a different candle for every month of the year. She printed her candle photos right on the flyers and cards so potential customers could see more of her products.

Summary

Image matters probably more in business than anywhere else. What better way to build an image than with digital pictures? Beyond digital pictures, you need a clear idea and a good business plan, plus affordable software, a color printer, and some custom paper. Creating items such as business cards, flyers, and business forms can even save you money. As your volume increases and you get more absorbed in daily business operations, however, working with a service bureau may be a cost-effective way of saving your time while ensuring the highest quality.

This chapter's ideas for using digital pictures should get you started, but it's up to you to take these ideas and your pictures to the next level.

PART

V

APPENDIXES

A Few Scanning Tips

`scantips.com`

Scanner maven Wayne Fulton has written a collection of informative articles on scanners. He covers, thoroughly and clearly, the basic concepts of resolution and tackles the issues of scanning materials from different sources and for different uses. He examines graphics software in depth along the way.

Adobe Photoshop Tutorials

`www.adobe.com/products/tips/photoshop.html`

This official Adobe Photoshop site, shown in Figure A-1, focuses on the kind of specific tips that users of this high-end software crave, on topics such as using layers to improve unevenly lit photos, minimizing background noise, and making the most of Photoshop's selection tools. One tutorial even teaches you how to simulate the appearance of something that's on fire. The tutorials feature award-winning authors and experts in the field of graphic arts. Some of the tutorials are in QuickTime (video) format. For more Photoshop links, check out AOL Keyword: **Photoshop**.

American Photo Mentor Series

`mentorseries.com/website/default.htm`

This Web site serves as a showcase for the American Photo Mentor Series program, which invites readers to travel the country and world to attend workshops taught by professional photographers. Put on your hiking boots, dust off your camera, and investigate this site to find out how you might be able to participate.

Figure A-1. Use the Adobe Photoshop site's tutorials to get useful tips.

AOL Decision Guides

AOL Keyword: **Personalogic**

Need a scanner, a printer, or a digital camera? Answer a few questions on the appropriate Personalogic-powered AOL Decision Guide, and the software identifies the equipment that best matches your needs. This guide even warns you if you have set your price too low or requirements too high. After you've identified a product, use AOL Keyword: **Shop@AOL** or **CNET** (Comparison Pricing) to find the best deal on the right product.

AOL Hometown: The Gallery

AOL Keyword: **Gallery**

`hometown.aol.com/hmtwnc9b/gallery.htm`

The Gallery showcases AOL members' pages featuring creative photography. Add it to your Favorite Places folder, because the topic attraction changes weekly. You can browse member's gallery pages as well as become a member of the Gallery yourself. Click the Gallery Web Boards link to read and post messages about using photographs in Web pages.

AOL Hometown: Photography Pages

AOL Keyword: **Hometown** (Hobbies and Interests⇨
Creative Pursuits⇨Photography)

With a few clicks and a digital picture or two, you can easily
create a Web site that shows off your pictures to the online
world. The photography pages of AOL Hometown allow you
to search for other members' work and to put your own photos online.

AOL's News Photos

AOL Keyword: **News Photos**

The Picture of the Day (click the Day link) captures current
events in a memorable way. The Pictures of the Week (click
the Week link or use AOL Keyword: **Pictures of the Week**)
features current entertainment, political, and sports photos
from photojournalists around the world.

AOL's Pictures & Albums Webcenter

www.aol.com/webcenters/pictures

This compact and useful page gives you access to AOL's
Pictures of the Week, online photo galleries, Kodak's invaluable Photo Tips (under Essentials), and decision-making guides
if you're in the market for a digital camera or scanner. As with
the other Webcenters available from AOL.COM (www.
aol.com), here you can find a select group of related
destinations, including online stores carrying picture-taking
and photo-related equipment.

Camera Review

www.camerareview.com

Looking for an analog camera — you know, an old-fashioned
film camera? Start here to see camera reviews, a short bibliography of photography classics, a dream-camera finder, discussion forums, and a well-organized directory of photography
Web sites.

CNET

AOL Keyword: **CNET**

www.cnet.com

What can one say about what seems to be the most linked-to Web site dealing with all aspects of digital imaging? CNET, a creation of a cable network and the "anchor tenant" of AOL's Computing Channel, has impressive original content: in-depth product reviews, shoppers' guides, comparison pricing tables, how-to articles, and message boards, plus the browsing and searching features that make all of this content usable. Be patient, though, because with so much material, the navigational paths are not always obvious, and some of the content is a year or two old.

Desktop Publishing Forum

AOL Keyword: **DTP** (AOL only)

Wondering what to do with your pictures once you have them in digital form? Check out AOL's Desktop Publishing Forum for in-depth information on all aspects of desktop publishing. In the reference center, you'll find a technical FAQ about scanning, originally published by the media coordinator at the University of Alabama's School of Medicine. (Also check out the review of "A Few Scanning Tips," earlier in this appendix.)

DigiCams.Net

www.digicams.net

This unassuming Web site, currently under construction (what site isn't under construction?), is packed with links to information about digital cameras, logically categorized for convenience. The site includes many reviews of digital cameras, plus frequently updated technical news from the digital imaging industry.

Tip

If you're in the market, read as many online product reviews as possible. Popular Photography (AOL Keyword: **Pop Photo**) and CNET (AOL Keyword: **CNET**) are other good places to start.

Digital Art Gallery

www.willmaster.com/gallery

This Web site features creative digital photographs and electronic art. Click Photography to view enhanced digital photographs or click Digital Art Slide Show to see a fascinating array of digital and traditional photographs mixed with electronic art.

Digital Camera

AOL Keyword: **DPT** (AOL only)

Whereas AOL Keyword: **Photography** (see "Photography Forum," later in this appendix) pulls together general photo areas on AOL and the Web, this AOL area has a narrower purpose: to introduce the benefits and features of digital cameras to AOL members and to suggest the kinds of activities possible with them.

Digital Camera Magazine

photopoint.com/dcm

The Web edition of *Digital Camera* magazine is chock-full of feature articles on digital photography. Find tips for buying a digital camera in Buyers Guide 2000, get up-to-date by checking out reviews of the latest digital photography equipment, and read a column about scanning or Adobe Photoshop. You can also subscribe to the hard copy of this magazine by filling out an online form.

Digital Camera Resource Page

www.dcresource.com

The Digital Camera Resource Page lives up to its name with a useful summary of what's notable and new on *other* digital-camera sites. This site adds value, however. Click Reviews and Info to see a review of digital cameras in matrix form, with a link, for each product, to the corresponding CNET comparative pricing tables. The site has a message board and a list of frequently asked questions.

In the Digital Photography Channel, under Digital Photo Tips & Tricks, you'll find a detailed summary of chats devoted to subjects such as preparing digital pictures for eBay (when you want to sell something).

Digital Photography

AOL Keyword: **Digital Photography** (AOL only)

This AOL "meta" area (it has lots of links to other sites) points you to diverse places on AOL and the Web where you can get help choosing a digital camera, learning how to use it, and sharing ideas and questions about digital cameras in the weekly digital photo chats. Check out the digital photo tips and tricks for some valuable tutorials.

DoubleTake Magazine

www.doubletakemagazine.org

A literary and photographic quarterly, *DoubleTake* is devoted to realistically documenting communities around the world. The strong, simple photography makes the site a good choice for classroom use with students from elementary school through college.

Eastman Kodak Company

www.kodak.com

This large, searchable photography Web site makes you want to dust off your old 35mm camera. Learn how to take better pictures by exploring the Taking Great Pictures area. The Digital Learning Center contains ideas for activities for kids of different ages (see Chapter 12). Especially useful is the guide to a dazzling array of new color films.

Focus on Photography

www.goldcanyon.com/photography

This site offers background information about traditional photography, including camera mechanics, photography history, and lighting techniques. It includes both a Webliography and a bibliography. The site's authors have prepared a quiz for you to take when you're done exploring the site.

Graphic Arts

AOL Keyword: **Graphics** (AOL only)

This teeming AOL community offers a large set of graphic arts resources. Chat about or take a weekly online class about digital photography. Read or post messages on the digital photography message board. Click the software libraries and find downloadable software for whatever you need. Participate in a weekly graphic arts contest such as an Art Jam, where participants create collaborative slide shows by using all sorts of graphics in a sort of creative tag team!

Graphics Software at About.com

graphicssoft.about.com

Whereas many sites collect links to other sites, this one generates expert opinions on issues of concern to graphic artists, including photographers. Learn about preparing images for the Web, converting between file formats, and choosing and using dozens of software packages. The products covered are also usefully grouped by vendor (Adobe, Macromedia, and so on) so you can read about complementary products that might be optimized to work with each other.

Hylas Search Engine

www.hylas.com

Hylas' mission is to be the number one provider of information about digital images. Think of the site as a usefully annotated directory of product information, with product reviews of its own. The site's guides can help you make an informed product choice in more than a dozen categories including digital cameras, digital camcorders, video-editing software, stock photography, and photo-capable printers. Vendors in each category are rated.

How to Build Your Own Digital Darkroom

AOL Keyword: **Digital Darkroom** (AOL only)

This area is a must-visit if you're in the market for digital photography equipment. Another "meta site," Digital Darkroom provides a highly selective set of pointers to recent product reviews in CNET and stores like Beyond.com.

Image Exchange

AOL Keyword: **Image Exchange**

Double-click the Members Showcase folder to view digital images created by other AOL members. You can also easily upload your own images, too. The images are divided into categories such as photography, painting, pottery, and weaving.

Journal E: Real Stories from the Planet Earth

www.journale.com

This Eastman Kodak–sponsored site is full of extraordinary photographs. Like DoubleTake, its focus is daily life in real communities. Visit the Kodak viewing room to see photographs by professional photographers and learn some of their techniques. This densely designed Web site, shown in Figure A-2, includes automated presentations that make use of audio and other forms of multimedia.

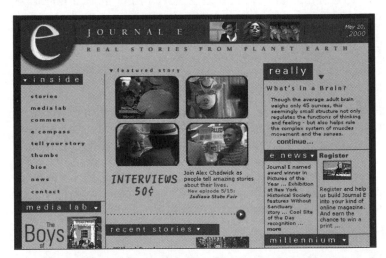

Figure A-2. Learn from professionals at Journal E, a festival of documentary images and good writing.

Kodak: Digital Cameras and Technology

www.kodak.com/US/en/nav/digital.shtml

From advice on getting started in digital photography to ways to store and display your digital photographs, this comprehensive Web site offers information on just about everything you need to know about digital photography. This site also features links to Kodak products such as digital cameras and scanners. Be sure to visit the discussion forum, where you can ask a question or make a comment about digital photography.

Kodak Picture Playground

alts1.kodak.com/US/en/corp/playground/
index.shtml

This is the fun epicenter of Kodak's large Web presence. Want to have a blast with your digital photos? Visit Kodak's Picture Playground and do simple digital-editing online. Upload your images from your computer and then reduce red eye or brighten up a dark picture. Turn pictures into puzzles or oil paintings, or apply special effects and make your boss look like a cartoon character.

Megapixel.net

megapixel.net

This monthly digital-imaging Web magazine, available in English and French, offers original content: detailed product information, editorials, and articles about digital imaging. Look up a digital photography term in the glossary. Join a discussion forum about digital imaging. And if you like the site, sign up to receive e-mail notification when a new issue is released.

Mugar Memorial Library: Finding Images on the Web

www.bu.edu/library/training/webimages.htm

This informative Web site from Boston University Libraries offers lots of tips on how to find digital images on the Web. This site features information on copyright issues, an often neglected

Find It Online

A number of other sites are beginning to offer online editing: upload your pictures and apply simple effects (cropping, filters, special effects, and the like). Here are three such sites: Shutterfly.com (www.shutterfly.com); CorelCity's Design Center (www.corelcity.com) and the Online Photo Lab (www.onlinephotolab.com).

A

Online Digital-Imaging Resources

issue when students and scholars use Web images in their research. The site offers a link to several image search engines and provides help with downloading images.

National Geographic

`www.nationalgeographic.com`

The National Geographic Society, publishers of *National Geographic,* long known for its spectacular photography, has a site on the Web. Click the Photography link to see breathtaking photographs in the Visions Gallery. Enter a photography contest and learn some photography tips. This site is a good place for kids, as well.

National Press Photographers Association

`sunsite.unc.edu/nppa`

The Society of Professional Photojournalists site features information for members, including competitions and classes of interest to serious photographers. For inspiration, spend time in the Member's Gallery, a large directory of pages featuring the often extraordinary work of NPPA members.

News and Photo Search

AOL Keyword: **News Search**

AOL provides an easy-to-use search engine that locates news articles and photographs. You can search all the categories or be more specific and choose a category such as business, sports, or entertainment. Or you can restrict your search to photographs. The help area gives tips on how to refine your search.

New York Institute of Photography

`www.nyip.com`

The New York Institute of Photography is a large correspondence school for photographers around the world. You need not be a student to learn from the site's tips, photo critiques, photo lessons, and digital photography FAQs. You can also find out how to take courses from the NYIP.

Online Classrooms

AOL Keyword: **Online Classroom**

AOL offers a variety of online classrooms, some of which cover graphic arts topics. These classrooms are often repeated weekly. For instance, the digital photography online classroom currently takes place on Thursdays at 10:00 p.m. ET. When you find the class you want, double-click its title and choose Join Class.

Paint Shop Pro

AOL Keyword: **PSP**

Paint Shop Pro is a very popular imaging-editing program for Windows and is available in a shareware version. This AOL area gives some valuable tips for using the software. Download the shareware version here and then use the tutorial folder to learn how to use the program. Discuss Paint Shop Pro in a chat or on the message boards. You may even want to participate in the weekly Paint Shop Pro Clinic.

Panoguide

www.panoguide.com

Ever wonder how panoramic photographs were made, those long photos showing a much wider stretch of horizon than you could ever capture in a single picture? Learn techniques for taking panoramic photos. Most important, get specific information about the software that lets you stitch together your own panoramas. The Gallery includes breathtaking 360-degree panoramic photographs.

PC Photo Review

www.pcphotoforum.com

What sets this site apart are the product reviews systematically solicited from readers such as yourself. Products are grouped into categories and hence easily found. For each product, reviewers submit a description of what they liked and didn't like, plus a rating on a 1–5 scale. Ratings are averaged and presented in a bar graph, making it easy to identify well-regarded products. Readers can also rank each others' reviews, a useful way of qualifying those extreme rants and raves that can skew results in a small sampling of opinions. You can also find professional reviews and comparative product specifications. And if you're in the market for used equipment, be sure to look at the classifieds.

Photographers on AOL

AOL Keyword: **Photographer**

This is the home for professional photographers on AOL. Learn about job opportunities, post a comment on the message boards, chat with fellow photographers in a weekly chat session, and learn where you can continue your education or attend seminars and tradeshows.

Photography at About.com

`photography.about.com`

There's probably no better way to learn to take pictures than to look at, and read about, the work of the great photographers. Here you can read about the inventors of photographic art, including Kertesz, Cartier-Bresson, Stieglitz, and Strand. Closely integrated in this site are in-depth articles about photo techniques and explorations of themes such as war photography, landscapes, and more. You'll also learn about traditional photo and darkroom techniques. This site is a feast for photography enthusiasts.

Photography Forum

AOL Keyword: **Photography**

This Kodak-sponsored forum, part of the AOL Interests Channel, is a hub from which you can explore AOL and general photo resources on the Web. Take a poll concerning digital photography, or chat about the big issues as photography goes digital.

Photo Secrets

www.photosecrets.com

This Web site offers travel guides for itinerant photographers. From here, you can order photography guidebooks, learn where to find the best places to photograph when traveling, and find links to other photography sites.

Photo.net

www.photo.net/photo

Philip Greenspun, the creator of photo.net, seems to have an infinite amount of knowledge on the subject of photography. He offers his knowledge with wit and makes even difficult-to-understand concepts easier to grasp. Especially useful are his articles on light, portraits, action, and making the most of a point-and-shoot camera. He also helps you choose film, filters, and, of course, cameras.

PhotoAlley.com

www.photoalley.com

Are you in the market for anything photographic? Visit PhotoAlley.com. More than an online store, this Web site features articles to help you get the most out of your photography equipment. You can also find a tips section with discussions about digital and traditional cameras and a full glossary of photographic terms. Be sure to visit the online community where you can join a discussion forum, receive feedback on your photos, and subscribe to a newsletter.

PhotoArts

www.photoarts.com/toc.html

This site, run by a New York gallery, hosts Internet photographic exhibitions that run either concurrently with actual exhibitions in other galleries or run on Internet-only galleries. It's a good place to get a sense of current trends in the photographic arts. Use the event calendar to find out about photographic events taking place near you.

Caution

Look hard for copyright information at any Web site from which you want to download photos for use in your own work, whether it's for school or business. Make sure that you secure the necessary permissions before using any such images.

PhotoCollect

www.photocollect.com

A New York photography gallery, PhotoCollect uses this site to display some of its best work, and many of the images on this site are extraordinary. The gallery also offers appraisal and other services to collectors. If you're a photographer, you'll find information here about how to submit your work for consideration. You can sign up to receive an e-mail message whenever this site is updated.

Popular Photography Online

AOL Keyword: **Pop Photo** (AOL only)

This online version of *Popular Photography* magazine offers extensive and reliable information about photographic techniques and products. Learn about new talent in New Exposures, view spectacular photographs taken by professionals and amateurs in the Gallery, and check out new products in the Products Guide. You can also read or post messages on the message board.

Tip

Want to share your photos with photo enthusiasts? Popular Photography Online gives you the chance to upload your photos and to view others' work.

Scanning

AOL Keyword: **Scanning** (AOL only)

Ever wondered what a TWAIN device actually does? Find out in the tutorials and tips folder of this Graphics Art area of the AOL Computing Channel. Find out how to use AOL to capture images from a digital camera or scanner. Also find out how to fix specific flaws in scans, such as color banding.

Short Courses

www.shortcourses.com

One of the most comprehensive sources of original content about digital photography, ShortCourses offers easily navigable online "courses" (long text articles with graphics) on digital video and information on choosing a digital camera, taking better digital photos, and related subjects. The voluminous content was written by David Curtin, author and associate of Ansel Adams.

Taking the Long View: Panoramic Photographs

`lcweb2.loc.gov/ammem/pnhtml/pnhome.html`

This Library of Congress site is part of the American Memory Collection. It features sweeping panoramas dating from 1851–1991, including a portrait of the New York Giants (1905), a badly damaged San Francisco after the earthquake (1906), a mostly rebuilt San Francisco (1914), and a 1914 panorama of the Elgin, Illinois watch factory. Browse the collection by subject, creator, or location, or search the collection by keyword.

Time-Life Photo Sight

`www.pathfinder.com/photo/index.html`

This starting page from Time, Inc., features photographs from the Time, Inc., photo collection (see Figure A-3). The photographs come from many of the magazines published by Time, Inc., including *Time, LIFE,* and *Sports Illustrated.* These photos are a great way to study the techniques of professional photographers. Each week a new Photo of the Week is featured. Be sure to take a look at the photo essays for some remarkable and memorable photographs.

Family outing, Birmingham, Alabama, 1956

Ed Clark/LIFE, copyright Time Inc.

Figure A-3. From Photo Sight's Popular Culture gallery, a family photo 1956-style.

"You've Got Pictures" Quick Start

AOL Keyword: **Pictures**

This handy guide answers your basic questions and helps you get started using "You've Got Pictures." For starters, you can locate your nearest participating developer by entering your zip code into the text box (AOL Keyword: **Photo Developer**). Make sure to subscribe to a weekly newsletter about "You've Got Pictures" as well as browse the list of frequently asked questions.

Appendix B
Glossary

A

album

A collection of digital pictures. Albums can be used to organize your digital pictures and to share them with others. Many home image-editing programs let you make digital photo albums.

analog

A way of representing information in a format that attempts to reproduce real sounds, images, and movement by capturing (for example) a sound wave's differing levels and properties. A telephone line that carries voice, with its ability to capture the nuances of pitch and tone, is an example of analog technology, as is a film camera, which captures a scene's continuity of color with a high degree of fidelity. See also *digital*.

angle

A camera's perspective on the subject (see Chapter 3). The camera angle can be altered to affect the composition and the mood of a photograph, as when you shoot the subject from the side, above, or below, rather than straight on.

animated GIF

A series of simple images, stored in a single GIF file, sequentially displayed to simulate simple animation on a Web page.

AOL Hometown

A large, topically organized community of Web sites where AOL members and non-members alike can post their Web pages. Anyone with Internet access and a Web browser can add, search, and view Hometown pages. Use AOL Keyword: **Hometown** or go to hometown.aol.com.

AOL Keyword

A word, abbreviation, or phrase that acts as a shortcut to get to a specific AOL area.

AOL Search

AOL's solution to finding information and people online. You can search AOL, a database of millions of choice Web sites, newsgroups, AOL's message boards, the White and Yellow Pages, and more. Click the Search button on the AOL toolbar to visit AOL Search.

aperture

The opening in a camera that lets light pass through to expose the film (or, in a digital camera, to "expose" the CCD). The size of the aperture is called the f-stop. See also *f-stop*.

archive

Files grouped for a purpose: to be compressed, transmitted, stored, or simply made available for viewing by others. Also, a collection of digital pictures on your hard drive or other storage device.

attachment

A digital picture, word-processing document, or other file sent with an e-mail message. When you use the built-in e-mail program in "You've Got Pictures," digital pictures are sent as attachments.

auto-focus lens

A type of lens that uses a motor to focus the lens automatically. Most digital cameras come with auto-focus lenses.

AVI

The standard format for Windows video files.

B

background

Part of a photographic image against which a subject is set. Should sometimes be blurred or cropped to prevent distraction from the subject.

backlit

A situation in which the light on a subject comes from behind. Must often be compensated for to avoid an underexposed (dark) subject, by using either a fill-flash (see Chapter 7) or an image-editing program's dodge tool (see Chapter 9).

bandwidth

The amount of data that can travel over a network in a given time. See also *bps (bits per second)*.

bit

Short for *binary unit,* also know as *digit.* The basic unit of computer storage, a digit can only be a 0 or 1.

bit depth

Describes the number of colors (or shades of gray) that any pixel can display and hence the number of bits needed to record colors. If eight bits are used to define a pixel's color, the pixel can display up to 256 colors. If 24 bits are used, more than 16 million colors can be displayed. Reducing bit depth is a simple way to reduce the size of files intended for Web use.

bitmap

A type of graphic file that stores information about colors and tones in small blocks called pixels. BMP, JPG, and GIF files are made up of bitmaps. See also *vector graphics.*

BMP

A file saved in a standard Windows file format for graphics.

bps (bits per second)

A measurement of the speed of data transmission. The higher the bps rate, the quicker your data travels to or from your computer.

broadband

Also known as high-speed network access. On AOL, the main types of broadband are delivered over either cable wires or phone lines, and a special modem is required. Broadband access greatly speeds up the rate at which data travels from AOL to your computer, but has less effect on the rate it travels from your computer to AOL. Visit AOL Keyword: **AOLPlus** for more about AOL's programs in this area.

browser

An application used to view information on the World Wide Web. AOL has a built-in browser and develops a popular browser called Netscape Navigator, which can be used with your AOL account.

byte

A unit of computer-readable data made up of eight binary digits or bits. Typically defines a single character, such as a letter or symbol, but can store other information. A byte is the standard measure of file size (the amount of space the file takes up on a hard drive or other storage medium).

C

cable release

A cable that can be attached to some cameras, allowing a photographer to release the shutter (take a picture) at a distance away from the camera.

CD (short for CD-ROM, compact disc read-only memory)

A standard method of storing and distributing software libraries, reference works, games, application software, and multimedia software.

CD-R (compact disc recordable)

Optical digital storage drive that lets you save files on a CD. CD-R disks can only be *written to* once. See also *CD* and *CD-RW.*

CD-RW (compact disc rewritable)

A new type of optical digital storage drive that lets you save files on the same CD many times, as you do with floppy diskettes or tapes. See also *CD-R.*

channel, on AOL

A major category of AOL content, a collection of related AOL forums. For example, the Interests Channel is home to the photography community on AOL; the Computing channel is where you can get detailed information about digital cameras, printers, and scanners.

clipart

A collection of digital images designed for use in Web sites, graphic presentations, and other documents. Easy Designer (see Chapter 13) includes clipart, as do image-editing programs such as PhotoSuite III (Platinum Edition) and many common applications such as Microsoft PowerPoint.

CMYK

Shorthand used in printing to describe any color as a combination of four different ink colors: cyan, magenta, yellow, and black. Used to describe colors for print publications. See also *RGB.*

color depth

See *bit depth.*

compositing

Technique of combining several images in one document for dramatic effects.

contrast

Range of brightness between the light and dark areas of a photograph or other graphic image; a high-contrast image has a wide range.

copyright

Legal right to publish and distribute an artistic or intellectual work.

crop

To trim a photograph or other graphic image down to the portion you want to edit, print, or display.

cursor

Small movable arrow on your monitor that you control with a mouse. The shape of the cursor varies with context, always indicating what is possible at any time while using a program. An insertion cursor is a thin vertical bar indicating that you can type text at that point, and the standard arrow cursor changes to a pointing finger when something can be clicked.

D

database

Structured and searchable collection of data in the true sense of data — discrete bits of information. Database products like Filemaker and Microsoft Access can be used to organize your digital pictures.

depth of field

In photography, the portion of the total depth of a photograph that is in focus. Wide-angle lenses offer greater depth of field than lenses of longer focal length. Any lens has a greater depth of field at a smaller aperture setting — an f-stop with a larger number (for example, f/22). A narrow depth of field can be a good way to emphasize a subject.

desktop publishing

The use of a personal computer to set type and add graphics to produce highly formatted publications such as newsletters and brochures, intended primarily for print.

digital

A way of representing complex images, sounds, video, and text (and more) into computer-readable patterns of binary numbers (1s and 0s). The purpose of digitizing is to make extremely diverse types of information (1) widely available to people and (2) easily manipulable and transmissible by computers. See also *analog*.

digital camera

A camera that captures images digitally rather than on film, using a CCD and computer memory. The digital pictures can be downloaded as files to a computer, where they can be edited, shared, and used in many ways.

download

To transfer information from one computer to another, usually from a remote networked computer such as a Web server to a personal computer, but also from other devices (such as cameras and scanners) to a PC.

dpi (dots per inch)

A way of measuring the resolution (sharpness, or amount of information conveyed) especially for printers and scanners. If you know an image's overall resolution in pixels, setting its dots per inch determines how big it will be on a monitor or page.

driver

The software that a computer uses to operate a piece of hardware such as a printer, a monitor, a scanner, or a mouse.

E

e-mail (electronic mail)

A message from one person to another via the Internet. Digital pictures can be attached to an e-mail message or inserted within the message. E-mail is available in many forms on AOL: "standard" mail (click the Read or Write icon on the toolbar); AOL Mail (at www.aol.com/aolmail); AOL Mail on the Web for handheld computers and Palm devices; and the e-mail integrated into "You've Got Pictures" to share digital pictures with one person or several.

emulsion

Light-sensitive chemical coating, especially on film, in film-based photography.

exposure compensation

Overriding your camera's light meter reading in response to difficult lighting situations, such as backlighting. Some cameras, including automatic ones, have an exposure compensation control that allows you to overexpose or underexpose in steps of f/1 or f/0.5 to compensate for such situations. Consult your camera's manual for advice on using this advanced feature.

exposure mode

Exposure is determined by two main factors: how long the shutter opens to let in light (shutter speed) and how wide the aperture is (f-stop). The faster the shutter speed, the better the ability to capture movement and detail. The higher the f-stop, the narrower the aperture and the greater the depth of field.

F

Favorite Places

On the Internet, *bookmark* is the generic term for a saved link to a specific site. In Microsoft Internet Explorer, the term is Favorites. On AOL, the term is Favorite Places. On AOL, you can save anything as a Favorite Place, including a newsgroup, an e-mail message, an AOL area, and so on.

file compression

Storing a file in a format that reduces its size to speed up transmission and reduce storage requirements. (1) On AOL, files are automatically compressed when you send more than one file as an attachment to an e-mail message. (2) JPG files, a common graphics format, can be compressed to download more quickly (see Chapter 13). JPG files are preferred on the Web because of their ability to represent complex images, yet also to be reduced in file size for quick downloading.

file extension

The abbreviation following a filename that describes the format the file is saved in. See also *file format*.

file format

A standard manner in which files are stored that enables an operating system to determine what application is needed to open them. The format is usually represented by a file extension following the filename, such as .TXT (text files), .BMP (bit-mapped graphics), .JPG, and .GIF (standard bit-mapped graphic formats for use on the Web).

fill-flash

Flash used as supplementary light to highlight the main subject and remove unwanted shadows (such as a backlit face cast in shadow).

film speed

The measure of a film's sensitivity to light. Typically a numerical rating, such as ISO100/400/1600; the higher this number, the more sensitive the film and the better it handles dimly lit situations. Slower film provides better, finer-grained images.

filters

(1) Electronic filters are common in photo manipulation programs like Adobe Photoshop and MGI PhotoSuite III to provide image-editing enhancements and special effects (see Chapter 10). (2) In traditional photography, glass or plastic rings are used to correct for unusual lighting and to alter color and contrast. Clear or *skylight* filters may simply be used to protect the lens. Special-effect filters may intentionally distort or multiply images.

FireWire

An easy-to-use (plug-and-play), very fast means of importing large video files from a digital-video camera into your computer for editing and storage. Also known as a 1394 serial bus. Now standard on the Mac, and a common option on many new PCs.

fixed-focus lens

A lens that does not have a variable focal length. Point-and-shoot cameras typically have a fixed-focus lens, as do many digital cameras.

flash

Brief, intense burst of artificial light used to illuminate the subject. Can essentially replace or augment sunlight or indoor lighting.

floppy disk

A relatively small, portable storage medium for computer data. It's not really floppy, and it's usually $3^1/2$ inches squared.

font

A complete set of characters (numbers, upper- and lowercase letters, and common symbols) in the same typeface and size.

foreground

The area of a photographic image closest to the viewer; the area in front of the primary subject.

freeware

Software made available to the public free of charge by the program's author, even though the author retains exclusive copyright. See also *shareware*.

f-stop

Aperture setting (for example, f/8, f/22, and so on).

FTP (File Transfer Protocol)

A standard method for transmitting files from one computer to another via the Internet. Often used to share large files or upload HTML files from a personal computer to a Web server.

G

GIF (Graphics Interchange Format)

A graphics file format common on the Internet and nearly universally supported by browsers. It can be formatted to enable a transparent image background, making it useful for Web pages. Most commonly used for solid-colored images, logos, buttons, cartoons, and similar, simple images.

gigabyte (GB)

One billion bytes (1,000 megabytes, MB). The capacity of hard drives, high-capacity disks, and CDs is measured in gigabytes. See also *byte*.

grayscale

A black-and-white representation of an image that can include many shades of gray.

H

hard drive

Primary file storage hardware on a PC. Uses magnetic storage media.

hardware

All the devices that can be directly connected to a personal computer, including scanners, digital cameras, hard drives, Zip drives, modems, video cards, monitors, and keyboards. See also *software*.

home page

(1) The opening page of a Web site. (2) A personal page. (3) In your Web browser, the Web page to which the browser automatically opens.

Hometown

See *AOL Hometown*.

HTML (HyperText Markup Language)

The script (code) used to format ASCII text files into documents usable by a Web browser; browsers download HTML files and display them as Web pages. (See Chapter 13.)

HTML editor

Software used to create Web pages. HTML editors automatically generate the underlying HTML so you can focus on the content — the words and pictures you want to communicate (see Chapter 13).

hue

One of three ways in which a color is specified — its position along the spectrum of all colors. See also *saturation* and *luminosity*.

I

icon

A small graphic image displayed on a computer screen, an icon represents a program (like Word on your Windows Start menu); a function (like Print, on the AOL toolbar); or a destination (like "You've Got Pictures" on the AOL Welcome screen). By clicking an icon, you open the application, perform the function, or jump to the destination.

image map

A *single* Web graphic that provides a *set* of links to different destinations.

inkjet printer

A type of color printer that produces good results on a wider variety of media (paper, canvas, sticker paper, stock paper, and so on) and for a more affordable price than a laser printer. The name comes from the nozzles that spray very small dots of color. See also *laser printer.*

interactive

(1) Software that lets you express your preferences by giving you the chance to make choices (click buttons), enter text (as in a search engine), and so on. (2) Software that lets you communicate with other people over networks.

Internet

A worldwide system of networked computers. Supports globally shared standards for sharing information, such as the Web, FTP, and e-mail.

interpolated (also enhanced or inferred) resolution

Optical scanner resolution fine-tuned with software to produce the effect of additional pixels and thus a sharper image. See also *pixel (picture element).*

ISP (Internet service provider)

A company that provides subscribers with a plain connection to the Internet, usually by modem, without original content or unique interactive opportunities.

J

Java

A computer language used to create small programs that can be downloaded over the Web, to create special effects, animations, and sophisticated mini-applications. On AOL, Easy Designer is a Java application.

JPEG or JPG (Joint Photographic Experts Group)

A graphics file format widely used on the Web. It compresses well, enabling transmission of large, complex graphics such as photographs, with more or less loss of image quality depending on the amount of compression.

K

Kbps (kilobits per second)

Measure used to describe relatively slow data transmission, such as via a modem. See *bit.*

L

laser printer

A printer that uses a small laser beam to transfer an image to a photosensitive surface (usually a drum), which is then sprayed with toner that is in turn applied to paper. Usually more expensive and higher in quality than an inkjet printer. See also *inkjet printer.*

LCD (liquid crystal display)

A type of display commonly used on laptop monitors, digital camera viewers, and other types of hardware. On digital cameras, an LCD viewer usually lets you view (1) a scene before it's captured, (2) an image after its captured, and (3) a menu of choices for setting exposure and managing pictures.

lens

Ground glass, sometimes plastic, that focuses light on film or, in a digital camera, a CCD surface (see *CCD*). Also used to describe a group of lenses that function as a unit, as is the case with most camera lenses.

light meter

A usually built-in camera component that measures light in order to help you produce properly exposed photographs. See also *exposure mode*.

link

On the Web, a link takes you from one document to another when you click it. On AOL, links take you to related AOL and Web pages.

luminosity

Measures a color's brightness. See also *hue* and *saturation*.

M

megabyte (MB)

A measurement of digital storage capacity equal to approximately 1 million bytes. See also *byte*.

megapixel

A way of measuring the maximum resolution of a camera's digital-picture files. A megapixel camera records more than 1 million pixels in an image, usually by recording at least 1152 pixels by 872 pixels. The resulting files are often required for good printout quality but are usually excessive for good Web quality. Some current cameras now top 3 megapixels.

message board

An AOL feature that lets members read and post messages to a public, online message board devoted to a specific topic. On AOL Search, you search AOL's message boards for discussions about many topics in digital imaging.

modem (short for modulator-demodulator)

A hardware device that takes digital computer signals, converts them to analog waves, and sends them across phone lines to another computer, where they are again digitized. Broadband (high-speed) connections require a special type of modem. Some modems go inside your computer, and others are external.

motherboard

The part of the computer that manages communications between the processor and other components.

My FTP Space

Online storage provided for AOL members, based on *FTP*. Used for storing Web files and other documents meant for sharing with other people on the Internet. (See Chapter 13.) AOL Keyword: **My FTP Space**.

O

operating system

Specialized software such as Windows 98 or the Mac OS that enables a computer to perform basic functions, such as controlling peripherals (printers, for example), managing files, and accepting information from input devices such as keyboards and mice.

optical resolution

Actual physical resolution that a scanner or printer is capable of recording in dots per inch (dpi). See also *dpi (dots per inch)*.

overexposure

Application of more light to capture a photographic image than a light meter reads as necessary for a correct exposure. Can be used intentionally to alter the image or compensate for difficult lighting situations, such as backlighting, that might fool the meter.

P

panning

Photographic shooting technique in which you move the camera to track a moving object; the background blurs, while the subject remains sharp relative to the background.

panorama

A photographic image with a broad angle of view, for capturing very wide horizons, large group pictures, and so on; usually created with software by compiling several photographs. Some cameras (like the APS, or Advanced Photo System) let you take panorama shots as a standard format.

PC (Personal Computer)

Originally, the brand designation of personal computers from IBM. Now used to describe any personal computer that uses the Microsoft Windows operating system. Sometimes used to refer to any personal computer.

PDF (Portable Document Format)

Created by Adobe, a popular file format used to present highly formatted documents, especially as word-processing documents, to publish on the Web. The Adobe Acrobat reader is freely available at www.adobe.com, but to create Acrobat documents, you must purchase the full Adobe Acrobat software.

peripheral

A hardware device connected to a computer, such as a monitor, scanner, or printer.

pixel (picture element)

The smallest unit of a bitmapped (standard) digital image, a small square made up of a specific color. The resolution (sharpness) of monitors, scanners, and digital cameras is measured in terms of the number of pixels across by pixels down (monitor); or dots (same as pixels) per inch (printer), or pixels per image (digital picture). The number of colors a pixel can display depends on its color depth, determined by the number of bits available to define a color for any pixel. See *bitmap*.

plug-in

Software created to work within another application, expanding that program's capabilities. (1) Browser plug-ins enable viewers to view additional Web content, particularly multimedia files (such as RealAudio, Shockwave, and Flash). (2) In image-editing software like Photoshop, plug-ins provide additional special effects and other enhancements that can be applied to a selection or an entire image.

processing

In photography, developing, fixing, and washing exposed film or traditional photographic paper to produce negatives or prints. Unnecessary in digital photography, where image editing takes place with software and a computer.

program

See *software*.

R

RAM (random access memory)

A computer's memory (measured in megabytes), used to run applications and display (or play) files. Many image-editing programs use hard drive space when working on large files.

real time

Almost-immediate communication over a network. On AOL, Instant Messages and AOL Instant Messenger support real-time communication.

removable media

Computer storage consisting of a drive (usually the personal computer, with a slot) and removable storage units such as floppies, Zip disks, or writable CDs.

resolution

The sharpness or fineness of a digital picture, either printed or on-screen, measured by the number of pixels in the image file. Also describes the sharpness that a monitor can display, a printer can output, or a scanner can capture. This intricate subject is covered in detail in Chapter 9.

RGB

A way of defining colors as combinations of red, green, and blue light, for on-screen use (because screens are lit from behind by moving beams of light). See also *CMYK*.

S

saturation

The amount of color. The lower the saturation, the grayer the color; the higher the saturation, the brighter and more intense the color. See also *hue* and *luminosity*.

scanner

A piece of hardware that converts a paper-based text or image, such as a photo or document, into a digital file that can be manipulated by using image-editing software or used on a Web page or elsewhere online.

screen capture

A digital picture showing all or part of whatever is displayed on a computer monitor.

screen name

Your way of identifying yourself on AOL and the Internet. Your Internet address is your AOL screen name followed by @aol.com.

screen resolution

Measures the number of pixels that appear on your monitor, usually as a vertical by horizontal measure, such as 640×480. Most monitors let you set resolution at various levels; the higher the *resolution*, the smaller but sharper any individual image appears on-screen.

search engine

An online tool that searches for Web sites and other types of content according to keywords you type in. AOL Search is AOL's integrated search engine.

selection tools

Indispensable in effective image editing, selection tools allow you to identify the part of an image to which you want to apply effects and changes, protecting the rest of the image in the process. Software varies widely in the number and type of selection tools provided, but common ones include rectangular and elliptical, magic wand, and freehand (also known as lasso).

serial port

A plug at the back of your computer that you use to attach a cable to modems, digital cameras, and other devices. Today, the USB port has superseded the serial port for many uses.

server

A networked computer shared by many users.

shareware

Software that can be downloaded and freely used for a trial period, sometimes with restrictions until the user pays a fee to the software maker.

shutter

Mechanically controlled camera opening that enables exposure of film (traditional photography) or digital card (digital camera).

shutter release

In both film and digital cameras, the button you press to open the shutter, capturing the light required to represent the image you want in your photo.

shutter speed

The length of time the aperture is open during exposure (see also *exposure mode*), usually represented as a fraction of a second (for example, 1/8, 1/250, 1/500).

slide show

AOL and other software publishers use the term *slide show* to describe the display of a series of pictures, often accompanied by sound. Microsoft PowerPoint is used to create slide shows, and many image-editing programs (including MGI PhotoSuite III and ThumbsPlus) create slide shows based only on your digital pictures.

SLR (Single Lens Reflex camera)

Common film camera type in which you compose a photograph through the actual lens that will take the picture. SLRs often use interchangeable lenses (of different zoom capabilities and *focal lengths*). Digital cameras that are comparable in quality and features to traditional film SLRs remain prohibitively expensive.

software

Any program (computer-readable instructions) that enables computers *to do something,* such as start up, manage a scanner, organize or edit pictures, browse the Web, send e-mail, and so on. Software is often divided into the *system* software that your computer uses (for example, Windows), and *application* software that you use to do something (work with numbers, words, images, and so on). Application software is created for specific system software.

sound board (or sound card)

Hardware component that enables a personal computer to record and reproduce digital sound.

still

A single frame of a video clip. Like digital pictures, stills capture a moment. With a digital video camera, however, stills lack the clarity and compositional controls of a digital picture.

stock photos

Collections of digital pictures made available for publication or other use, often for a fee. Many such services are available over the Web.

T

telephoto lens

Lens with a longer-than-normal focal length and narrow field of view (for example, 105mm).

template

A fill-in-the-blanks document that you use in AOL's 1-2-3 Publish and in many graphics programs, where templates are also called *wizards,* to quickly create a highly formatted yet personalized document.

text

The most common way of representing simple English letters, numbers, and

characters on computers, also known as ASCII (American Standard Code for Information Interchange) text. In most programs, saving a document as text creates an ASCII file with a .TXT file extension (format). Web pages are text files that carry a .HTML extension.

text-only

Files that contain only standard, near-universal text characters. Excludes colors, text formatting, and graphics. Text-only files can usually be shared easily among different types of computers.

thumbnail

A small version of a digital image, viewed on-screen. Often used to ease locating and organizing graphics files by allowing multiple images to be viewed on-screen simultaneously.

TIF (Tagged Image File)

A graphics file format used with both Windows and Mac operating systems that retains a great deal of image information but at the cost of producing large files.

toolbar

A row of icons or buttons in application software that provides ready access to the program's major functions.

TWAIN

Software that lets you import an image from a scanner or digital camera directly into a graphics application. What this means is that you control key hardware functions, such as downloading pictures from a digital scanner or initiating a scan, from within the sofware.

U

underexposure

Application of less light to capture a photographic image than a light meter reports is necessary. Can be used intentionally to alter the image or compensate for difficult lighting situations that may result in meter error.

upload

To transfer a file from your personal computer to another (usually larger) computer. On AOL, you use AOL Keyword: **My FTP Space** to upload files for anyone with Internet access to *download*.

URL (Uniform Resource Locator)

The address of an Internet resource. Begins with one of several standard prefixes that identifies the type of Internet resource, such as http://, ftp://, or news:. Must include the computer's name, which identifies the site (www.aol.com), and sometimes a directory path and specific file on that computer. Web site URLs begin with http://, but on AOL, you can leave that part off when entering a URL in the box on the AOL navigation bar.

USB (Universal Serial Bus) port

A newer personal computer plug designed for nearly any peripheral device. USB devices, such as printers and scanners, can be plugged into each other. Most digital cameras can use USB ports, but require a special, inexpensive cable to do so.

utility

A broad term for software accessories that improve your computer's ability to carry out a specific function such as compressing files or viewing an unusual image format.

V

vector graphics

Graphic image files saved as mathematical formulas to represent lines and shapes, by using a continuous line rather than a series of pixels as with bitmapped graphics. Web pages display bitmapped graphics (JPGs and GIFs). To construct vector graphics, you need to use a special graphics program such as Adobe Illustrator, Macromedia Freehand, or CorelDRAW.

video adapter/card/board

Known by these and many other terms, this hardware enables the computer to import camcorder or digital-video files for editing, playing, and sharing on a computer.

viewfinder

On a traditional or digital camera, the window that you look through when composing your picture. Usually differs slightly from the actual area captured in a photo. Most digital cameras offer an LCD viewfinder in addition to a standard viewfinder.

virus

A program that you can inadvertently download with other software or as an e-mail attachment; a virus is designed to change files on your computer, often with malicious intent.

W

WAV file

Standard Windows sound file format.

wide angle lens

A lens with a shorter-than-normal focal length and wide field of view.

WYSIWIG (What You See Is What You Get)

Pronounced "whizzy-wig." Used to describe a graphical software user interface in which the editing view closely approximates the final printed or on-screen appearance.

Z

Zip

(1) A generic term for file compression. (2) Extension of a set of zipped files. (3) A Zip drive is a type of storage medium that holds more data than a floppy — 100MB or 250MB, instead of 1.5MB.

zoom

(1) In photography, changing the lens's focal length to see more or less of the subject closer up. (2) In image-editing software, you zoom into a picture to do fine edits and zoom out to view the overall image.

zoom lens

A lens with a variable focal length, letting you capture more or less of the main subject.

Index

C

Continued

AOL's Complete Source for Your Digital Imaging Needs!

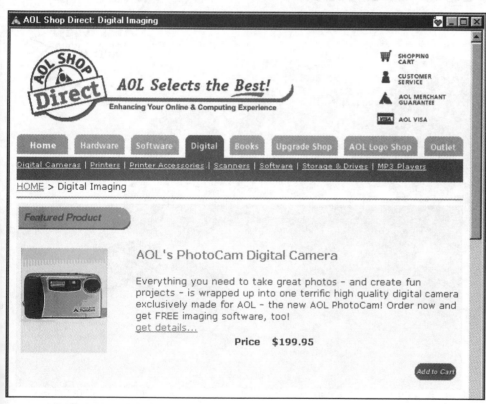

Visit the AOL Shop Direct Digital Shop and check out our departments:

- Digital Cameras
- Scanners
- Digital Software
- Printers and Printer Accessories
- Storage and Drives
- Video Accessories

All this and more to help you get your pictures online and share them with family and friends!

So easy to use, no wonder it's #1

AOL SHOP Direct
AOL Selects the Best!
Enhancing Your Online & Computing Experience

The Fast, Easy Way to Share Your Photos Online!

Order Today!
1-888-299-0329

AOL's PhotoCam

Everything you need in one great package to get you started with digital imaging. Just point, click, connect and send! Save money and time. There is no film or developing cost. It is easy to share your photos with family and friends through your e-mail or view pictures on your TV/VCR with the video output connector. AOL's PhotoCam includes an easy to use manual, MGI's PhotoSuite III SE, 8MB of built-in memory to shoot and store up to 128 pictures, beautiful black vinyl carrying case, 4AA batteries, USB and serial Connectors, and more. Available for PC.

$199.95 (s&h $8.95)   #0014769N00011712

AMERICA
Online.

Just Point, Click, Connect and Send!

So easy to use,
no wonder it's #1

Please allow 1-3 weeks for delivery. Prices and availability are subject to change without notice.

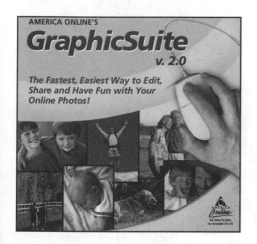

Smart Scanning Made Simple!

Order Today!
1-888-299-0329

SCAN
Scan photos, business documents, articles, even 3-D objects directly into the award-winning PaperPort Deluxe software.

COPY/PRINT
Create clean, crisp copies by sending scans to your color or black-and-white printer.

E-MAIL
Scan an image or document and immediately send it to others as an email attachment.

CUSTOM
Configure this button to send your scanned page to the application or device of your choice - a second printer, your favorite image editing software, or to our desktop publishing software.

CANCEL
Instantly cancel any scan in progress.

Visioneer OneTouch 8100 Scanner

The Visioneer OneTouch 8100 scanner is one of the easiest scanners in the world to setup and use. It has five convenient buttons that make faxing, copying, OCR, emailing and storing images easy to do. With one touch, save your favorite pictures or documents and store them on your PC. The Visioneer OneTouch gets you one step closer to sharing your pictures with family and friends online, designing your own Web page, or creating greeting cards, calendars and more. Features 600 x 1200 dpi optical resolution, 42-bit internal color and 5 button hardware controls.

$179.95 (s&h $10.95)   #0014770N00012009

So easy to use, no wonder it's #1

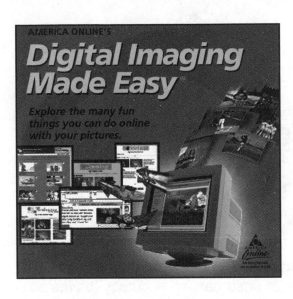